WE SHOULD BE SO LUCKY

ANDREW LOW

WE SHOULD BE SO LUCKY

WHY THE AUSTRALIAN WAY WORKS

Prospect Editions

Prospect Editions

First published in 2025 by Prospect Editions,
an imprint of Prospect Publishing
2 Queen Anne's Gate, London, SW1H 9AA
www.prospectmagazine.co.uk

ISBN 9781068318603
Available as an ebook, ISBN 9781068318610

Copyright © Andrew Low, 2025

The right of Andrew Low to be identified as the author
of this work has been asserted by him in accordance with
the Copyright, Design and Patents Act 1988.

ALL RIGHTS RESERVED.
No part of this publication may be reproduced, stored in a retrieval system
or transmitted in any form or by any means, electronic, mechanical, photocopying,
recording or otherwise, without prior written permission of the author.

Cover design by Two Associates
Text design and typesetting by Typography Studio

CONTENTS

INTRODUCING AUSTRALIA — XI
   The Australian Way — xiii
   The changing world — xv
   Why the Australian Way works — xviii
   Lessons of the Australian Way — xxi
   Lessons for Australia — xxvii

* * *

I. WHAT MAKES AUSTRALIA DIFFERENT

WHAT IS AN AUSTRALIAN? — 3
   Egalitarians — 6
   Individualists — 10
   Indulgence over restraint — 12
   Short-term focus — 15
   The safety nation — 18
   Competitive achievers — 21
   The need for balance — 22

SUBURBIA AND SPORT — 27
   Cities — 29
   Sport — 31
   Giving it a go — 34

FAIR GO	37
What is a fair go?	39
Innovation and having a go	40
The arts	41
SCEPTICAL PRAGMATISM	45
Wages and unions	49
Cohesive community	51

II. THE AUSTRALIAN DREAM

THE FIRST AUSTRALIANS	55
Recognition	58
Australia Day	59
Closing the gap	61
BORN BY BALLOT NOT BATTLEFIELD	65
A unique democracy	68
Current challenges	74
BOUNDLESS PLAINS TO SHARE	79
The immigration debate	84
Cohesion in a multicultural society	86
Somewheres and Anywheres	89
Making it work today	91

III. AUSTRALIAN QUALITIES

HEALTHY	95
Does it work?	97
How does it work?	98

    Primary care and diagnostics   100
    Other factors   102
    Keeping it going   103

WEALTHY   105
    Superannuation   112
    The complexity myth   113

WISE   123
    Australian universities   124
    Australian schools   127
    Losing the advantage   128
    Can the Australian Way return?   130

DIVERSE   133
    States and cities   133
    Gender   136
    Disadvantage   137
    Fragmentation   138

DEMOCRATIC   141
    Democracy and balance   142
    The alternative model   145
    The future   148
    Technology and social media   149

IV. AUSTRALIA'S PLACE IN THE WORLD

ISLAND NATION
    The fear of invasion   157
    The psychology of perceived distance   159
     163

Climate and population — 163
Australia's approach — 164

THE CHINA CHALLENGE — 165
What does Australia have to fear? — 171
China and the United States — 174
A core-interests playbook — 175
Which China? — 176
Underestimating power — 179

AMERICAN UMBRELLA? — 181
Australian views — 185
The US in Asia — 187

ASCENDANT ASIA — 191

DIPLOMACY IN THE 21ST CENTURY — 201
Britain — 202
The republic — 206
Europe — 207
Diplomacy in the 21st century — 209

V. THE LUCKY COUNTRY

MAKING IT LAST — 213
Economic backsliding — 214
Energy and climate — 216
Housing — 220
Tolerating mediocrity — 222

STILL LUCKY, STILL WORKING — 225
Why nations succeed or fail — 227

Sharpening the saw	228
Still lucky, still working	229

* * *

Notes and Further Reading	233
About the Author	269
Index	271

INTRODUCING AUSTRALIA

Imagine a country whose people enjoy the highest median wealth in the world and also a life expectancy two years longer than in Britain and five years more than in the United States. Imagine that same country goes for almost 30 years without a recession and then bounces back from Covid with its rare AAA credit rating reaffirmed and a national budget in surplus. A country where average incomes (GDP per head) are 30 per cent higher than in the United Kingdom, and median wealth is almost twice as high, and with the world's top-ranked healthcare system for its mix of effectiveness and equity. A nation where populist politicians remain on the margins and rated as one of the two "best places to be born in the lottery of life."

A country that is a huge beneficiary of the shifting centre of gravity of the world towards its region in Asia, yet also with close ties to Europe. An ever-tighter American ally when China is reasserting its historic primacy in the region. A country that, for all the success and prosperity that open engagement with the world has delivered, sometimes has bouts of insular parochialism. An innovative country with a world-leading quality of life but where political debate is often negative, bruising and focussed on the trivial.

More than half a century after Donald Horne coined the phrase "the Lucky Country" in a book with that title, most Australians still respond to the persistent evidence of their remarkable and unusual national health and prosperity by shrugging that Australia is simply lucky. In this book, I will challenge that notion and explore the essence of Australia in the 2020s, what really underlies this so-called "luck," and what it means for Australia's future.

This is a subject important not only to Australians. For a G20 country of increasing strategic importance (with a GDP larger than South Korea's and Spain's—or almost Switzerland's and Saudi Arabia's *combined*), Australia is not well understood. Locals, focussed on their internal debates and inclined to hold the rest of the world at arm's length, have not been front footed in explaining the uniqueness of Australian institutions (or even thought much about them).

My story is only one of more than 27 million Australian stories, but I've been fortunate to have now lived a lot of different Australian lives—as an immigrant, in the city, in regional Australia, and as part of the large Australian diaspora in Asia and Europe. I have worked for leading companies in the private sector, with government, think tanks, and world-class arts organisations. I'm not a professional academic or a politician, though this book draws on the insights of both. Having grown up in Australia and then spent about half my adult life living and working in Asia, Europe, and North America, the perspectives in this book come partly from the "outside looking in", providing another lens through which to view Australia. It's easier to see the shape of the mountain when you're not standing on it.

The success of a country is mostly determined, according to the Nobel prize-winning authors of *Why Nations Fail*, by the quality and inclusivity of its institutions—government, the justice system, education and civic associations—and the way they work together cohesively (or don't). Australia's values and institutions are quite unique, yet there is a large disconnect between how effectively these institutions work in practice and how little this is recognised. Even in Australia, very few people would guess even two or three of the facts in the first paragraphs of this chapter; Australians focus on what's wrong and they underplay the differences between their system and European and North American models. Yes, Australia has had some luck; countries, like people, need a little luck to succeed. But it has been the unique institutional environment that has made the difference. Australia's institutions, values, and culture are distinctive, and they are much stronger than is understood; far from perfect, they are nevertheless extremely adaptable, and arguably deliver better outcomes for the average person than almost every other place on Earth.

The portrait of Australia that emerges today is more optimistic than that painted by Horne's *The Lucky Country* in 1964. He underestimated some of the underlying strengths of the Australian institutional framework, which has carried the country forward, even in times when individual leaders have been poor. But it's also because Australia has changed a lot in 60 years. The world became smaller, with television, cheap jet travel and the internet collapsing the "tyranny of distance". The world's economic centre of gravity also moved into Australia's time zone. The first- and second-order impacts of immigration were not yet so evident in the 1960s, and the transformative social and economic reforms of the 1980s and 1990s were still in the future.

The Australian Way

The Australian Way has several key elements. A unique voting system—combining compulsory voting, ranked-preference ballots and rigorously independent electoral process—which steers politics away from polarisation and enhances the legitimacy of the result. A unique mix of public and private provision in health, education and national savings that has delivered equity without constraining innovation and excellence. Australia has remained relatively pro-trade, pro-immigration, pro foreign-investment and pro-competition when most countries have retreated from these key drivers of economic success. Judicious financial regulation has avoided the banking crises seen in other countries, and workers enjoy strong bargaining power to spread the gains from economic success. Sophisticated financial and legal systems underpin relatively high rates of both domestic and foreign private investment, and a liquid and floating currency has delivered resilience to external shocks.

Above all, the sceptical pragmatism of Australians combines a willingness to try new things (unburdened by the weight of tradition or class hierarchies, and fuelled by being particularly early adopters of new technologies) with a small-c conservatism that prefers evolution to revolution. This mix enables continuous adaptation without the convulsions that many other western countries have experienced in recent decades. At a time when the leading democracies of the world are polarised, gridlocked and seen by many of their citizens as ineffective and sometimes even as illegitimate, it is important to realise that there are liberal democracies that are working.

This is all even more important in a world where the current leadership of China, a country I have come to know well over the past 20 years, promotes an alternate model for the many countries who remain on the fence as to whether liberal democracy or more state-driven and authoritarian models of government have the greatest practical ability to improve people's welfare.

Australians are self-critical and they are especially frustrated right now. Government has been slow to deal with major challenges such as housing affordability, while real disposable incomes have fallen more sharply in Australia since the pandemic than in other Organisation for Economic Co-operation and Development (OECD) countries. This should not, however, obscure the country's remarkable relative success over the longer term. Australia stands out starkly—both as a place and an idea—among the more than 70 countries where I've lived, worked or visited. It has never been more timely or important for Australians, as well as others, to know what has made Australia work: not only because of what other countries can learn, but also so that Australians themselves understand what goes into the secret sauce and don't throw out the recipe.

The changing world

For more than half of the past 20 years, I lived in Hong Kong and travelled between operations that covered 15 countries from India across to Japan and down to Indonesia (making more than 200 trips to a dozen cities in mainland China alone). So I have closely watched the rise of the countries to Australia's north. It's been invigorating and revealing to see the increasing prosperity and confidence of these countries as they've made their people richer and their nations more influential on the world stage.

The rise of Asia has been very positive for Australia, and there is far more potential that is yet to be realised, but the story comes with a caveat: China's more aggressive nationalism, just as it becomes the rising power in the Asia-Pacific, alongside the relative (though sometimes overstated) easing of the once unilateral power of the US in the region. Until the Second World War, Britain was Australia's major security and economic partner. When Britain couldn't help with repelling Japanese threats to Australia, the US stepped in and became Australia's protector, as well as its economic driver—as for most of the world. Now, though, for the first time in Australian history, Australia's major economic partner is not the major security partner. Worse still, in 2020 the major economic partner, China, decided to punish Australia, imposing trade sanctions and a freeze on ministerial contact, and going so far as to table 14 grievances it wanted "fixed." Australia stared down that attempt at coercion, but it's grown harder for Australia to take full advantage of the trade and investment opportunities with China while also being a close friend and strategic partner of the US.

Australia is exceptionally complementary to China when it comes to trade and investment: agricultural and mining products from Australia feed and power China, and Chinese people pay Australia for education and tourism. Meanwhile, Chinese manufacturers enable Australians to enjoy clothes, electronics, renewable energy, and a world of lifestyle products at a fraction of the price they would otherwise pay. And yet the Australian Way is egalitarian, individualist, free-trading, decentralised and short-term focussed—entirely different to the current tenets of the Chinese state, with its centrally planned collectivism, top-down decision-making, long-term focus and pursuit of group harmony over individual aspiration. (In practice, a great many Chinese people actually feel quite comfortable with the Australian Way, and Chinese success over the past 45 years has in fact owed much to their people's ingenuity in getting around many precepts of the party.)

The Australian relationship with China has helped to make both countries richer and more interesting, but has also brought about a more contested balance of power in Asia that has pulled Australia from the periphery of global politics to the frontline. Together with a second-term Donald Trump presidency that will do less to protect global rules, it makes it necessary to think more about Australia's place in the world and the new dynamics of global power. This tension now shapes Australia's foreign policy: trying to ensure that global norms and institutions reflect Australian values, while recognising the realities of hard power and maintaining free and open trade, including with China.

More subtly, it is also forcing Australians to better articulate and define Australian values in a way that was unnecessary when an

American-dominated globe could be taken for granted (or when, earlier in Australia's history, they were simply transplanted British values). An alternative power centre to the US forces Australians and other democratic nations to consider more deeply the liberal democratic system, one that previously passed without much notice, and what culture and values are integral to their own identity. To what extent will Australians be prepared to "live and let live" if the economic benefits are strong? What is "non-negotiable"? If Australian values are not in line with China's new political orthodoxy under Xi Jinping, then are they the same as American, European or Singaporean values? Or are they something quite different and exceptional? If Australia is being squeezed in a geopolitical competition, then how does Australia compete? And will it succeed in a new strategic environment in the same way it has in the environment of the past half a century?

At the same time as the balance of the world changes, many people within Australia and its fellow mature democracies (let alone in many non-aligned and developing countries) are questioning whether liberal democracy and capitalist markets provide the answers to the problems that concern them, be that climate change, housing affordability, technological change or new patterns of work and social interaction. The consensus descriptors of political systems in most developed countries involve words like "polarised" and "dysfunctional" rather than "inspiring". Surveys show that many young people have less faith in democracy and the way the economy works than previous generations—perhaps not surprisingly, when incomes have stalled and homes are ever more out of reach.

The good news for Australia is that the solutions to both domestic and foreign policy challenges are already deeply embedded in the institutional and cultural foundations of the country. Australia is uniquely well positioned for the 2020s and beyond—if it can avoid mistakes. Recognising why this is the case is not just useful for Australians but is part of the broader debate across the world about what systems and practices work. Political commentary in what is colloquially called "the West" focusses a lot on how power is dispersed within countries, but the strongest tale of our times is how global power has become more dispersed. Medium-sized countries, including Australia and many others in Australia's geographic region, will have substantial influence on how the world develops, and their options are not confined to which superpower to follow.

Why the Australian Way works

The first section of this book will ask "What is an Australian?" The culture of a country evolves far more slowly than its economic and social circumstances, and its values in turn shape institutions (which then reinforce those values in a positive, or negative, loop). Sociologists have identified six distinctive personality traits of Australians, and I'll argue in the first section of the book that these are especially adaptive for the economic, social and demographic trends of the 21st century.

Traits of *Individualism* and *Task-focus* drive innovation, an under-stated entrepreneurialism, and the willingness to compete and succeed in global markets. An unusual degree of *Egalitarianism* and *Safety-focus* mean that policy prioritises health and wealth for ordinary people, helping to maintain a degree of social cohesion that is not intuitive for an individualistic and ethnically diverse society. Even the fifth and sixth Australian traits of *Short-termism* and *Indulgence,* often decried as wholly negative, drive a focus on rapidly actionable and human-centred wins, rather than monuments and quests for national glory. There is a deeply suburban streak in Australia, a fixation on giving everyone a "fair go", and a sceptical pragmatism and conservatism that ward off the perils of ideology and utopian thinking.

The second section of the book will describe what most contemporary observers would regard as the three pillars of the modern Australian identity. The first is the imprint of the world's oldest continuing cultures, Australia's indigenous peoples. The next is the institutions and norms of British settlement, with the late-19th-century liberalism that flowered during the period in which Australia wrote its constitution, improved by Australians during the 20th century, to the point that it now represents a uniquely distinctive expression of liberal democracy. The third is the waves of immigration that have resulted in Australia having the highest proportion of overseas-born citizens and the most pro-immigrant population in the OECD. Skilled immigration has supplemented crucial capabilities, stimulated entrepreneurship and balanced the parochialism and autarky that would otherwise prevail in a country with no land border with another nation and distant from other major population centres.

Australia's framework of laws captured the best of the evolved British legal and parliamentary system in 1900 (and of the US and other systems that emerged in the 18th and 19th centuries); Australia became a country when the liberal ideals of the Enlightenment were at their most influential. Australians then actively changed and improved this framework to develop a robust system that is arguably the most responsive of any country to the needs and wants of the average person. Waves of immigration, particularly since the Second World War, have then created a hybrid culture that is Mediterranean and Eurasian in lifestyle, food and outlook, while still anchored in those key institutions and public norms of the British settlement.

The third part of this book examines the health system (a particularly important strength of Australia), the education system and the economy. It was vital for Australia that, in the 1980s and

1990s, the country was able to turn around its then-declining economic trajectory. A country is only as strong as its economy allows. Not only does a more prosperous country give people better lives, but it can also afford to be more independent in how it relates to other countries and sustain an environment that allows liberal democracy and the arts to flourish. As in other countries, old shibboleths of protectionism and government subsidies to individual projects (rather than government help being transparent and non-discriminatory) are creeping back into Australia, hidden within seemingly benign notions of "self-reliance", "strengthening supply-chain security" and "promoting domestic manufacturing", but—for now—there remains enough appreciation of Australian economic history that Australia has a chance to resist another detour from prosperity.

The last section of the book puts Australia in the context of a changing world, and the resulting challenges, threats and opportunities. The re-emergence of China and India as part of a broader shift of relative global weight towards Asia is perhaps the most obvious. Western elites have belatedly realised that China is not becoming "more like us" as it gets richer; in fact, Xi Jinping has taken the country in the opposite direction. Australia is in a pincer movement between two rival superpowers, both of which are of huge importance to its future, but who increasingly see each other as high-stakes strategic competitors. Australians are also realising that not all Americans think like them either, and Australia needs to deal with the diminishing capacity, and sometimes appetite, of America to defend and promote the global world order which it set up after the Second World War.

Yet Australia also sits in a region with stronger economic growth, more optimism and a greater sense of distinctiveness than the "old world order". Australia is an integral part of the Indo-Pacific region, closely bound to high growth in the Association of

Southeast Asian Nations (Asean), India and the Pacific, and the background and mindset of its population increasingly converges with the locality, though Australia is also an unusually enthusiastic proponent in its region for values of free speech, universal democratic elections and rule of law, about which some neighbours are more ambivalent.

Indeed, the unique combination of institutions in Australia arguably now represents liberal democracy's best package. The democratic and judicial foundations of these institutions may have come from European philosophers and American revolutionaries, but Australians have tinkered with and improved them to the point that they are now far more effective and fit for purpose in the 21st century than the longer-standing systems from which they derived.

Lessons of the Australian Way

There are lessons that can be drawn from a detailed analysis of Australia's unique character, history, and experience, especially for those countries who are similar in culture and values but have not done as well in recent years for the average citizen. The most obvious comparison is to the UK, where I have lived and worked and which I know best. But understanding the Australian Way will also have applicability in North America, Europe and in many other countries in Asia, Africa and elsewhere that value well-spread prosperity and individual flourishing.

1. Update democracy for the 21st century

The Australian voting system combines compulsory voting and preferential voting (where voters number the candidates in order of preference and the lowest counts are eliminated until someone has more than 50 per cent of the vote). Electoral boundaries are set transparently by an independent non-partisan commission, and most electorates are contestable. By contrast, the current UK and US systems regularly allow people to get elected with votes of only 20–30 per cent of the people eligible to vote. This breeds alienation and amplifies the extremes of the political spectrum. In a polarised world with threats from inside and out, the perceived legitimacy of election outcomes is also crucial. The Australian experience shows that combining compulsory and preferential voting can help the centre to hold and to keep extremists in a box.

Australia's written constitution, clear federal structure and elected upper house of parliament also serve the country well and have contributed over recent decades to its stronger economic and social outcomes than the UK. Contrast the Brexit vote (where there was no clarity over what Brexit actually was or how it would be implemented) with Australian referendums, where precise legislation must be spelled out and passed by parliament so people know what they are voting for, and where the hurdle is transparent and requires broad support (a simple majority of the whole country plus a majority of the six states).

The relationship of Australian states and the national government is far from perfect, but it has greater clarity and is more effective than the messy, unresolved devolution that seeks to fit England, Wales, Scotland and Northern Ireland into a UK. The smaller Australian states also elect the same number of senators to the upper house as the larger states, which helps them to "level up", avoiding the centrifugal forces that push a country apart. The fact that these senators are elected also gives this upper house more legitimacy than the mix of patronage and inheritance that puts people into the UK's House of Lords. The Australian senate also has more power than the House of Lords, and legislation is properly tested, often amended, and sometimes rejected.

2. Diagnostics and a mix of public and private in healthcare

People in the UK are rightly proud of the original vision of the National Health Service to ensure that when you get sick you don't have to worry about the bill. But the NHS has become a sclerotic bureaucracy, trying and failing to deliver healthcare to an older and more demanding population through centralised government monopoly. Conversely, the largely private American system leaves many people without adequate healthcare. Australians therefore enjoy lifespans of two to five years longer on average, and with much less variation in health between rich and poor. And all for a lower cost, relative to GDP, too.

Like the other countries who outperform in healthcare, Australia has a mix of public and private in the system to combine a minimum level of care for all with the incentives necessary to drive innovation and performance. About half the hospitals in Australia are privately run, and more than half of Australians have private insurance cover (encouraged by a mix of carrots and sticks that make it attractive for higher-income earners to contribute to the system). It's driven several of the world's best medical research precincts and enabled a focus on mental health and disability care that is more proactive and better funded than in other countries.

Private provision of services also supports Australia's other great strength in healthcare, which is in diagnostics. In contrast to the hospital-heavy approach of the UK, Australia has much more available primary healthcare (patients choose their GP, and the doctor is paid for the time they spend treating patients—rather than on "registering" them, as in the UK), so issues are identified and treated earlier. There are five times as many MRI and CT scanners in Australia, relative to population, as in the UK (many of them bought and operated by private doctor-run businesses), and more and better-paid doctors and nurses.

Australia's system is not perfect (there is duplication between states and the federal government, and a well-intentioned national disability programme was badly designed), but the overall lesson of Australia (as in Singapore, France and the Nordics) is that a well-calibrated mix of public and private care, with incentives for early diagnostics, allows for better resourcing and targeting, and delivers for the average person in a way that the NHS and the US system no longer do.

3. Invest in society and cohesion

Government shouldn't be a player on the field, competing with and crowding out private enterprise, but sports-loving Australians understand that it has an important role to play in both setting and enforcing fair rules for the game *and* nurturing the field of play and the health and skills of the people who play it. With the notable exception of schools, where the UK has done a much better job than Australian states in addressing declining achievement, Australia has generally done a better job of improving its civic architecture than the UK in recent decades.

The UK has run down its police, courts and prisons (thereby undermining confidence in the "rule of law" that underpins a trust in society, rather than people turning to personal networks or populists to protect their families). Funding for the police and courts has not been reduced in Australia, so people feel safer than in the UK, and a substantially higher minimum wage and strong worker protections have also led to fewer people falling between the cracks of society. Regulation of companies and financiers is more independent and less reliant on the "good chap" approach than it is in Britain, with fewer losses and scandals as a consequence.

Australia's federal system, multiple capital cities and strong state governments have made for much more successful efforts to "level up" different geographies (no one city or geography is politically or economically able to dominate), and societal cohesion has been less undermined by the way economic transitions have been handled. Contrast the way the Australian car and refining industries were wound down, with generous compensation packages and retraining for workers, against the damage done to mining communities in the UK and factory towns in the US, where communities were not assisted through the change. It is no wonder that support for trade is lower in places where its impact on specific communities is not cushioned.

Australian governments have also been quicker to act on transparency of political donors, on foreign interference in politics and university research, on corruption and on stopping illegal immigration (which can radicalise parts of the population when they think that control over borders has been lost). There are independent anti-corruption commissions federally and in each state in Australia, with state premiers having been brought down for not declaring a gift of an expensive bottle of wine or not reporting suspect conduct by a boyfriend, behaviour that would not even raise eyebrows in recent UK and US legislatures.

4. Reform from the centre

The 19th-century Britain that gifted countries like Australia a then-state-of-the-art parliamentary democracy and incorrupt common-law system was known for its pragmatism. While other nations indulged in ideologies and revolutions, Britain was the nation of shopkeepers and incremental improvement through liberal democracy, trade and centrism. British thinkers outlined most of the underlying principles of how to make a society prosperous. But the main exponents—and beneficiaries—of these great British insights are now in Asia, Australia and a handful of other open economies.

Australia's three decades of success started with a Labor government that brought about Thatcher-style reforms without the harder edges and with more support for those left behind, while subsequent Liberal conservative governments demonstrated a razor-sharp focus on meeting the needs of middle Australia, including with whatever tax cuts or handouts were required. Whichever party deviated from the competent and pragmatic centre was quickly removed from office. Meanwhile, the UK has become a more polarised place. On the left, there was the radicalism of previous Labour leader Jeremy Corbyn and a continuation of strike-led industrial disputes (in contrast to Australia, where unions have skilfully entrenched themselves in the setting of wages and the management of retirement savings, so they exercise more influence but without the same heat). On the right, pragmatic and analytical Thatcher reforms hardened into dogma, and a splintered Conservative party became preoccupied with issues disconnected from the average worker.

The way back to "delivery-focussed" pragmatism would be greatly helped by some of the changes in constitutional and voting arrangements noted above, ones that force policymaking into the centre ground, but they also require a change in mindset. The UK needs to relearn many of the lessons on how to make a country prosperous and fair that it once taught to Australia.

5. The devil is in the detail

The UK parliament is an impressive sight, with its grand gothic columns and politicians quoting classical philosophy. In the US, the rhetoric soars to even greater heights. If only this were the key driver of good public policy. Australian parliaments are grittier, robustly argumentative and more dedicated to horse-trading over the fine detail of legislation (particularly in an elected upper house, where the government has not had a majority for 37 of the past 40 years).

Granular problem-solving has served Australia well. There is not much wrong with a Politics, Philosophy & Economics (PPE) degree from the University of Oxford, but it provides, at best, some broad principles to help analyse issues. And it can often seem that the British political scene remains stuck in university-debate-society mode, rewarding the performance rather than refining the policy. A more Australian style, sceptical and with a clearer eye on economics and policy detail, would improve the policies that impact British lives.

Of course, applying things that work in Australia is not only a means of improving public policy in the UK. The great power of the US is also threatened by issues of internal governance and social cohesion, the legitimacy of its political system is doubted, and polarisation is rife. A demonstrably fairer approach to voting and healthcare and a return to open economic policy, accompanied by investment in social capital, would make America stronger at home and abroad. Australia's experience can also provide input to other countries seeking a mix of economic prosperity, opportunity and agency for their peoples.

Lessons for Australia

Analysing how and why the Australian Way has worked is not only relevant for other countries. Australians, too, need to reflect more about what has worked so they understand and maintain this secret sauce. Again, there are five obvious takeaways from the Australian experience for Australians themselves.

1. Australia is not just 'lucky'

The popularity of Donald Horne's book, along with a more general tendency to not take themselves seriously, has led to Australians downplaying their success as mere luck. If you ask why the country went 30 years without an economic recession, most will reply, "We were lucky, as China needed our natural resources." Asked why the country is safe, uncorrupted, and offers great opportunity to live your own life, they will attribute it to the weather or to some passive gift of British inheritance.

These explanations are shallow and misleading. Having lots of national resources as a country has been shown, counterintuitively, to lead to lower incomes rather than higher ones. This phenomenon—which academics have dubbed the "Resource Curse" or the "Paradox of Plenty"—has natural resource abundance driving up the exchange rate and making other exports uncompetitive, while elites tend to capture or spend the windfall, and fight over the spoils, rather than investing in education, other productive investment and fiscal efficiencies. This curse of resource wealth is only avoided where the cultural, political and legal underpinnings of a country are strong enough to withstand it. (Norway being perhaps the other successful case besides Australia.)

The reason mining and gas took off as industries in Australia, and not in the many countries with comparable raw resources, had to do with technical, financial and diplomatic expertise that allowed Japanese and other investors to make long-term bets on the industry. More broadly, the reality is that Australia's economic strength is built on its world-leading institutions, an education system that was (at least until recently) one of the world's best for the average person, and on Australia's economic and social resilience, adaptability and openness to trade and investment.

Australians had to invent and nurture their unique electoral system, their independent judiciary and central bank, institutions such as the Productivity Commission, the mix of public and private health and education spending, and the superannuation system, among other economic and social reforms of the 1980s and 1990s. The efficiencies and competitiveness of many Australian sectors had to be created, and profitable mining and gas projects built by engineers and financiers, with foreign capital attracted by dint of political stability and legal clarity over the long term. To attribute these things to luck not only does a disservice, but it can also lead to a dangerous mix of complacency and meddling with the formula.

2. Australia could still screw it up

The values and institutions that have made Australia successful are not guaranteed to last. There are many global examples of checks and balances being eroded and democratic norms being undermined. Continual effort is required to call out extremism (on both left and right), evolve the system and reinforce values. The public has to see results, and there is a need for civic education about how and why the system works, even more so when a larger portion of the population is now drawn from countries where there is no history of liberal democracy and for whom many Australian values may not be intuitive.

Australia's success has also been based on education, movement of people (both into Australia and out into the world to pick up skills and ideas from overseas) and on a high level of broad property ownership that reinforces care for the community, economic responsibility and social cohesion. A chronic failure to build enough homes threatens this culture, and education standards and skilled immigration have been undermined in recent years.

Australia's historic success, and unusually high level of wages for low-income workers, has also been built on cheap and abundant energy. Australia has (rightly) committed to a rapid transition to renewable energy, but has failed to get planning and environmental approvals and skilled immigrants in quickly enough to build renewable generation, batteries and transmission lines at the rate that it is shedding fossil fuel supply. This will make it a highwire act to "green the grid" without power shortages and higher prices, especially with big AI-driven increases in how much power is needed. There is also a risk of more general backsliding on the economic reforms of the 1980s.

3. It's the productivity, stupid

The political strategist James Carville famously said that elections are won over "the economy, stupid". And economics tells us that, when it comes to growth, "productivity isn't everything, but in the long run it's almost everything". Australia's experience certainly bears this out, particularly when you look at median wealth (the net amount accumulated by someone right in the middle of society), rather than the usual GDP measures that are skewed by a small number of billionaires up top. At the end of the 20th century, median wealth was similar in the US, Britain and Australia. Then, as the reforms of the 1980s and 1990s played out, Australia sprinted ahead, to the point that the median wealth of Australian adults went up to almost twice what it is in Britain and three times what it is in the US. This is arguably the best measure of prosperity for ordinary people.

But, unfortunately, making the economy more productive isn't fun for a government; it's hard work and will annoy people attached to the status quo. Productivity can also sound to voters like making them work harder (though, in reality, it's more often about being smarter and getting more from the same inputs). It's tempting to try to shortcut all that hard work. Why not instead use the government's money and power to launch a "moonshot" that magically summons people to do futuristic things and directs investment to where the state's crystal ball sees opportunity. But stagnation in Australia's growth started when the country stopped caring about productivity (or at least not caring enough to dust off the hundreds of excellent studies that the Productivity Commission and others have done into how to make Australia work better for the average person).

The global rise of protectionism and centralised industrial policy is likely to lead to failures throughout the world. But for a country like Australia their risk is particularly pernicious, as it could undo the gains of the last quarter century. Even countries with hierarchical cultures and long-term orientation usually fail when they try big, centralised projects. The evidence is overwhelming that state-led "moonshot" projects hardly ever succeed and they drain resources and effort from things that do. This is even more true of a country like Australia, where the culture is short-term, individualist, and egalitarian. Australia's strength has been adaptability, fast-following on what is invented or works overseas, and in having the skills to take advantage of opportunities through a strong education system for the local-born and through targeted skills-based immigration from around the world.

Whenever Australia has tried to implement big, centralised plans, especially those driven by government, the results have been disastrous. The damage is not only in the direct waste of money, but from the way that incentives in the private sector shift from building and competing to lobbying and stifling competition. There is also, almost inevitably, cronyism—and even corruption—when bureaucrats start to allocate money to individual private businesses.

4. Avoid binary choices

The more complex geopolitical environment will challenge Australians, who are used to having a single "big brother" and have done whatever they need to do to cling to that country in what's been called a "fear of abandonment" (including fighting in many wars that didn't threaten Australia, in the hope that the favour might one day be reciprocated). Today's world has multiple centres, strong middle powers, a prickly but powerful China and an unpredictable US. The instinct of many Australians (idealistic, underinvested in their own defence and never previously involved in conflict on the home front) will be to stick to the century's old formula of trusting everything to the most powerful ally, rather than becoming more self-reliant and playing a more nuanced balancing game that older countries and others in the Asian region will play.

Australia has more in common with the US than China, and Australia is a great beneficiary of the world order that America established and still, to some extent, underwrites. If and when it is really forced to choose, Australia should and will take the American side. But Australians will have to be thoughtful about when and where it needs to take sides. There is no need to damage the Australian economy prematurely or to ratchet up tension for the sake of it. Australia helps itself, as well as its region and its friends, when it chooses carefully when to back the US unequivocally, when to mediate and push back against unhelpful views, and when to work independently with other partners and friends (as it has in the World Trade Organisation and did in completing the trans-Pacific trade deal that the US started but wouldn't finish).

Australia also doesn't have to make a false binary choice between Asia and Europe. Stronger engagement, more two-way investment, and integration with Asia, India and the Pacific is essential for Australia, and an enormous opportunity. But in a complex world of digital trade, cyber and AI competition, and conflicts over values in international bodies, there is also much to be gained by maintaining and strengthening links with like-minded liberal democracies in other places too. Australia can walk and chew vegemite at the same time.

Australia is far from the only country having to deal with greater complexity in geopolitics; so are most European and other Asian countries. But Australia does so without some of the others' historical perspective, and with a sometimes-naive sense that its robust egalitarian and values-driven approach will prevail simply out of good intentions.

5. Reinforce the global rules

Australians are keen rule-followers and operate best in a world where the rules are clear, well understood and enforced. The US-led world order after the Second World War was a boon to many countries, and it was perfect for Australia: a security umbrella making the seas safe for trade, the promotion of human rights, the World Trade and World Health Organisations, and global standards and supply chains. But rising powers chafed at the inherited order, and have started to co-opt, undermine or replace its institutions, while US support for them has also wavered. Australia needs to be extremely active in shaping this changing landscape across numerous interactions all over the world. An active foreign diplomatic core is essential, but Australia will also need to involve its million-strong diaspora to make sure that its influence can be meaningful. It is not just multilateral institutions; Australia needs to nurture and shape the growing number of groupings it is in, from security alliances to trade agreements, the G20, Asia-Pacific Economic Cooperation (Apec) and Asean Plus, among other forums. Australia's proactivity in shaping the agendas of these organisations is often underestimated, but it will need to be redoubled. The battleground is messy, the work gritty, but it will need to be prosecuted with vigour to maintain a world order that works for Australia. Some Australians criticise their leaders travelling to so many global summits, but the new world order demands more, rather than less, such contact. For a country like Australia, diplomacy needs to be better resourced and to become a national endeavour.

Australia is the great repudiation of the idea that countries succeed through the purity of their blood or through a great leader or colonial conquest. Despite its faults and challenges, Australia also shines as an exemplar of the effectiveness of democratic institutions at a time when authoritarian governments profess them ineffective. Autocracies can point to systematic failures of governance in many powerful democracies, but it is much harder to deny the usefulness of a system that has made a country founded in an arduous environment into a place so objectively prosperous and offering such a strong quality of life and opportunity.

It's a country with difficult soil, challenged by harsh weather and a lack of water, and a long way from the historical centres of power. A country populated by disparate indigenous groups, then convicts, their jailers and others finding refuge from trouble spots around the world. Conventional wisdom would not forecast such a country to lead the world in multiple measures of health, wealth and happiness, yet sceptical pragmatism, strong and inclusive institutions, free but fair markets, and liberal democratic accountability have made it happen for Australia—and can do the same for others too.

PART I

WHAT MAKES AUSTRALIA DIFFERENT

WHAT IS AN AUSTRALIAN?

[Australians are] immensely likeable—cheerful, extroverted, quick-witted and unfailingly obliging. Their cities are safe and clean and nearly always built on water. They have a society that is prosperous, well-ordered and instinctively egalitarian. The food is excellent. The beer is cold. The sun nearly always shines. There is coffee on almost every corner. Life doesn't get much better than this.

BILL BRYSON, *Down Under*

In the weeks before the Australian border was slammed shut by Covid, I took a trip. First in a taxi to Sydney airport, followed by a stopover in Hong Kong, and finally on to London. The cab driver told me his story: of growing up in Iraq, and then, when Saddam Hussein launched an invasion of Kuwait and he was called up to fight, using the confusion of the times to escape into Turkey and eventually to Australia. He talked excitedly, in a broad Aussie accent, about his love of cricket, his children going to university, and his appreciation of the equality and incorruptibility of Australian institutions compared to what he'd grown up with: "Mate, this is the greatest country in the world!"

On my Hong Kong stopover, I met up with some former colleagues from the time I ran the Macquarie Capital business in Asia.

It reminded me that when I first moved to Hong Kong, my equivalent at Goldman Sachs told me that, throughout a decade doing the same job in Asia, he had found Australians to be the best at cross-regional roles. Your head of India should always be Indian, your head of Korea should be Korean, and so on. But Australians, more so than Americans or Europeans, were good at the roles that cut across countries, having enough humility to appreciate differences between cultures and enough curiosity to "dive in" to new places and learn. At Macquarie, this proved true, and we were able to mix some amazing local hires in the 13 countries in which we operated with outstanding Australians who mostly proved to be as adaptable as my opposite number had suggested (the magic ratio proved to be about 80 per cent locals and 20 per cent Australians). From a standing start, we were able to build a very valuable business; at one point, Asia accounted for a quarter of Macquarie's net income. But Macquarie was taking off everywhere at that time, and it's not just in Asia that an Australian background travels well. Australians have run the world's largest investment bank, the banking and property portfolios of British kings and queens, and one of the world's largest media conglomerates; expatriate Australians are disproportionately prominent everywhere, from Hollywood to Silicon Valley to United Nations development agencies.

When I got to London, I went straight to a dinner that the lord mayor was hosting to raise money to support relief for the Australian bushfires. There were hundreds of expat Australians in the room, all successful in very different professions (from barristers to bankers, pop musicians to television comedians) and all united in wanting to support communities in regional Australia that many had not grown up in or had not visited for many years. As well as concern for fellow Australians, everyone shared that unique Aussie sense of humour, and an informality, put in even sharper relief in the sumptuous surrounds of Mansion House.

These three encounters across three countries made me reflect about what it means to be Australian. You can't define "Australian" by race, like some countries do, and you can't define it by birthplace, or even by the physical place where a person now lives. The common thread of "being Australian" is a personality—a set of values and ideas that are shared by that tribe relative to others.

A land surrounded by sea will naturally evolve a culture distinct from that of the various ancestors who migrated there, whether 65,000 years ago or more recently. A culture that reflects not only a unique geography and experience, but also the unique mix of different peoples in that melting pot. The economic and social circumstances of nations can change over decades, even just years, but national character and personality evolve very slowly and persist for a long time.

I wondered if this Australian culture could be measured in the same way as the surveys I completed as a first-year psychology student, which told me how I compare to others on individual personality measures. Fortunately, it turns out that you can measure "national personality" in the same way, using six dimensions developed by the social psychologist Geert Hofstede, and there are surveys taken over a long time that show how the average Australian compares to his or her peers in other countries. These six dimensions are: power distance (the strength of a social hierarchy); individualism versus collectivism; task-orientation versus people-orientation; uncertainty-avoidance (the desire for safety); indulgence (versus self-restraint); and the degree of long-term orientation.

According to these comparisons, Australians are *individualistic* and *indulgent* compared to the rest of the world, far more *egalitarian*, and with the most *short-term orientation*. Australians are particularly focussed on *risk avoidance and safety* but are nonetheless more sharply *task-* and *achievement-oriented* than a caricature image might suggest.

Of course, cultural norms are only averages. The Hofstede portrait won't fit every Australian, and each person will be more or less than the average on at least one of those measures. But differences in averages do say something about how Australia has taken a unique shape, and sharp differences between countries can also illuminate the challenges of communication and national strategy.

Egalitarians

The largest cultural difference between Australia and most of its Asian neighbours is in what Hofstede calls *power distance*. It's a measure of hierarchy, and particularly whether those people lower on society's totem pole willingly acknowledge inequalities in status. It turns out that the great Aussie egalitarianism is not a myth. Not only are Australians much less hierarchical than their Chinese, Japanese and Asean trading-partner neighbours, but also much less hierarchical than Americans, Europeans and pretty much everyone else on the planet who isn't from New Zealand. Australians are allergic to deference.

The people that came to Australia from the British Isles (in the 20th century, as well as earlier) were mostly working class, cockneys, northerners and Irish, rather than the upper classes. They were happy to adopt a British parliament, legal system and culture, but most had no interest in importing a class structure, nor the complex manners of their prior homeland. If the world has progressed from a focus on gods to a belief in half-human-half-gods (Ancient Greece and Rome) to the rule of kings, followed by the rule of groups of aristocrats and then property-owners, Australians took the next step and made it about the ordinary citizen. It's a measure of Australian exceptionalism that it's difficult to even find the right word in the English language for this Australian focus on the welfare of the middle of society; references to the "average", "ordinary" or "common" person can't help but seem slightly condescending, showing up the implicit assumption in the English language of a natural hierarchy. Even today, there remains a gap between the very positive way Australia is seen by the vast bulk of British people and a lingering sense among some British elites that there is something a bit "common" about a society oriented entirely to the needs and wants of the everyday person.

In no other country do taxi drivers have the front seat rolled back so you can sit next to them, or do former prime ministers queue to watch the cricket or get photographed in Speedos on the beach. One prime minister went missing on a swim in the ocean with not a security guard in sight (the naming of Melbourne's Harold Holt Memorial Swimming Centre is a typically ironic Australian tribute). Only the Kiwis are in the same bracket when it comes to informality and the sense that Jack is just as good as his master and should address her accordingly. There is an inscription in the rock on the eastern-most point of North Bondi that reads, "I am better than no man and no man is better than me." It's a pithy summary of the Australian ethos.

Australian egalitarianism is not expressed as a political or legal philosophy, although its influence in the institutional framework is clear. Rather than a bill of rights, Australian egalitarianism expresses an instinctive reflex towards both levelling and inclusion, enforced with sharp humour to puncture any attempt to rise above the crowd. Sledging is as Australian as Vegemite. Mateship (a companionship grounded in equality and mutual loyalty) is also part of the egalitarianism of Australians, though they are now also attuned to the negative side of a mateship culture sometimes defined more by the exclusion of the "non-mates" than in the binding of those who are. This is also the egalitarianism of the "tall poppy syndrome"—that latent desire to cut down anyone seen as rising above the pack—which can act as a discouragement of excellence and drive talent overseas.

Even the organisational hierarchy in an Australian business is just there for convenience. Managers are expected to be accessible, and even very junior people expect to be informed and be able to express their opinions. Studies of plane crashes around the world often link accidents to more-junior crew members or engineers not willing to challenge a mistake, but anyone servicing a plane in Australia would have no compunction calling out a problem; Qantas regularly gets rated as the safest airline in the world. I saw the difference starkly when running businesses for Macquarie in Asia and Europe (where local hires found the flat structure and bottom-up strategy and planning at this Australian-run company refreshing and invigorating, but also sometimes confronting), and then later for a subsidiary of a Chinese company (where decisions were always top-down and everyone knew their place).

Part of not having hierarchy is that Australians don't mince their words or hide their feelings to maintain "harmony" and "social stability". There are some countries where Australians' blunt outspokenness and aggressive informality will be welcome, and some neighbouring countries have historically had to work to understand their bigger and richer neighbour. But the most important relationships, particularly those in Asia, are with countries that are now bigger and wealthier than Australia. The only way to communicate effectively is to be aware of the different cultures and adjust the way messages are delivered. Australians complain that others should talk robustly and openly like they do, but, sadly, it's also a truism of power between states that the small need to work harder to be understood by the big than the big need to work to be understood by the small.

The differences in culture between Australia and other countries should be a reminder that we don't all hear the same meaning even when words are literally translated. The cultural differences between Australia and China have become much more noticeable as conversations become more complex than what price to charge for a shipping container of iron ore or coal. The two largest countries in the world, China and India, are at the absolute other end of the power distance spectrum to Australia, preferring a clear hierarchy, no public confrontations, a long-term focus and communicating subtly and indirectly. Japan is not only Australia's second-largest trading partner, but also one of the main destinations for Aussies going overseas—a country that consistently rates as one of the places for which Australians have the most affection. Japanese people have a well-documented sense of power distance. They care deeply about politeness and appropriateness. Harmony and order are given great importance in Japanese culture; it can't always be assumed that what is said is all that is meant.

Australians who approach a senior Chinese, Japanese or Indian person with characteristic Aussie virtues of robust, direct and challenging speech can easily come across as rude and arrogant. Hofstede comparisons show that leaders in China and India seek obedience and tend to be less open to feedback than Australian (or US) leaders, who try to persuade, collaborate and show more vulnerability than would be considered appropriate by leaders in a country where people are more comfortable with hierarchy and an unequal power distribution. It's hard to imagine the status-conscious leaders of most countries saying proudly, as did Australian prime minister John Howard, "I can't think of a nobler description of anybody than to be called an average Australian bloke." The first Australian prime minister is not remembered, like Washington, by having a state, city and airport named after him; instead, Edmund Barton gives his name to a garden suburb of 1,400 people in Canberra.

The egalitarianism of Australians is also a reason for Australia's uniquely responsive political institutions. There is a universal tendency for families with wealth and power in any society to try to perpetuate it, but in Australia those attempts to tilt the playing field in their favour usually meet with fierce resistance (except when it comes to inheriting real estate). The political philosopher John Rawls famously suggested a thought experiment to determine whether a society is "just": would you wish to be born in that country if you didn't know what circumstances you would be born into—rich or poor, male or female, privileged or disadvantaged? It's arguable that Australia, perhaps only rivalled by a handful of northern-European countries, would satisfy this construction. Through most of the world, the risk of being in the bottom half would be too high to roll that dice.

Individualists

Australia is one of the most individualist countries in the world on the Hofstede scale. Whether it is early Australians spread over an enormous land mass for tens of thousands of years, emancipated convicts remaking themselves, or gold-rush settlers in the 19th century, Australians have always had a vast country to explore—and, for up to a quarter of Australians in each generation, the sense of freedom that comes from being very far from one's birthplace. Until relatively recently, Australia provided the chance for reinvention and redemption—a prospect that fascinated Charles Dickens, who sent both his sons to live in Australia, and adopted it as the place for characters like Magwitch to move from convict to wealthy benefactor. Australia still offers space, tolerance and sufficient prosperity for the average person to follow their own path.

According to Hofstede's analysis, individualist societies are more loose-knit than others, with an expectation that people will generally look after themselves and their families first. Promotions and opportunities at work will be based on merit rather than nepotism or sectarian considerations. More interdependent societies tend to be structured around groups that take care of people in return for loyalty to a collective, but Australians want to make their own decisions and push back against groupthink. Employees are expected to be self-reliant and demonstrate initiative; in return, they demand greater autonomy and individual acknowledgement and feedback. The dream (and often reality) of "working for yourself" is more common in Australia than the desire to be a "salaryman" or an efficient cog in the wheel of a well-run corporate machine.

Australians are feisty, self-directed and focussed on living the life they want for themselves and their families. The bounds of conformity that previously repressed individual expression in Australia have substantially loosened, as international travel, the media and the internet widen the breadth of possibilities available to even the most suburban or rural of Australians. There is more scope in Australia to find your own tribe than in almost any other country. People move freely between suburbs and from the country to the city or the city to the country, to find the friends and colleagues who best match their interests. Booming broadband has allowed each individual Australian to choose their own online communities too, and a global media basket (daily France24 news bulletins for my mother to keep her French language skills honed; WeChat and Weibo accounts for Chinese speakers; and, for others, a mix of American, European and other social media memes, newspapers, magazines and video snippets).

Outside the traditionally English-speaking world, Hofstede's measured scores for individualism fall away very quickly. Australia's average levels of individualism are almost at the opposite end of the spectrum to those of Australia's major trading partners in China and Japan. As a manager of businesses in Asia, I was conscious of the greater expectation that the company would look after people and guide them. This was very different to an Australian expectation that employees be self-directed, self-driven and quick to provide evidence of why they merit promotion. It may be that the ability of Australians to pursue their own dream and their own individual path is a moral and institutional strength, but it also requires explanation to others and a sensitivity to the different vocabulary of more-collectively-oriented cultures.

Indulgence over restraint

Is it a surprise that Australian scores for *indulgence* beat even the US and Canada, let alone the British, Chinese and Japanese? A land with lots of sun and light, long stretches of beach and plentiful food and resources has that effect. Australia has also enjoyed a history that's distinctive, compared to almost every other nation, for its degree of personal and national security and generally high levels of employment. Modern Australia has never been invaded nor wrecked by intergenerational internecine conflict. The half of Australians who are first- or second-generation immigrants are particularly conscious of the opportunity, security, and lifestyle that they enjoy in Australia compared to what they left behind and are keen to enjoy their good fortune.

All of this makes Australians—more than almost everyone else—enjoyers of life. They religiously observe and celebrate their weekends and value a good time. Hofstede's opposite of the "indulgent" culture is the "restrained"; the latter are the cultures that socialise their people to control their desires and impulses.

Australians are here for a long time as well as a good time. With an average life expectancy of more than 83 years, Australia is only marginally behind the world leaders in Japan (at 84 years) and well ahead of most European countries and the US. But Australians also expect to pack a lot of enjoyment into that lifespan. Immigration has injected plenty of continental European and Asian vim into what was sometimes a very solemn British settlement, and Australia is now happy to own the wholehearted enjoyment of life that a good climate and relative prosperity allow.

It's true that watching Australians have a good time is not always pretty. Binge drinking and drunken violence (particularly domestic violence) remain problems. Even when not dangerously antisocial, there are many Australians who embrace a "larrikin" culture ("uncultivated, rowdy but good-hearted"). Originally applied to street-fighting hoodlums in Sydney, the term has been diluted over time so that the sense of larrikinism is now more associated with the laconic humour of *Crocodile Dundee* star Paul Hogan or the Anzac diggers. There is no mistaking the unique disdain for propriety that can still be found in pubs, mining sites and sporting grounds across the country. The greatest legacy of the larrikin is that Australian sense of humour, which exceeds even the earthiest of most other countries. Comedians in Australia say things that would be well beyond the pale anywhere else—sometimes cleverly so, sometimes cringeworthily.

The 20th-century notion of good times and quality of life has now evolved. Australia's major capital cities are consistently rated among the world's most liveable, and other towns and coastal peninsulas would argue they offer even better quality of life—from laid-back barbeques to forests and waterways. The beach remains central to the Australian experience, and everyone has their favourite piece of the vast coastline, but the sun worship has become more southern European as time goes on; even away from the beaches in the suburbs, there is now a culture of cafes, coffee, avocado on toast and watching the promenade that wasn't there a generation or two ago. There remains a particular focus on sport (always a key part of the Australian ethos) and also on a very democratised and participatory practice of the arts.

Indulgence isn't necessarily bad; you only live once. Our individual allotment of days is unknown, so why not enjoy long holidays on the beach and travel the world? Why not enjoy playing and watching sports, indulging in the best food and wine you can afford, and consuming what you want, rather than hoarding away cash? At the same time, Australia's propensity for indulgence has also resulted in an unusually high rate of gambling, binge drinking and consumption of drugs such as cannabis, cocaine and ecstasy, with negative impacts on health and culture. Australia has the highest-per-capita gambling losses in the world, more than twice those in the US—with electronic gaming machines (pokies) that are more numerous than ATMs and spread their tentacles (unlike in other countries, where they are usually only in casinos) out into the poorest and most vulnerable suburban communities.

Australian men are also more likely to be obese than their counterparts in any other OECD country apart from America, and Australians have one of the highest average rates of household debt (although relatively high levels of personal debt are offset by relatively low levels of government debt). Australia's AAA credit rating illustrates that the country is not unusually leveraged overall; Australians just like to spend on the things that individuals want to spend on, and don't like to delegate those decisions to governments or sacrifice personal consumption for grand public projects.

Australians want what they want—and want it right now. The country is one of the most heavily tattooed nations, but also a leader in tattoo removal. Australians are the highest per-capita users of IVF fertility treatment, but also of vasectomies. It's not surprising that Australia has excelled in the Buy Now Pay Later (BNPL) sector, and that the largest takeover in Australian history was of a company called Afterpay.

Short-term focus

For thousands of years, Australians have needed to continuously adapt to capricious weather patterns. It's the only continent with no regular seasonal rain pattern in a year, agriculture being hostage instead to the El Niño–La Niña oscillation and unpredictable waves of drought and flood. Does this explain why Australians have such a low cultural score for "long-term orientation"? Or is it that, until recently, Australia has largely been a country responding to big pictures drawn by other nations with larger populations, newer to modern nationhood and still defining a distinct identity? Australia ranks lower on "long-term orientation" than the US, Canada, and New Zealand, a long way below the British, and even further below Singapore, Indonesia and China (the latter of which has the longest-term perspective of all).

Australia is a culture that values the "here and now," dealing with the immediate fix, and less keen to make detailed future plans and assumptions about what we will be tomorrow. In the main, as Horne observed in *The Lucky Country*, Australians are adaptors and improvisers, not long-term planners. Australians are quick to borrow, reluctant to delay gratification, and Australian investors historically prefer dividend-paying companies to those with longer-term growth potential. Expanding a business into Asia has too long-term a pay-off for Australian-listed companies and the institutional investors who bankroll them, so only private equity and family-run businesses (with a handful of exceptions) have really given it a proper shake. Australian companies underinvest in R&D, and many tech-company founders are relatively quick to sell their company or float on the stock exchange and cash out.

Australians often reproach themselves for this relatively short-term focus. Sometimes that's appropriate: Australia could have done a better job scaling up new clean-energy sources with a clearer, consistent and long-term plan, and infrastructure would not be so expensive to build if rail corridors were purchased and plans made a long time in advance. Many Australians thrilled to the "big-picture vision" that former prime minister Paul Keating drew for Australia, but that kind of thinking remains the exception rather than the rule in Australian politics. Even a politician with Keating's powerful rhetoric was unable to bring many Australians along with his vision.

Fortunately for Australians, it's also true that people usually overstate the importance of long-term plans and grand ambition. The future is essentially unknowable, and the further you look ahead, the more things will change. Rapid improvisation and adaptability are actually more important. World history is a tale of unintended consequences, where grand plans have been set in motion only to clash with reality. "No plan survives contact with the enemy," says the field marshal; "Everyone has a plan until they get punched in the mouth," says the boxer. Our human minds love the soaring vision and the grand design, but real life is not a static problem to be solved, nor a blank sheet of paper; the quick pivot and flexible strategy usually beats the Maginot Line.

The long-term total return of the Australian share market (over the 120 years since federation) is the highest (including dividends as well as capital gains) of any measured stock market over that period. The average annual return, capitalising dividends every year, from buying Australian shares has been higher over that very long-term period than buying international shares. It turns out that quickly and effectively recycling and reallocating capital as things change is far more effective, when paired with a stable liberal democracy, than long-term bets on red or black. Australia's attempts at big, bold, very long-term plans have mostly ended up as a mess. The ambitious building of a national broadband network, a national disability scheme and most defence procurements have all ended up costing multiples of what they were supposed to cost—and have been far less efficient than smaller, more targeted and flexible interventions would have been.

Writers such as Nassim Taleb (in books including *Fooled by Randomness*, *The Black Swan* and *Antifragile*) and Paul Ormerod (*Why Most Things Fail*) have highlighted how humans overestimate our ability to know what's around the corner. Just as shapes in the clouds resolve themselves into recognisable forms, we think we see patterns in "randomness", and we fail to anticipate or prepare for "black swan" events. They advocate being flexible, building systems that are "antifragile" and resilient and responsive to unpredictable events. Australians, specialists in adaptation and sceptical of grand long-term visions, are relatively good at this. They see what works and adapt quickly.

Australian governments do project population, health needs, infrastructure, defence procurement, climate, city planning and numerous other things out to 2050 and beyond. The thinking that goes into these plans is useful, and the overall shaping of priorities important. The Covid-19 experience put focus on the areas where longer-term thinking is helpful—having resilient supply chains (not all "eggs in one basket") and ample stockpiles of essential pharmaceuticals and energy. But the pandemic also made many Australians lose sight of the nation's comparative advantage, which lies in openness and rapidity of reaction. There has been a revival of the pre-1980s belief that governments and bureaucrats can direct and should subsidise and "incubate" on the basis of multi-decade guesstimates about what might be "future industries". But centralisation, rigidity in workplaces and markets and long-term planning are the antithesis of resilience and antifragility; well-intentioned attempts to "futureproof" the country often end up undermining the resilience, productivity and adaptability that matters most. Safety doesn't lie in making big bets on the future, but in making sure that people are well educated and can move easily, that companies and bureaucracies can adapt rapidly, and that labour practices are flexible.

Australia has prospered by playing to its strength. Australians are adaptable: tweakers, tinkerers and solvers of the problem on the plate at the time. Australia is attractive enough a place to live that it's been able to rapidly import talented people, input and ideas as and when they are required. This will only become more and more important as technologies develop. Even when it comes to more predictable longer-term challenges such as artificial intelligence, the rise of China and climate change, the exact way things play out is far from certain, as it depends on unknown future events and on the actions of many other actors beyond the control of Australians; adaption and refocussing will be required. Australians are better at a series of quick dashes than the long march. In a world of rapid change and unpredictable outcomes, this is the right way to be.

The safety nation

Australia is the "safety capital of the world": a land of curfews, rules, regulations and fluorescent hi-vis vests that all make Aussies think they have successfully been able to avoid risk. Australia sits on this measure above the US, Canada and Indonesia, and well above the UK, China and Singapore. The comparative surveys show that Australians generally don't like ambiguous or unstructured situations and reach for stricter laws, safety and security measures, what Hofstede calls "uncertainty-avoidance". Many Australians would use a less academic description: Australia is a bit of a nanny state, even if nanny turns a blind eye to betting.

The strict measures imposed to eliminate Covid in Australia (while other nations tried merely to ensure that their hospitals could cope) were just one example of the extreme lengths that Australians are prepared to go in the interests of safety from harm. As the commentator Bernard Salt has noted, even new Australians quickly become fully invested in protecting the haven status that Australia has enjoyed: "We are obsessed with anything that protects our lifestyle, and we are prepared to trade our freedoms in order to protect that way of life."

Australia was the first country to make wearing seat belts compulsory in cars and went on to make bike helmets compulsory—not only for motorbikes, but for pushbikes as well. Australia quickly adopted smoking bans in public (even outdoor) venues, random breath testing and regulated fencing around swimming pools; none of which, even now, are universal among democratic peers. Traffic infringement fines are inevitable, and the National Disability Insurance Scheme takes a few thousand dollars from every Australian each year to provide high-standard and expensive care for anyone with a physical or mental disability. Australians almost unanimously celebrate the 1996 buyback of guns that almost entirely halted mass shootings and have embraced sun-protection and anti-smoking initiatives. Australians fall easily into line with measures to protect health, ones which Americans and Brits often push back on.

Perhaps it was the care required to coax agricultural productivity from unhelpful soil, the lethal animals or the insecurity of European immigrants finding themselves on the other side of the world that made Australians proactively address risks that arose on the frontier. It is also true that Australia developed an almost universal voting franchise more quickly than other nations, which has given particular power to Australia's middle classes for pushing their priorities to the fore. Either way, Australia has developed a culture that is less comfortable muddling through ambiguity than the Europeans and Chinese, and international visitors are surprised at the strict regulations within which these outwardly feisty Aussies seem content to live. The safety-first orientation of Australians is an article of faith in economics as much as in social and personal lives. Australia has the highest minimum wage of any significant country, compulsory long-service leave and was one of the first countries to provide sick leave, the extent of which has become more and more generous over time.

The focus on safety is partly connected to the Australian focus on quality of life and egalitarianism. Older nations with less favoured histories may accept that getting rich and being a powerful country will lead to collateral damage for some of the herd, but Australians want to have their cake and eat it too. There is a zero-tolerance approach to death and injury at work, an unusually strong and growing focus on mental health, and a widely held belief that every risk can be tracked and eliminated. Nowhere else puts as high a monetary value on an individual life. Australians are mostly prepared to pay, whatever the cost, for security from harm, insulated from the cost of such protection by an enviable prosperity and lifestyle.

Life is sweet in Australia's shock-proofed bubble, but the single-minded focus on safety-first does have a flip side. Innovations are slower to get to market as they are repeatedly tested for any undesirable side effects. Regulation and red tape proliferate, and make it hard and slow to build homes, transport and renewable energy. Australian corporate boards spend a greater proportion of their time on risk than those in other countries, and new innovations are seen through the prism of what can go wrong rather than what opportunities they might bring. A desire to protect the capacity of the health system in the face of Covid-19 quickly morphed into a quest to fully eliminate the virus in Australia, sometimes ignoring the—less in-your-face-and-on-TV—collateral costs to mental health, education and cancer diagnoses. Being wrapped in cotton wool can also feel sterile; many Australians escape overseas, from France to Thailand, to take the risks considered normal there. Barry

Humphries once said, "To live permanently in Australia is rather like going to a party and dancing all night with your mother."

Australians can emerge onto the world stage unprepared for how tough it is in countries that aren't able or interested to eliminate all conceivable risk. Australian companies, and some citizens, can find themselves unprepared for the less-protected environment in the rest of the world.

Competitive achievers

The final dimension of the Hofstede cultural comparison is the measure of a society's drive for competition and achievement, where a successful life is defined by being "the best in the field". It's described as the difference between being primarily "task-oriented" or more "people-oriented" in the way society works. The traits measured are things like assertiveness, materialism, self-centeredness, power and individual achievement. America, China, and the UK are the most "task-oriented" societies, but Australia is not far behind. Cultures as disparate as Canada, Indonesia and Singapore don't score as highly on this dimension of achievement orientation and, relatively speaking, place more emphasis on liking what you do and caring for others.

A large proportion of the Australian population may be descended from "England's green and pleasant land", as in the classic Wiliam Blake poem and hymn, but Dorothea Mackellar's classic evocation of an Australian "sunburnt country" evokes a far tougher place. A "wide brown land" not only of "beauty" but of "terror", whose "sweeping plains", "ragged mountain ranges", and "jewel-sea" contain both "droughts and flooding rains". Australians revel in telling foreigners not only about cuddly marsupials, but also about a profusion of killer sharks, spiders and crocodiles. Ten of the world's most poisonous snakes are in Australia, though most

Australians will never see one, and anti-venoms have reduced fatalities to one or two people a year (there's that safety-focus again). Australia's beloved beaches are populated with box jellyfish and blue-ringed octopus, as well as sharks, all of which can make stony Mediterranean beaches seem inviting. The hardened adventurer of *Crocodile Dundee* myth is less common in today's safety-obsessed Australia, but you can still discern some of the toughness—whether on the sporting field, in business or among young Australians venturing to every corner of the globe.

Australians may be proud of the safety net provided to their fellow citizens, but the nation has a value system, reflected from school into workplaces and personal life, that is "harder" and more achievement-motivated than most other countries; it more closely resembles that of Australia's biggest trading and investment partners in China and America than they might readily admit.

Australians enjoy an image of the laid-back and leisure-seeking. But, in reality, the business culture is sharp, Australian average working hours are longer than in most countries, and political decision-making tends to be relatively less Oxford debating society or ideological and more tough-minded and oriented towards problem-solving. There is a robust and forthright culture in decision-making in Australia that doesn't allow problems to be avoided or side-stepped, as they are in countries where people are more polite and leave more things unsaid.

The need for balance

The Australian uniqueness, as chronicled in Hofstede's cross-cultural surveys of national personalities, contains both things to be celebrated and things of which to be wary. A smart country, like a smart person, will understand what it does well and what it does not, and where and how it can learn from others. When Australians play to their strengths, they embrace being fast followers of tech innovations, flexible exporters that can pivot between markets as required, and a nation skilled at allocating capital to the most efficient use that can be determined with the information available at that time. When Australians compensate for weaknesses, they work with the Japanese and Germans to develop massively long-term resource projects and hydrogen pilots, and put effort into longer-term infrastructure and foreign policy frameworks that are less conducive to being reactive and require a thinking that's less intuitive to Australians.

The same balancing act is appropriate for "indulgence", for which the Hofstede surveys give Australia a high score. It is very much in time with the 21st century to be strong on entertainment, hospitality, tourism, and wellness and pampering businesses that leverage the love of a good time, but you also need a health focus and regulation to counter the side effects of over-indulgence, gambling and substance abuse. The same thing goes for the egalitarian spirit, which at its worst can undercut effort, innovation and achievement, and yet, very positively, elevates people who in other countries would merely be part of a background choir to the elite.

What Australia has in its favour is that its mix of traits balances well. The combination of egalitarian and safety-focussed culture drove the country to introduce old-age and invalidity pensions and a minimum wage in 1907, as one of the first acts of the Australian federation. At the same time, an achievement-orientation and a safety-focus create the right sort of tension. Too much safety without achievement-focus—and a country stagnates. Too much achievement-focus and not enough safety-focus—and a country can experience economic growth without human security.

One combination that works particularly well for Australia is the balance of individualism and egalitarianism. Countries that are egalitarian and communitarian tend to stifle entrepreneurial spirits;

at worst, they become authoritarian and moribund. Countries that are individualist but not egalitarian become polarised between winners and losers, leading to instability. Australia's individualist and achievement-oriented culture provides the spark, while egalitarian ways ensure that the benefits are reasonably spread and that the opportunities are open for the best talent to step forward regardless of background.

You can see the individualist and egalitarian impulse in how the housing market harnesses the pride of individual homeowners to invest in and improve homes. You see it in the open spaces available to all, from urban parks and beaches to national parks and long-distance walks; almost every inch of the most prime harbour and beachfront land in Australia is in some way accessible to all. It's evident in the Australian health system, which works so well because egalitarian Australia provides high-quality and efficient health care for everyone, regardless of their capacity to pay, while also allowing private doctors and hospitals to work within that system and pursue breakthroughs in diagnostics and treatments, an expression of the Australian individualist impulse.

A big challenge for Australia is to ensure the risk-averse side of the Australian character doesn't suffocate innovation. Amazon, Tesla and Uber didn't take off on the western side of the US just because they attracted the best talent (though the openness to immigration that allowed this was certainly critical). The willingness of "lighter-touch" regulators to accommodate their disruption, and to not strangle new competitors and new business models at birth, was just as important. In the same way, the Chinese magnate Jack Ma has said that Alibaba grew as it did mostly because it launched in Hangzhou, far away from the bureaucrats in Beijing. Technology became a mainstay in India because it was too boring to attract the smothering protection that the government gave other sectors.

The Australian character (egalitarian, individual, competitive, short-term-focussed, safety-conscious and indulgent) contains negatives as well as positives, but, overall, Australians undersell their culture as well as their institutions. By channelling the positive and redeeming the negative, there is a positive circularity, where character shapes institutions and then institutions reinforce character to maximise the potential of Australia.

SUBURBIA AND SPORT

> *The real life of this nation [is] in the homes of people who are nameless and unadvertised, and who, whatever their individual religious conviction or dogma, see in their children their greatest contribution . . . the home is the foundation of sanity and sobriety; it is the indispensable condition of continuity; its health determines the health of society as a whole.*
>
> ROBERT MENZIES, former Australian prime minister

Australia is the country of Bunnings DIY hardware stores, *MasterChef* and *The Block*. Of backyards, sausage sizzles and McMansions. *Neighbours* and *Home & Away* soap operas exported Australian suburbia to the world, and television like *Bluey* and *Kath & Kim* and movies like *Muriel's Wedding* and *The Castle* still resonate with a quintessentially suburban Australian experience. I have lived in a small town, the outer suburbs and in the inner parts of Sydney, and they all feel suburban rather than having the intensity of big cities in other parts of the world. Gritty urban or outback stories still feel several steps removed from the average person's experience in Australia.

Australians have never been the rural frontier people often celebrated in the country's own myths. Almost 70 per cent of them live in the six largest cities and a further 20 per cent in the satellite cities and "sea change" and "tree change" areas within a two-hour drive of these large cities. This leaves only 10 per cent of Australians in the vast interior of the country. But neither are Australians a particularly urban people; the five million souls who live in each of Sydney and Melbourne are spread across such a vast footprint that there is much less of the energy created by real population density in cities such as New York, London and Paris. Instead, even in large cities, Australia's values are still those of the suburbs. Australia adopted quarter-acre-block living and suburban consumer lifestyles even more rapidly than Americans. Australians, clustering in the suburbs, also led the world in adopting secular education, chasing material comfort and embracing the weekend—a time to be spent in house, beach and garden instead of at work. The dream was—and largely remains—a house (financed with a mortgage) with a garden, privacy, domestic comfort and weekends with family. Most Australians still follow a predictable arc of life: marriage, kids, paying off the mortgage, saving enough money for a decent retirement, and then passing the house (or the division of money from its sale) down to the kids.

Robert Menzies's record 17-year run as Australian prime minister was foreshadowed by his "forgotten people" speeches during the Second World War, which included the praise of suburban homes quoted at the start of this chapter. Australian homes are now much more diverse than the standard nuclear families he envisaged, but the appeal to an ordinary "home and family" remains the core of Australian political discourse. Barry Humphries and others have satirised this "vast and unexplored suburban tundra" with characters like Dame Edna Everage, but it has equally been celebrated. Australia has certainly not become any more rural in the last 20 years, although electoral boundaries favour the countryside, and the smalltown-based National party is part of the centre-right Coalition, a political grouping with the Liberal party, which gives rural areas a voice in national affairs that's disproportionate to the actual number of people living there (the same, to be fair, is true in most democracies). Australia does now also have the beginnings of real urban centres, and Australians make more than 19 million trips overseas. This heightened exposure to an ever-growing number of different countries inevitably broadens the peripheral vision of even the most insular of people. The two-year shutdown of international borders during the Covid pandemic upset this broadening of the national mind for a time and revived parochialism, but overseas travel quickly bounced back.

Cities

Among all the western European and US cities, only a handful are larger than either Sydney or Melbourne. At five million people apiece, Sydney and Melbourne would rank equal third in Europe (behind only Paris and London) and be among the top five in the US. The combined Brisbane–Gold Coast–Sunshine Coast is projected to throw up a third similarly sized metropolitan area not long after they host the 2032 Olympic Games. Though more spread out, the big Australian cities are each larger than Rome, Berlin, Milan, Stockholm, Zurich and all the other major cities of the European Union. Greater urban spaces have spurred productivity, creativity and world-class arts and technologies. They have also led to a more diverse range of social attitudes, an affinity with global peer cities (sometimes as much as with those Australians outside of the cities) and an interest in more vibrant and edgy entertainment, lifestyles and stimulation than suburban Australia can provide.

But any challenge to suburban values needs to contend with another unique feature of geography—Australia's very low population density. Across the whole country there are only three people per square kilometre. In the same area of space, there are 36 people in America, 286 people in Britain and a whopping 8,123 people in Singapore. Even though 87 per cent of the Australian population clusters around the coast, the density of Australian cities is still very low by global standards. The centres of Sydney or Melbourne have only a fraction of the people in central Paris or New York, let alone Hong Kong or Singapore. Australia has had unusually low population density for more than 65,000 years of human habitation, and even steady immigration hasn't materially impacted the spaciousness of the country. A sense of space is seen as a birthright in Australia, and reflected in the large public spaces in the centre of cities and the rings of bushland and almost uninhabited coastline that still surround them.

There has nonetheless been a slow osmosis between the Australian values of the suburbs and the often offshore-influenced values of the urban core. The Australian backyard barbecue has evolved new ethnic and vegetarian options, kids playing cricket on the street will be joined by Lycra-clad cyclists, and a greater diversity of faces is starting to appear on television. When the time came for Australians to vote on same-sex marriage, the liberal attitude of allowing other people a "fair go" was more powerful than the residual suburban traditionalism.

The Aussie weekend breakfast is a nice summation of how offshore and urban influences have slowly permeated into a suburban ethos to create something unique (and which, like Australian coffee-making, has become an export too). Almost every suburb and major street in an Australian city, and many towns, gets a Saturday and Sunday morning influx of casually dressed families (often with prams or carrying sporting equipment to or from a park) with their variety of coffee orders. The values would be recognised by Donald Horne (egalitarian, casual and family-friendly, combining individual expression with a shared experience), but the venue is not a pub and the food would be unrecognisable to a 1960s Australian—smashed avocado; the eggs benedict and croissant fusion known as a "sunny benny"; deluxe brekkie burgers with halloumi; bircher muesli with chia seeds; vegetarian fritters.

What brings all the tribes of Australia together is an essential moderation, built around core values that are as evident now as they were to Horne in the 1960s: the "fair go", a willingness to "have a go", a focus on quality of life, and a sceptical pragmatism.

Sport

Sport has an exalted position in Australian society, one that might only be rivalled in America. Sports stories always make up a substantial slice of a news program in Australia, and often they lead. Sports commentators are as well—or better—known than their peers in journalism, and ghost-written memoirs of sports personalities fill the bookshelves. It is almost obligatory to begin a business meeting on a Monday with some comment on the major sporting events of the weekend. Female participation, and the profile of elite women in sport, is also immeasurably higher than it was even half a decade ago.

The intensity with which sport is regarded in Australia is a sign of the achievement-oriented nature of Australians noted in the previous chapter. It also suits an egalitarian and lifestyle-oriented character. Sports and exercise featured prominently in the Australian response to Covid. Exercise routines, indoors and outdoors, far from people, were at the forefront of people's minds and at the pointy end of the debate around the trade-off between safety and broader mental and physical fitness. As former prime minister

John Howard has said, "You don't really understand what makes the Australian nation tick unless you understand the great affection Australians have for sport."

Australia almost always finishes in the top ten of the Summer Olympics medal count (most recently coming fourth for gold medals in Paris), despite ranking only 55th in population size. The significantly stronger performance in many sports, compared to what population and an individualistic mindset would imply, also points to the Australian focus on technology—both physical devices and training methods and programmes—to improve performance. It is perhaps more obvious in sport than in other arenas that Australian culture doesn't rely on "luck" but is one that focusses skills and resources on improvising and improving outcomes. Several other countries have copied the Australian Way in improving sporting outcomes, with great success—a path that doesn't rely on coercion of young people into sports based on body-type, in the way of authoritarian countries, but that channels technology and the passion of individuals and their local communities.

It may be less intuitive, but Australia's sporting obsession has also helped to shape the way the economy is run. A nation reared on sporting contests has a visceral understanding that a good game demands both the freedom of players to engage in competition and a strict set of rules of the game, with an umpire or referee who makes sure they are enforced. Australia's very high level of prosperity for the average person has a lot to do with a relatively bipartisan view that government should be a strong regulator of fairness and competitive equality, but shouldn't be a player on the field. This nuance (the difference between making businesses play fair and the state stepping in to own and run businesses) is often lost in countries that can't see past the binary of "more government" or "less government". In Australia, it's less about how much government, and more about whether the government is inserting itself in the play or is acting as an umpire/regulator to keep the contest fair.

One example is Australia's much-praised superannuation (retirement savings) system. Australians can choose from hundreds of competing funds (including both profitmaking subsidiaries of banks and insurance companies, but also non-profit "mutual" industry funds) or can manage the money themselves (if they are so-called "sophisticated investors"). But this competitive, privately driven market doesn't mean that government is absent. Not only does the government mandate 12 per cent contributions from employers, it publishes transparent league tables of fund performance, closes down the worst underperformers, promotes portability and consolidation of people's accounts via the tax system, and sets clear rules for fund governance to ensure that people in charge are pursuing the "best financial interests" of their members to maximise the retirement pot.

The Australian love of sport also feeds a cohesive national character. Firstly, because sporting clubs (from netball and rugby to yoga classes and surf lifesaving classes for young "nippers") are exactly the sort of civil engagement that binds communities together. Australians are not "bowling alone" and still interact, at least to some extent, across different social backgrounds in a common pursuit. The Australian sporting codes are not representative of any one demographic group, although some might say that rugby union and rugby league are exceptions to that rule. The CEO and the office cleaner will both be at the Australian Rules Football game and be equally as passionate about the results. Secondly, sport is also a common pastime to be pursued with passion, yet where the stakes are ultimately not monumental. A shared interest in sport provides cohesion without dampening individuality; it allows a community without being a commune.

Giving it a go

While many of the solid values of such a suburban life serve Australians well, Horne noted that they can also lead to a culture of conformity and self-satisfied torpor. Even immigrants coming from hard-scrabble parts of the world can relax into the pleasures of Australian life and lose the energy and effort that's required in places less lucky. If life is sweet, and known to be sweet—"How good is Australia?" asked one former Australian prime minister rhetorically at every opportunity—then it's tempting to focus on removing every risk and every possible discomfort. This risk aversion in Australia is one of the reasons that so many Australians go overseas, keen not only to learn, but to test themselves away from the ubiquitous guardrails of home. The skills, businesses and ideas these people bring back to Australia are crucial, though the benefits of a global education are typically undervalued by those who have stayed home, and returning expatriates often find it hard to fit back in on their return.

Back at home, Australians, compared to other people, are keener to achieve, but also more focussed on wanting to be safe. An obsession with safety is clearly not a bad thing and is part of the reason why ordinary people in Australia have such a good quality of life in ways that are not just economic. Obsessing about safety can, however, become a problem when it is mixed with fear. Taking prudent protective measures is good, but not accepting risk is detrimental when every new investment, every start-up and every adventure in life involves taking a risk. For example, Australian boards and governments spend more time assessing the risks and ethics of AI than in other countries, but much less time on the opportunities. Protecting workers is also rightly a key priority, but priorities can become self-defeating if hundreds of pages of prescriptive workplace regulations squeeze out the investment necessary to provide long-term job security.

Losing its competitive edge will not serve Australia or individual Australians well. Like individuals, nations need to get out of the comfort zone from time to time and take well-judged risks to prosper. A constant challenge for Australia, relaxed and comfortable as it is, will be to avoid a retreat into insularity that might see the country revert to the blandness and protectionism of the 1960s version of suburbia. Australians will have to trust in their flexibility, resilience and abilities, and "have a go", whether it's in business, sport, the arts or any other part of life. This is the better angel of the Australian character—and why Australia has been successful.

FAIR GO

> *[Australian characteristics include] their non-doctrinaire tolerance, their sense of pleasure, their sense of fair play, their interest in material things, their sense of family, their identity with nature and their sense of reserve, their adaptability when a way is shown, their fraternalism, their scepticism, their talent for improvisation, their courage and stoicism.*
>
> DONALD HORNE, *The Lucky Country*

Australia was founded in a spirit of liberalism, both economic and social. The ascendant philosophy, as expressed by late-19th-century thinkers such as Jeremy Bentham and John Stuart Mill, was one that embraced both markets (believing free exchange and trade make people wealthier) and liberal democracy (because well-informed citizens can be better trusted to advance their personal and collective interests than unelected rulers).

Britain first embraced free trade and markets in the few decades before the first elections in the Australian colonies—but this was not just a period of economic growth. Adam Smith was as much concerned with morality as he was with money. He advocated empathy and trust as the bridge between personal liberty and respect for the liberty of others. The great anti-slavery advocate and Christian social reformer William Wilberforce had a particular interest in Australia, and his humanitarian ideas of equality, liberalism and egalitarianism were adopted by the many prominent Australians who knew or were inspired by him in the years leading up to federation. That great humanitarian Charles Dickens was also a great fan of Australia (characters such as Micawber and Magwitch enjoy opportunities that would never be available to them in England, and he encouraged two of his children to emigrate to Australia) and was in turn widely read and influential in the colonies.

Australia inherited a system of institutions that was a wonder of Europe at that time: rule of law, parliamentary supremacy and protection of individual rights. This is one reason why Australia has enjoyed such a durable liberal democracy. Geography and relative freedom from war and threats are others. But a further—and underappreciated—reason is that Australians took democracy seriously, improved on the UK model, and always had a sense that good governance could deliver better results for people's lives. Horne was right that Australia was lucky to inherit a great platform of institutions, but wrong to suggest that Australians have simply coasted on this inheritance.

The notion that everyone has a right to a "fair go" is integral to that Australian system—an ideal built on Christian and Enlightenment beliefs about the equal value of each individual, then turbocharged in the formative years of a country that became a nation in the heady days of 19th-century liberalism and was peopled by working-class people, migrants and seekers of a safer and better place. Many countries pay lip service to the notion of equality (as to liberty and fraternity), but it is—if anywhere—only in New Zealand and parts of northern Europe that egalitarian individualism thrives as it does in Australia.

What is a fair go?

There are different ideas of what a fair go looks like, though. The age-old question of equality of opportunity versus equality of outcome has been a regular debate in Australia, and different prime ministers have struck different tones over time. Is it true that you must "have a go" then "you'll get a go", or should you expect to be delivered "fairness" regardless of what talent and effort you are able to bring to the game? Horne noted that, in the 1960s, "The general Australian belief is that it is the government's job to see that everyone gets a fair go [and they] see a government—which they both trust and despise—as an outfit whose job is to help them when they need help." Those sorts of fair goes were distributed by a range of tribunals, workplace arbitration authorities and the Tariff Board. It was a cosy system, but Horne could already see the problem with it when he was writing 60 years ago: "It is a common human demand to want to feel safe and a sensible one if it works. But the concept of the fair go has no international currency [and] renders Australians naïve when faced with nations who do not share their kindness."

The fair go was therefore redefined in the 1980s and 1990s, and the demands for government to "do something" still remain, but the shared bottom line of the fair go is to have the opportunity to succeed according to what each individual perceives as success. Australians now mostly accept that the world will do it no favours (there was no fair go when Britain dumped Australia for Europe in 1973, nor when the Chinese government ordered their citizens to stop buying Australian exports a few years ago), so Australia has learned to be competitive and resilient.

The argument about what constitutes a fair go is ongoing. The desire of people and businesses to be cossetted persisted in Australia, under the surface, through the country's reform years in the 1980s and 1990s (just as communist ideology lay under the surface throughout China's reform years), and it won't take much encouragement to have protectionism re-emerge in new clothes, be it discouragement of foreign students, reducing skilled migration, or subsidies for schemes that have failed the test for private-sector funding.

What does, however, still burn the Australian soul—rightly—is when opportunity is denied. Every Australian should have the education to be equipped for life; should face no particular barriers because of background, sex or other factors; and have assurance that their health and basic living standards are insured against those vicissitudes of fortune against which hard work is no protection. That is a fair go. Australians expect no less.

Innovation and having a go

Every 21st-century economy in the world is obsessed with being more creative and innovative. As British author Matt Ridley has pointed out, Australia has always generated great innovations, disproportionately to the size of its population—the world's first feature film and the technologies that underpin WiFi and Google Maps, for example. Medicine has been a particular strength: from the first electronic pacemaker and ultrasound scanner to penicillin, spray-on skin for burn victims and the cochlear ear implant. True to the safety-first approach, Australians also invented—and then first deployed—the inflatable escape slide and raft on planes, and the black box flight recorder. That's to say nothing of the McCafé, counterfeit-proof polymer banknotes and the refrigerator (the first commercial user of which was a Bendigo-based brewery).

Australians are adaptive tinkerers who also travel and copy what they see, who tweak and quickly adopt what works elsewhere. The clever application of disruptive innovation to solving problems has been stymied only by the risk aversion, noted in Hofstede's character assessment, that can result in good ideas being stillborn or sold offshore at an early stage. And while it is true that innovation reforms in 2015 increased tax breaks for early-stage investors, promoted Stem education and boosted government R&D funding, these policies were not sustained for long enough to fundamentally change this culture. Ridley also cautions that, while funding good research is important, the real rewards of innovation go to those who can make an invention practical, reliable and available. There were at least 21 people who "invented" the idea of the lightbulb, but only Edison tried 6,000 different filaments until he found the perfect one. A small country doesn't need to invent everything to productively apply it, but most innovation is now capital-light, and Australia should be both willing and able to scale and export homegrown inventions rather than let others do it.

There is, though, sometimes a pessimistic view expressed that Australia is somehow "weaker" for buying and copying things from overseas instead of making them domestically. Not true. Australians make up around 0.3 per cent of the world's population, so even if they were ten times better at inventing things, there would still be 97 per cent of what Australians want and need being invented somewhere else in the world. Australia's real strength is being unusually open and well-travelled enough to rapidly find those new ideas and products, wherever they are, and adapt and tweak them to make lives better in Australia. The country can and should continue to bat above its weight as an innovation nation, but Australia also needs to recognise and accept that skilled people, immigrants, and good relationships around the world is the true and proven path to prosperity.

The arts

We often think of innovation in the context of research and business opportunities, but nowhere is the creativity of Australians more apparent than in the arts. When I first migrated to Australia, there was much talk of a "cultural cringe" and a disbelief that Australian arts organisations could go head-to-head with the best of the rest of the world. Forty or so years later, this is no longer the case. Just as Australian winemakers have a reputation for blending grapes to engineer higher-quality wines, while "old world" winemakers cling to the purity of their terroir, Australian arts companies are increasingly able to do strong and original work through their willingness to mix music, dance, cinema and the visual arts, as well as by mining Australian indigenous and migrant heritages.

There was almost no government funding of the arts until the 1970s, but now the three levels of government invest billions every year, and creative and cultural activity is a major employer, nourishing the economy as well as souls. There were more than 22,000 new book titles published in Australia in 2019 with 72 per cent of Australians saying that they read for pleasure. Meanwhile, 68 per cent report having recently attended a live cultural venue or event. Unlike my experience in Hong Kong, where cultural life revolved around greatest-hit events such as Art Basel or the sporadic visits of famous musicians, Australia has creativity baked in at every level of society—and increasingly so—from schools and local drama and dance companies to major performing companies and film schools.

It is perhaps this democratisation of the arts that most distinguishes Australia today and shows how far confidence has come since Horne was writing in the 1960s. The self-conscious mimicry of European "high art" is now very rare, and the most quintessentially Australian arts experience is a festival: there are a rolling series of events every week across every corner of the country that encompass every kind of music, painting, comedy, and theatre experience, open to all-comers. The ABC is Australia's equivalent of the BBC and has a similar history of nurturing the arts and promoting a distinctive Australian perspective on the world. Like the BBC, this role became diminished in recent decades amid the quest for commercial ratings, but it can be reinvigorated in a digital and streaming-driven world where delivering quality niche content becomes economic again.

Even the most quintessentially European art forms have been Australianised: opera is performed open-air in a park beneath the Sydney Harbour Bridge, and the Australian Ballet boasts a racially diverse and eclectic cast and programme that stands out from the monochrome classicism of ballet in older global cities. Australia's Bell Shakespeare Company interprets the timeless insights of the Bard through a new-world prism, and in an Australian vernacular (including a reimagining of *Macbeth* in the Noongar language), and the Australian Chamber Orchestra marry traditional technical virtuosity and collaborations involving dance, film, and cabaret.

This is an arts world far removed from the slavishly derivative one of the 1960s, when Australia's most original talents packed their bags for London. Horne attributed the disinterest in cultural activity in Australia at that time (including the complete lack of a film industry, few books published and a paucity of theatre) to a mismatch between the subject matter of European art and literature (infused with war, suffering and class conflict) and the actual Australian experience (peace, security and egalitarian suburbia). But those filmmakers, playwrights, writers and artists who have channelled authentic Australian stories (from *Muriel's Wedding* and *Neighbours* to the bringing to life of indigenous history, art, and experience) do capture both Australian and international audiences.

As I've recently started writing and developing film and television productions, I have started to appreciate how important this industry is in Australia and how fast it is growing. Australians have long been disproportionately successful in Hollywood, from actors such as Cate Blanchett, Nicole Kidman, Margot Robbie and Hugh

Jackman to multiple Oscar-winning directors, designers and other crew people; a success that Baz Luhrmann has attributed to the very Australian attitude of "taking the work seriously, but not taking yourself too seriously".

The increasingly strong flow of film projects between Los Angeles and Australia has also rapidly increased the skill levels of the local industry; we are now seeing more Australian locations appearing in international movies, as well as a wide range of Australian stories getting global distribution, from children's content such as *Bluey* to television series such as *Colin from Accounts* and independent films such as *Talk to Me*.

Australia's film and television industry is not only a strong export-earner but one of the fastest-growing sectors of the economy at home, having more than doubled in size over the past five years, as world-leading cast and crew, studios, post-production and special-effects companies service both global tentpole movies and uniquely Australian storytelling.

SCEPTICAL PRAGMATISM

Deeply inlaid scepticism is a genuine philosophy of life, a national style [whose] influence can be detected throughout Australian society.

DONALD HORNE, *The Lucky Country*

Putting Horne in a different vernacular, Australians have a good sense of smell when it comes to bullshit. Australians will quickly ridicule most abstract and utopian plans, and have little truck with ideology or dogma. People in Australia may be energised by the bouncy, self-promoting Americans—many Australians appreciate a culture that is always "on" and has faith in upward mobility and opportunity (whether via start-up or hip-hop), even when that country no longer provides it for many—but, in their hearts, Australians are realists to the point of being naysayers. Australians are pragmatists at heart—more interested in what works in practice than an elegant ivory-tower theory. Australia misses opportunities, but rarely runs headstrong into a true dead end; there are too many people prepared to critique and call things out before the visionaries have finished their work. Most Australians would agree with Helmut Schmidt that "people with visions should see the doctor".

Australia was born non-deferential and adaptable, as it had to be as a settlement with as many convicts as officers and a long way from the rulers of the time. Zealots were not welcome. Australians are mostly "small-c" conservative. As Michael Oakeshott said about the conservative philosophy, Australians tend to prefer "the familiar to the unknown, the tried to the untried, fact to mystery, the actual to the possible, the limited to the unbounded and the near to the distant." Aussies scrutinise the proposals of politicians and commentators for self-interest, and instead ask, "What's in it for me?" On all but eight of the 45 occasions the country has been asked to change the constitution, the majority declined to do so, honouring the view of Australia's founders that the most fundamental of changes should only occur once the reasons for reform are completely clear and compelling and (in practice) both sides of politics agree.

The reason the British monarch remains, technically at least, the head of state is not that most modern Australians feel particularly attached to British royals—it's that the current system has essentially worked okay, and Australians aren't motivated to fix things until they're broken. When a republic referendum did get put to the people, most Australians wanted a republic but couldn't reach a consensus about precisely what that form of republic should look like. Presidential or parliamentary? A minimal change to the governor-general's role or a whole new system? Australians stuck with an imperfect status quo that works tolerably well rather than risk something new.

An advantage of Australia's written constitution is that the detail of an amendment must be spelled out in legislation before the public vote, and a majority of states must also vote in favour to ensure broad appeal across the continent (something missing in the UK Brexit vote, where English views on Brexit prevailed over those of Scottish, Northern Irish and London voters). Indeed,

Australia's system would make impossible a situation in which a marginal simple majority of those voting on the day could mandate a separation from the EU in an undefined form whose meaning was different for different people and changed over time. Whatever your views of the Brexit outcome, nobody would claim the ensuing years as a triumph of smooth process and predictable outcomes.

However, the small-c conservatism of Australians shouldn't be seen as making the country naturally "big-C" Conservative. Australia's origins as a country were a reaction against traditionalist notions of hierarchy, class and dogmatic morality. Australians are very happy to embrace change and new ways to live when there is a rational and persuasive reason to do so. Australians easily embraced cross-cultural marriage and female suffrage, and the community endorsed same-sex marriage well before parliament caught up.

Those who claim to hold big-C Conservative views (often very un-conservative and society-warping ideas imported from the US) sit a long way from the mainstream of sceptical and practical Australians. These more radically reactionary "Conservatives" offer nostalgic, rose-tinted dogma. Like their mirror on the radical left, they entice with the promise of certainty, security and tribal belonging—at least for some. Australians have shown that, on the whole, they prefer balance; they understand it's a Faustian pact to seek comfort and security in tribal tropes that provide less freedom, fewer new ideas and a retreat from the open and liberal society that's made the country so prosperous. Australia is not the country of the great leap, but it is very good at the small steps.

It's this tendency towards moderation that best explains the success of Australia. The Australian right is less inclined to defend class privilege than Britain's Conservatives and to fight culture wars than the American Republicans. The Australian left indulges less than Britain's Labour party in Marxism and extreme "redistribution", and has mostly avoided going down the rabbit hole of identity politics to the extent of the American Democrats. The echo chambers of polarised social media and news media try to push people to the extremes, but the ordinary Australian is unconvinced and remains where they have always sat—in the middle.

We now know that human beings have several significant systematic cognitive biases, including declinism—the belief that things are getting worse when they are actually getting better. Numerous studies have demonstrated how bad even well-informed people are at guessing what's really happening in the world. People systematically believe that poverty, violence and natural disasters are increasing, and that the global population is exploding. In reality, the proportion of the world living in extreme poverty has halved in the past 20 years, fewer people are dying in natural disasters, population growth has levelled off, and the chances of a violent death or major injury are only a fraction of what they were a hundred, let alone five hundred, years ago. Our brains are hardwired to crave drama and sense danger—a craving satisfied by a 24-hour social and other media—even though that leads our judgement astray. The past was less rosy than we remember it; the present is far better than we think.

People who believe the world worse than it is will choose either apathy or radical change. If the world is going to hell in a handbasket, then you'll either want to throw your hands up in despair or you'll figure that we might as well give that demagogue, populist or revolutionary a go. What have we got to lose? The snake oil salesman who feels our pain is surely preferable to those mainstream politicians who tinker at the edges instead of making our country great again. Revolutionary change seems necessary to turn things around—but revolution doesn't work. The purported cure is always worse than the diagnosed ailment. Not just in the old saws of history (Robespierre, Lenin or Pol Pot's promises of a new order), but in public policy more generally. It is to Australia's credit that attempted revolutions don't gain traction, and the country is relatively good at avoiding the environment that would feed such false "solutions". Positive change comes from the centre, when they are engaged and passionate about their society, not from the angry fringe.

There are times when the typically Australian utterances "No worries" and "She'll be right" are a cop-out, an evasion that encourages complacency and laziness—but not always. Sometimes, believing in our ultimate ability to withstand the vicissitudes of life and adapt to what the world throws at us is entirely legitimate.

Wages and unions

The pragmatism of Australians shows itself in some unusual places, including in the unique way in which wages are set for Australian workers earning less than about US$100,000 a year. As a reaction to bitter industrial disputes in the 1890s, the newly formed Australian government opted for an "independent arbitrator" to be established to rule on wage claims. The powers of this centralised body have gone through many iterations during the 20th and early 21st centuries, but the principle of a centralised body (now the Fair Work Commission) setting wages has persisted. The rigidities of a centralised system were tempered in the 1980s with introduction of "enterprise bargaining" at individual company level, and successive governments from the left and right have either strengthened or loosened the ability of individual workers and workplaces to make their own deals between employee and employer. The closest comparable to the Australian system is in Singapore, where annual wage levels are set after tripartite discussions between government, employees and unions.

This system has enabled unions to maintain a much stronger influence than the current level of union membership would suggest. About 12 per cent of Australians are union members, only marginally more than in the US and France, and about half the proportion of British and German workers who belong to unions. However, unions are involved in the Fair Work Commission process for centrally determined wages, and therefore have influence well beyond their own members. Pragmatic union bosses of the 1980s also entrenched union representation on most of the new superannuation funds which now dominate the ranks of institutional stock market investors and have maintained a strong hold on the Labor party. This has enabled unions to successfully prosecute their agendas without having to resort to the level of direct industrial confrontation that has characterised wage and benefit disputes in places such as France and the UK.

Australia proves that you can have high wages, worker safety and lots of time off work, and still have a strong economy. Businesses adapt to higher wages by introducing more labour-saving technology (Australia was an early adopter of electronic banking, supermarket scanners and driverless mining vehicles) and they adapt their working practices to make them safer (Australia has almost no fatalities at work, a big difference from almost every other country in which I have worked).

However, it needs to be appreciated that a high-wage, good-conditions economy can't do all things. For instance, many Australians dream of having more basic manufacturing and more downstream processing of minerals, though you can only compete in these sorts of things if you have lower wages and accept more environmental and other risks in the workplace.

The other risk for Australia in industrial relations is the complexity and ambiguity that comes from having thousands of pages of government legislation. Businesses will still invest and can still make money when they pay well and offer good conditions (albeit needing to choose from a narrower range of industries). But what stops private investment dead-cold is uncertainty and complexity. Australia's best advances were win-win reforms in the 1980s and 1990s, by which wages went up but workplaces also became more flexible and co-operative. Prescriptive government edicts since then have too often put grit in the wheels, and lead to lower productivity, less jobs and lower incomes in the longer term.

Cohesive community

How has Australia managed to have relatively strong social cohesiveness while remaining individualist and multicultural? I think the answer lies partly in the prevailing culture of moderation and sceptical pragmatism. Australians are able to air their views and differences with an expectation that they will be challenged, but also that the challenge is not a "life or death" matter. The average Australian doesn't believe that there is an absolute answer to every question; they allow for doubt and new information to emerge. Colours can be nailed to the mast, but also taken down and put on a different mast.

It is easy (and common) to criticise moderation and the middle of the road. Extreme views are much sexier and make for much better television and readability. What political party doesn't love its warriors, the uncompromising men and women who "aren't for turning" and prosecute a black-and-white view with fervour? Humans lionise simplicity: our minds are programmed for three-word slogans and clear lines that cut through messy complexities and compromises. It takes sceptical pragmatism to avoid the seduction of a revolutionary plan that promises to fix a problem once and for all.

For countries that are poor or broken, it may sometimes be true that big, bold plans and larger-than-life leaders are required, but not for a country that already delivers the highest net wealth and best healthcare in the world to its citizens and that has a world-leading quality of life and protections for individual liberty. Bold and radical plans are worse than unnecessary for that country—they are dangerous. Constant and incremental improvement and adaptation, tested by rigorous debate and analysis, are the proven way to make lives better. If humans constantly see things as worse (and getting more so) than they are, then the best antidote to counterproductive revolutionary zeal is a healthy dose of sceptical pragmatism. A society that instinctively distrusts big bold initiatives and sweeping plans to "fix things" will more often be right than wrong.

PART II

THE AUSTRALIAN DREAM

There is our ancient heritage, written on the continent and the original culture painted on its land and seascapes.

There is its British inheritance, the structures of government and society transported from the United Kingdom fixing its foundations in the ancient soil.

There is its multicultural achievement: a triumph of immigration that brought together the gifts of people and cultures from all over the globe—forming one indissoluble commonwealth.

We stand on the cusp of bringing these three parts of our national story together.

NOEL PEARSON, indigenous leader

THE FIRST AUSTRALIANS

Isn't it reasonable to say that if we can build a prosperous and remarkably harmonious multicultural society in Australia, surely we can find solutions to the problems that beset the First Australians—the people to whom the most injustice has been done.

Former prime minister PAUL KEATING
in his "Redfern speech"

The time has now come for the nation to turn a new page in Australia's history by righting the wrongs of the past and so moving forward with confidence to the future . . . a future where we harness the determination of all Australians, indigenous and non-indigenous, to close the gap that lies between us in life expectancy, educational achievement and economic opportunity.

Former prime minister KEVIN RUDD
in parliament's apology to indigenous peoples

The most noticeable change in Australia in the last decade and a half is the increasingly central place of the descendants of the indigenous people who occupied Australia before British settlement in 1788. Almost every public occasion in Australia now begins with a "Welcome to Country" by one of these descendants, or an "Acknowledgement of Country" in which a non-indigenous person acknowledges prior custodianship of the land upon which the event occurs. Indigenous place names for the 150 or so territories occupied by different indigenous peoples are prominently displayed, and their ancient histories and cultures are increasingly celebrated. The Aboriginal and Torres Strait Islander flags fly next to the Australian flag in government buildings and public spaces. The first pillar of Australian identity is more and more about the storytelling and artistic culture of those Australians, whose ancestors are thought to have been on the continent for at least 50,000 years.

Late in 2023, Australians voted on a proposed constitutional amendment which would have put the 3 per cent of Australians who identify as indigenous even more squarely at the centre. It sought firstly to formalise the recognition of indigenous people in the constitution (which has near universal support in Australia), but also proposed to add to the constitution a permanent "Indigenous Voice", which would be a body elected or appointed only by those who can claim some degree of indigenous descent, and which would advise parliament on any matter that could affect them. After a robust public debate about the powers and process proposed for the Voice, the proposed amendment was defeated by 60 per cent to 40 per cent, with people in the wealthy inner-city core and in many remote indigenous communities voting in favour, but most voters in suburban and rural areas against.

Indigenous people in Australia, as in many other countries, have suffered in the two-and-a-half centuries since Britain took possession of the continent. As well as violence in frontier areas, voting rights were not universal until the late 20th century. While Aboriginal men could vote in Victoria, New South Wales and South Australia (where Aboriginal women also voted after 1895, well before women of any race could vote in Europe), this right was restricted in Queensland and Western Australia. It wasn't until 1962 that the federal government legislated to also make voting universal in those states, and not until 1967 when it was made clear in the constitution that the federal government could overrule the states on indigenous issues and that indigenous Australians must all be counted in the national census.

The 1970s then saw mining royalties start to flow to indigenous communities, now worth billions of dollars a year. Then, in the 1980s, a number of Land Rights cases, notably the High Court's Mabo decision, granted some form of native title over around 36 per cent of Australia's land mass (often with associated cash payments). Indigenous land rights, in varying forms, now apply to about half of the country, and this is expected to rise to 60 to 70 per cent of the land mass as current claims are settled. Over $6 billion a year is spent on programmes focussed specifically on people of indigenous heritage.

Indigenous history is now integral to every school curriculum. The Welcome to Country has also brought the different indigenous peoples of particular parts of Australia into the everyday consciousness in a way they weren't before. When I came to Australia, the Art Gallery of New South Wales didn't think it was worth collecting indigenous art; this same art now dominates their annual prizes and corridors. Indigenous representation in federal parliament is now proportionate to the 3 per cent of Australians who identify as indigenous. The federal minister for indigenous Australians is herself indigenous, as were her two predecessors from both sides of politics.

And yet, despite these many advances, indigenous Australians still live, on average, about eight years shorter than other Australians (similar to the life expectancy gap for indigenous people in North America, but a greater gap than in Norway and Sweden). Low birthweight births are twice as common; indigenous children are less likely to attend preschool; fewer indigenous children have achieved the minimum standard for literacy and numeracy; the unemployment rate is almost three times that for non-indigenous people; and almost half of indigenous people aged 15 to 24 are neither in employment nor some form of education or training. The situation is worst in more remote communities, where a fifth of people have only completed school to Year 9 level, and less than 2 per cent have a university degree. Indigenous women are 32 times as likely to be hospitalised due to family violence as non-indigenous women.

These are damning statistics, and a blot on a country that has otherwise been so successful in providing such a high standard of living and quality of life to the average citizen. It is no consolation that the statistics for indigenous people in the US and Canada are similar.

There has been real progress in recent decades, but it does not mean that Australia has done enough; the gap of disadvantage is still too large. Many of the things that have made other Australians successful have not found their way into indigenous communities.

Recognition

While a constitutionally entrenched national Voice body was not supported in the 2023 referendum, some states have set them up, which will allow a test of whether they better inform government decisions and provide greater legitimacy in the eyes of indigenous communities that might otherwise see policy as externally imposed. There have already been problems with such bodies, but—if they are properly representative and appropriated oriented—they could potentially provide stronger support for difficult decisions around dealing with the alcohol, abuse, imprisonment and truancy that are harming indigenous communities.

There have also been arguments made for treaties that retrospectively address European settlement, but these attract less support, being seen as "looking backward rather than forward" and not taking account of the heterogeneity of indigenous Australians. Many are already living day-to-day in the same places and conditions as the broader Australian population, and most Australians who now identify as indigenous have mixed heritages of indigenous and non-indigenous ancestors. Even those who still live in traditional communities comprise hundreds of different groups with a spiritual connection to specific land languages and views about issues that affect them. The voice of indigenous Australians is not a monolithic one; it reflects an extension of ancient identities and particular cultures, languages and heritages.

Australia Day

The movement towards full reconciliation is an evolution. For example, it slowly became clearer that the Australian national anthem was historically incorrect, as well as insensitive, in making a reference to Australians being "young and free", a turn of phrase focussed only on post-colonial Australian history that didn't do justice to the long history of indigenous peoples across the land. The consequent change, in 2021, from "young and free" to "one and free" was pragmatic and appropriate, in the same way as the previous change from "Australia's sons" to "Australians all" when the gender-specific language started to grate. This is the adaptive and pragmatic reforming culture of Australians at work: preserving the rhythm and tradition of the national anthem while making it better embrace all Australians who sing it.

Another symbolic issue that's become controversial in recent years is the celebration of Australia Day. National days are, by their nature, arbitrary. They are about setting a narrative about "who we are". For Americans and the people of many other countries, it's the date of their blood-soaked independence. For the

French, it's the date the Bastille was stormed. Australia's current national day, 26th January, harkens back to 1788, when British settlement was proclaimed in Sydney. The British institutions and culture that took root in Australia at that time are a key foundation of Australia's identity and success, and the practice of having a blitz of citizenship ceremonies on Australia Day brings the immigrant experience into this celebration as well. But there is an obvious and insoluble problem with acknowledging and respecting indigenous culture and history while still celebrating the date on which some people's ancestors started to be dispossessed of land or worse. Arbitrarily designating that day as the national day has now become divisive, the exact opposite of what a national day is supposed to be.

The increasing disquiet over celebrating a date associated in many minds with the start of colonialism has led to several alternative dates being proposed, and to the current date becoming, uncomfortably, a day (for different people, or even for the same people at the same time) of both celebration and sombre reflection. With no one alternative date attracting majority appeal, and most of the population eager to celebrate the positive aspects of Australia during the height of summer (when barbecues, beach days and boats mark the occasion), it may be that Australia moves toward a typically pragmatic solution: to designate Australia Day as not being a specific date but simply the last Monday of January. Other holidays, such as Easter and Lunar New Year, are not on a fixed date, and Australians who are currently attached to 26th January and want to celebrate their country without equivocation are not going to object to their holiday moving a few days either way.

Closing the gap

Recognition and "truth telling" about history are important, but they are not sufficient to improve the lives of First Australians. The toughest issues are very practical and involve hard and granular work. A bipartisan "Closing the Gap" strategy, established in 2008 to address indigenous disadvantage, has had some success but hasn't worked quickly enough. In 2019, the Closing the Gap approach was overhauled to give indigenous people a much greater say (as the then minister for indigenous Australians, himself a descendant of the Noongar people, put it, "For too long, government has done things *to* indigenous Australians, as opposed to working *with* them.") and to include the states and territories. The initial failure to include the states was a glaring omission, given their primary role in health and education, both fundamental to indigenous well-being. However, it did also lead to much greater complexity, blowing out the clarity of the original seven targets into hundreds of "indicators" which will be harder to effectively monitor.

There has been some progress: the proportion of indigenous children staying in school until Year 12 went up from 45 per cent in 2008 to 66 per cent in 2019; indigenous university enrolments have more than doubled (albeit from a small base); and the rate of pre-school enrolment is close to catching up with non-indigenous children. Life expectancy has increased through anti-smoking initiatives (including reducing smoking during pregnancy, which is a major cause of birth problems), immunisation, better primary health care in remote areas and lower sugar products and restrictions in alcohol sales in remote community stores. However, during this same time, life expectancy and child mortality also improved among non-indigenous Australians, and so the gap remains. Efforts to improve school attendance, literacy and numeracy, and to increase indigenous employment, were mostly unsuccessful.

The current paradigm of addressing indigenous disadvantage has also been criticised for being overly centralised and for preserving a paternalistic and bureaucratic approach. Aboriginal communities are often not allowed the basic underpinnings of private land ownership, educational excellence and public safety that have allowed other parts of Australia to flourish. It can be said that key foundations of the Australian Way have not been available to the thousand or so remote towns in which many indigenous people live.

Traditional lands are typically owned in collectives, and the large cash contributions deriving from native title are held in community trusts which are controlled by traditional leaders. The inability of individual Aboriginal people to use this cash for starting new businesses (or, in many cases, to benefit from the types of microlending that fuelled growth in East Asia) extends even to the basics of home ownership. Most Aboriginal people do not own their own home in regional communities, and often live in poverty, dependent on centralised, community-controlled organisations for their housing, income and other needs. I have studied how giving individual property rights to people previously under communal ownership underpinned the economic development of China. Allowing 99-year leases of homes to individual indigenous Australians, or strata ownership in regional communities, would allow these Australians to enjoy the same sorts of opportunities and responsibilities that have made their compatriots so prosperous. There is increasingly a recognition that a collective and paternalistic approach has not been successful, and that individual people in these remote communities need to be given the agency to create businesses, make their own decisions and own their own family homes.

Indigenous Australians living remotely are also hurt by poor education, which traps people in cycles of disadvantage and makes it impossible to successfully transition into paid employment. This starts with school attendance; it has been estimated that more than half of indigenous children don't attend school for the minimum period (around 90 per cent of school hours) that's considered necessary to have an effective education. This feeds into a lack of literacy and numeracy and substantially lower completion of schooling. Not only do high rates of missing school lead to poor educational outcomes, they also statistically increase the risk of drug and alcohol use and going to prison. Several state and territory governments have shirked responsibility for improving education in indigenous communities—and thus shirked responsibility for breaking indigenous children out of disadvantage.

The lack of small businesses-forming in indigenous communities, and overall low levels of private employment and commercial activity, is partly a result of the lack of private capital and home ownership and insufficient focus on educational standards and outcomes. But these places are also held back by unsafe communities. The impact of crime not only crushes businesses, but clearly has an awful cost to the individuals in those communities, with disproportionately high rates of hospital admissions for assault, of young Aboriginal people in custody, and suicide.

Rates of disadvantage remain stark, and progress should be faster. But there are now stronger challenges being mounted to the flawed approaches of the past, and a much greater determination within Australian society to address the complex issues that need to be solved. The Great Australian Silence that Brian Stanner referred to in 1968 is no longer; there is now as much research into this part of Australian history as any other part, and a vigorous debate about how the positive and negative aspects of the Australian story are both done justice in the telling.

The first colonial governors sought to treat indigenous people and British subjects equally, but the vile actions of settlers in many parts of frontier Australia betrayed these ideals, as they did in so many colonial societies. The coming of the tall ships in 1788 began a process of dispossession and disruption that has led to much pain and many social problems for indigenous people. Yet the institutions of that settlement—law courts, property rights, liberal democracy and education among them—have worked in broader Australia and could enable indigenous children in the 21st century to have all the same opportunities and freedoms as every other Australian. For hundreds of years, these elements of the Australian Way were denied to remote indigenous communities, with Christian missions and bureaucratic overreach (and even the removal of many Aboriginal children from their families) giving way to paternalistic policies and welfare dependency under the purview of mostly white government officials. There is, fortunately, finally a focus on giving indigenous people their own agency and on practical steps that empower small business and safe and educated communities, which has the potential over time to redress this stain on Australia's history.

BORN BY BALLOT
NOT BATTLEFIELD

There has been strong, continuous, benevolent government in Australia but no ruling class. When the [British] governors ruled, the rich landowners and squatters thought they would take over when self-government was granted. But when that happened, they were quickly defeated, and democratic politics began.

Government [in Australia] is without social character; it is an impersonal force. That makes it possible for egalitarian Australians to give it the great respect which its record deserves. Australians are suspicious of persons in authority but towards impersonal authority they are very obedient.

JOHN HIRST, *The Distinctiveness of Australian Democracy*

On a hot November night in 1854, more than 10,000 miners in Ballarat resolved at a public meeting that "it is the inalienable right of every citizen to have a voice in the laws he is called upon to obey [and] that taxation without representation is tyranny." It was the same demand on the British governor that had been heard in America

70 years earlier. The expensive 30-shilling-a-month mining licence was resented by well-educated gold rush immigrants imbued with the ideas of the English Chartists, as well as of the French and American revolutions, and who were not allowed to vote or own land in the colony of Victoria. The stand-off between miners and government soldiers culminated in the bloody battle at the Eureka stockade where at least 30 miners are thought to have been killed.

The demands may have echoed those of the Boston Tea Party, but the British response and consequences were very different. Thousands of people marched in Melbourne in support of the miners, and those miners put on trial for sedition were acquitted by juries. A royal commission castigated the administration of the goldfields and recommended a general amnesty and voting changes that effectively universalised the right to vote for Victorian men. The leader of the rebellion went on not to jail but to become speaker of the parliament. Victoria's legislative council became arguably the most democratic legislature in the world at that time.

There is still disagreement about how much the rebellion itself accelerated change, as elections had already been held for the legislative councils in each colony and the push for greater democratic representation was already underway. The elections before Eureka were only open to those with property and educational qualifications, like British elections of the time, but the momentum in Australia for greater self-government and a further widening of the franchise was strong.

However, the very fact that Eureka still looms large in Australia's history shows how otherwise remarkably free of violence the steady path to Australian democracy and independence was. Australia's national anthem has no "bombs bursting in the air" (US) nor exhortations that "impure blood water our fields" (France) nor that "millions of hearts with one mind brave the enemy gunfire, march on!" (China). Instead, Australia's anthem asks rather simply that Australians "rejoice" at the beauty and natural resources of the country and at the opportunity and freedom it offers. One of the most resonant songs about the Australian experience is the Peter Allen song adopted by the airline Qantas that "no matter how far or how wide I roam, I still call Australia home"—a form of patriotism that embraces global travel at the same time as it lauds the comfort of the home country.

Like other British colonies, Australians had to struggle for their independence. It was Australia's good fortune that the American War of Independence was fought between Captain Cook sailing into Botany Bay in 1770 and Governor Phillip returning to establish a colony at Sydney Cove in 1788. By the time the Australian colonies were sufficiently developed to demand self-government (and no taxation without representation), there was no need for armed insurrection nor the throwing of tea into Sydney Harbour. Seventy years after losing the American colonies, the British parliament and public had learned a lesson and were willing to grant a peaceful transition to self-government and independence within the British empire.

Australia was therefore "born at the ballot box not on the battlefield"—and through the efforts of people who represented the liberal zeitgeist of 19th-century Britain. Australia's founding narrative of nationhood is of colonies merging into a federation by Act of British parliament after a decade of consensus-building. There was no "people taking up arms" to define Australian independence. The great fortune of timing was also that Australia emerged over the same 100-year period that saw the emergence of universal education and the push for equality of opportunity. Democracy came in Australia through the persistent lobbying of British parliamentarians and civil servants, the advocacy of a free press and through gathering liberal coalitions of supporters. Since then, British influence on Australian institutions has faded slowly away until the

Australian system became almost entirely distinct: by evolution rather than revolution.

A unique democracy

In the first few decades of the 20th century, Australia added several improvements to the British system of parliamentary democracy, which arguably explain the greater stability and success of the Australian system. None of them are unique, but the combination of all four features *is* unique among modern democracies.

I. Federation

The first difference from Britain is that Australia is a federation, modelled in this respect on the US model. The six states that came together received representation via an elected senate, with equal representation from each state, in place of the unelected House of Lords and confused relationship that still exists between the UK national government and the partially devolved territories of Scotland, Wales and Northern Ireland.

While sometimes a source of frustration for the national government, the Senate has provided the intended reassurance for smaller states that their interests won't be overlooked, and it has driven substantial financial transfers between states that have not always been edifying but have maintained more equality across the nation than would occur otherwise.

The proportional representation model of voting in the federal Senate has also been a shock absorber, allowing those who feel unhappy with the major parties to put alternative voices into parliament. As always, a balance needs to be struck between representation for significant minority views and handing over the balance of power to marginal candidates—the relatively low threshold for election to the Senate in smaller states has elevated some unusual characters. But when minority parties genuinely represent a material constituency, it is a feature rather than a bug for governments to have to deal with checks and balances and to build coalitions and alliances to pass legislation.

When the federal government failed to return income-taxing powers to the states after centralising them during the Second World War, it shifted the balance of power towards Canberra. Covid showed up the limitations of this, as states continue to provide most services (including health, education and policing, and even created internal borders within the country). A "National Cabinet" formed by the prime minister and state premiers tried, with varying degrees of success, to coordinate policies, but different states still took different approaches.

In part, this was understandable. Western Australia has very little services trade with other Australian states or people overseas; its people live off the mining products that are shipped out in boxes. By contrast, Sydney is prosperous because of services provided by its people to others in the state, interstate, and overseas, and most Sydney people have close family offshore. Leaders of those states would naturally come to different judgements about the complex balancing that's required in a pandemic.

Covid also led some states to impose lockdowns, curfews and other measures that were not proportionate to the risks or supported by medical evidence. The official inquiry later noted the "lack of compassion and too few exceptions based on needs and circumstances".

In normal circumstances, though, the combination of state power and what economists call "vertical fiscal imbalance'" (the federal government collects most of the revenue and the states do most of the spending) provides a way to spread money across the nation and leads to a more levelled-up country than either the US or UK systems.

2. Compulsory voting

The second and crucial Australian improvement to the inherited system was compulsory voting. Australia is one of only nine countries among 166 electoral democracies that enforces compulsory voting. Australians are appalled that their major security and trading partners elect their leaders with small turnouts and shrunken rolls so that they govern with support from only a minority of the country. There has been a bipartisan view in Australia that democracy needs to measure the views of the whole country and that democracy gains legitimacy when it does so demonstrably.

Compulsory voting also has very practical benefits. It reinforces the natural moderation of Australians by forcing the political parties to appeal to the centre—and means that elections in Australia tend to be closer than in most other democracies, while still delivering definite outcomes. Elections in Australia are won not by "bringing out the base", but by those who can win over the most citizens. Money paid to American consultants seeking to turn Australian elections into US-style campaigns, to rev up an angry minority, is wasted, and governing away from the centre is quickly punished at the ballot box.

The merits of compulsory voting have recently been debated in the UK, with reservations expressed that it is somehow "undemocratic" to "force" people to vote. But there are already many things that people are expected to do as part of being a citizen, from jury duty to paying taxes to ensuring that your kids attend school, so it would be strange if the most fundamental task of choosing your government were considered a bridge too far.

It should also be noted that the requirement in Australia is to turn up at the polling booth—there is no obligation to cast a vote for someone if the candidates are all unappealing. In practice, though, the act of coming to vote causes people to pay more attention to the contest; the number of spoiled ballots is very small, as it turns out that almost everyone does want to make a choice once they are in the voting booth.

3. Preference voting

The third distinction of Australia's electoral system is the use of preferential voting (what is called "ranked preference voting" in the US and the "alternative vote" in the UK). This allows voters, in a contest involving more than two candidates, to number not only their preferred candidate but also their second, third and other choices. (In some senate elections there has been the option to number more than a hundred preferences for those who care to do so.) The candidates with the lowest number of votes have their "preferences" distributed to the remaining candidates until all but the top two have been eliminated.

The main advantage of preferential voting is to avoid electing candidates loved by only a small part of the population—and loathed by most. In a first-past-the-post system, such as the UK's, someone who gets only 20 to 25 per cent of the votes cast can still win if there are multiple candidates and no one clear competitor. This bias towards extremist candidates is amplified even further in the US through primaries that allow candidates with low support to edge out people in their own party in a narrow and unrepresentative vote, and then be the only candidate from that party that is presented to the wider electorate.

To win a preferential voting election, you need to not only get a large proportion of first preferences, you also need to be acceptable to more than half of the electorate (either as their favourite or as a second- or third-best of the rest). This helps to keep out extremists and to pull elections back towards the middle. Angry voters can express a protest by voting according to a "single issue", but at the same time indicate their preference among the mainstream candidates who will survive the ongoing redistribution of votes. This lends legitimacy to elections as well as moderation to outcomes.

4. Electoral process

Australian elections are run at arm's length by a well-respected and properly funded independent election authority, according to uniform rules across the nation. The Australian Electoral Commission remains a global benchmark for independent management of the electoral process and is often called on for assistance in countries with much less experience of running elections. Electoral boundaries are drawn up on the basis of population and geography without partisan interference. All voting uses paper ballots, and these can be—and are—recounted multiple times in the presence of scrutineers from all parties to ensure that results are not only legitimate but seen to be legitimate. Australia is also one of the only countries in the world to vote on a weekend—while most other English-speaking countries vote on weekdays, meaning that many are unable to get to the booths because of work or study commitments. In Australia, you can vote at any booth in your state, or interstate, or overseas in consulates, or by post, all ahead of time.

And we should not forget that some other innovations of Australian elections have by now been so widely adopted that they no longer make Australia unique: for instance, secret ballots (once known as "the Australian ballot") and allowing women to both vote and stand for parliament (Australia was almost two decades ahead of the UK, and the female voting franchise only came to Switzerland in 1971, nearly 80 years after South Australia).

Compulsory and preferential voting help to both express and reinforce another characteristic of Australian democracy: the belief that voting should be the best possible expression of the will of the whole people. A compulsory, preferential vote means that anyone elected in Australia has been clearly identified by more than half the voters as their number one choice (usually), or at least as the least-worst person to represent them. This has become particularly important in the current age, when the legitimacy of election results is under challenge from rising social media and offshore misinformation.

Australia's system was not designed, like the US system a century earlier, to protect local rights against the monarchy, but to advance the utilitarian cause of the greatest good for the greatest number. The Australian constitution is a procedural one, full of the practicalities of how a nation of many different people and dreams can live and make decisions together. It is not full of rhetoric nor does it involve a "bill of rights" for law courts to interpret over the head of parliament, but instead it lays out the mechanics for a democratically accountable government to get things done. There is a deep adherence to the idea that the view of the majority should be respected (in sporting terms, the umpire's decision is final). The way in which Australians contested both the republic and Indigenous Voice referenda is telling: they were hard-fought battles, but the results were instantly accepted, and the issues largely disappeared from the headlines once the majority had ruled, in stark contrast to the continuing litigation of the Brexit referendum in the UK or recent electoral contests in the US.

Australians mostly see the state as a shared vehicle to promote individual well-being; it is not inherently good or bad, but merely a tool. Government can sometimes get good things done for the Australian people, but it must be constantly watched through a sceptical prism lest it stray. Any individual putting their hand up for election must also be viewed sceptically. The electoral system should be designed to best poll all the people and ensure the state doesn't stray too far from what the people want. This is not the case even in those countries which Australians might consider democratic peers. Electoral boundaries in the US are distorted and partisan, registration to vote there is contested, and the electoral college system has put two of the past five presidents into office with a minority of the national vote. The first-past-the-post voting system in the UK encourages messy "tactical voting" and means the make-up of parliament often diverges radically from the proportion of people who support particular parties, while the House of Lords remains a hodgepodge of inherited and partisan appointments.

Australia was not simply "lucky" to inherit a western system of democracy—its people also substantially and proactively improved it.

Current challenges

Australia is now one of the world's oldest democracies, one of less than a dozen countries in the world that have consistently been liberal democracies since 1901, the year when Australia came into being as a single country. There are now more than a hundred countries that elect their government, compared to 11 at the time of federation. There was a surge in the number of democracies after the First World War, which then retreated with rising nationalism and America's withdrawal from the world in the 1930s and 1940s, then another surge after 1945, and an even bigger one after 1989 when the Soviet Union disintegrated—to the point that more than half of the world's population outside China was living in a democracy, before flattening off in the last decade. South Korea and Taiwan made durable transitions in the middle of that extended period, and Indonesia became democratic in the late 1990s. It is worth remembering, as countries struggle to develop a culture of liberal democracy, that it is a much newer concept for almost all the rest of the world.

"The so-called liberal idea . . . has outlived its purpose," said Vladimir Putin in 2019. It was a typically mischievous gloat, and an ironic counterpoint to the premature declaration of the end of history by Francis Fukuyama after the end of the Cold War. It was also equally wrong. The Australian experience, among other countries, shows clearly that liberalism may not have extinguished all other philosophies from the world, but it remains the most successful in making people richer and happier. It is no coincidence (not that Putin would acknowledge it) that the Eastern European countries that left the Soviet Union have grown at two to three times the rate of Russia in the two decades since, or that Ukrainians look west, not east, for a better life.

Simply being the most successful way to organise a society is not enough to ensure that liberalism will always and everywhere prevail; there have been plenty of setbacks in recent years. But for every country that becomes less of a liberal democracy there are others that are becoming more open to markets, the rule of law and the popular will. Authoritarian states can survive for a long period, but the inevitable alternative to the peaceful and legitimate transfer of power is violence. Democracies deliver better individual healthcare and are less likely to execute people, regulate religion or censor the press. Wars between two real democracies are almost unknown; in fact, there's a case to be made that only an open democracy can allow progressive reform and leadership change to take place without there being bloodshed at some point. There is a very strong correlation between the strength of liberal democracy (measured through indices of both economic freedom and voice and accountability in government) and economic well-being—with Australia (among the top ranked in both) being one of many good examples.

What underpins liberal democracies is a belief that individual humans are capable of making their own decisions, and that institutions of government need to protect this individual agency rather than operate society from the top down. Individualism is a crucial value in Australia, as the second chapter discussed, so people instinctively embrace the institutions that allow its expression—independent courts, free markets and an open media. It is not a utopian idea; individual liberty also requires structural checks and balances to make sure that someone exercising their own individual freedom doesn't steal it from others, as well as to preserve a sense of public well-being and toleration.

Australia was one of the first places in the world to experiment with a universal franchise, something that even the great Enlightenment thinkers considered too risky. Educated elites have been sceptical of democracy since Aristotle, thinking it inherently unstable. And yet democracy works, not because the day-to-day opinions of the majority are always right, but because democracy allows mistakes to be corrected, and, over the longer term, the informed and considered judgement of people about their own best interests is sound. The ability to quickly "course-correct" is democracy's greatest strength. Hearing the individual reasons why people vote the way they do may often be dispiriting, yet the wisdom of crowds somehow mandates a government that best represents the collective view as to who can do the best job of looking after the broader interest at that time.

It is a sign of how far democracy has come that few now admit openly to being opposed to the principle. Leaders will hold elections, even when heavily rigged, to provide the pretence of "democracy"—and even North Korea calls itself the "Democratic People's Republic of Korea". Still, even in places where elections are fair, there are competing visions of democracy: the direct one driven by a single elected leader who assumes a mandate to speak for "the people", or the representative constitutional one in which the leader operates in a system of checks and balances provided by the legislature, the courts and a free press. The direct version is populist; it's exciting and promises action and cut-through. The representative version is greyer, pragmatic and consumed with detail.

But the representative version is also more robust. We've seen that countries can move from democracy to authoritarianism not only by military intervention (as was mostly the case during the Cold War), but increasingly through a slow process of subversion of the balancing powers of liberal democracy—courts, independent media and non-government entities—to break down key norms that, together with the separation of powers set out in a constitution, preserve checks and balances. These norms include the mutual toleration of rival parties as legitimate, even when you disagree, and the concept of forbearance (that the ruling party doesn't use its period of control to entrench a partisan advantage in the system itself).

The evidence suggests it is the representative-constitutional type of democracy that works best, particularly in the medium to longer term. On this score, Australia has real advantages compared to most other developed countries. A two-chamber parliamentary system avoids setting up the slippery-slope dynamic by which a president with authoritarian ambitions can use their personal mandate to progressively undermine all sources of power or oversight. It helps that the prime minister is not also the head of state, so there is no blurring of the "nation" with the person who happens to exercise political power at that moment. And, in general, parliamentary systems have proven to be more stable than their presidential equivalents. Australia's electoral machinery and courts are also among the most independent from government globally, so the type of partisan voter suppression and gerrymandering that occurs in parts of America and other countries is not possible under the Australian system.

Australia has a federation, two elected houses of parliament that represent diverse geographic viewpoints, a very robust press and a depoliticised, independent legal system. When working properly, the party system balances out the idiosyncrasies of 227 members of parliament in Canberra (more than a thousand around the nation) representing people with very different views of what Australia should be. There is a high bar for constitutional change, alongside compulsory voting and a culture of challenging leaders rather than deferring to them.

Australia's governance arrangements are by no means perfect. Nevertheless, a mix of luck and good judgement has given modern Australians one of the least-worst ways of governing a country that has been seen in any place or any time in history.

BOUNDLESS PLAINS TO SHARE

> *In Australia, there is no hierarchy of descents. There must be no privilege of origin ... the commitment to Australia is the one thing needful to be a true Australian.*
>
> BOB HAWKE, former prime minister

About 20 people gathered at the Hornsby Council building on 22 July 1982 to take the oath of allegiance to become citizens of Australia. For my parents, my brother, my sister and me it was the last stage of a journey of becoming Australian that began when my family left the diamond mining town of Oranjemund in Namibia, first for the Endeavour Migrant Hostel in Coogee as newly arrived immigrants in 1977 and then to Mount Isa in outback Queensland for five years before we returned to live in Sydney.

Once a month, and sometimes twice, every council area in Australia conducts these ceremonies. The first Australian citizenship ceremony in 1949 symbolically naturalised seven non-British European immigrants from each of the states and the Australian Capital Territory. By 2019, the top five nations from which immigrants became citizens were India, the UK, the Philippines, China and Pakistan. When I became a citizen in 1982, we still sang *God Save the Queen* and pledged our allegiance to Queen Elizabeth II, but new citizens now sing *Advance Australia Fair* and pledge their "loyalty to Australia and its people whose democratic beliefs I share, whose rights and liberties I respect and whose laws I will uphold and obey."

Lamingtons—the famous chocolatey sponge cakes—continue to be served at more than half of Australian citizenship ceremonies, as they were at mine, and these days the indigenous history of Australia is almost always acknowledged and recognised too.

My own Australian journey started at the Endeavour Migrant Hostel in Coogee. Before my family landed there in 1977, it had been mostly a waystation for "Ten Pound Poms"—that is, post-war British migrants—and for waves of southern European immigration. By then, however, there were also South Americans, as well as the Vietnamese escapees who were starting to come through after the fall of Saigon, a trend that accelerated in the years after we moved out. We were thousands of people following in the footsteps of another *Endeavour* that landed not too far away, at Botany Bay, and in the far earlier footsteps of the Gadigal people, who came to this part of Sydney well before Great Britain existed as a country. The few months that people stayed at the hostel were used to learn English (or, in my case, "Straylian"), integrate into schools and, with my brother and sister, to ride skateboards down the long driveway and chase Christmas beetles from the water fountains, soaking up the sun and the very particular light that defines Australia.

Being an immigrant is much more common in Australia than the rest of the developed world. One in four Australians is a first-generation migrant like me, and almost half of the people in Australia have at least one parent who was born outside the country. But the pace of immigration is far from a flood. In a typical year, less than one immigrant comes to Australia each year for every hundred people already in Australia. About half of these people come under a points system that rewards key skills needed in

Australia, English language proficiency and other criteria. Most of the rest come under family programmes, and there is also a small refugee intake. Australia has been a strong immigration nation for all its modern history. This has not only been an essential underpinning of economic growth and prosperity, it has also been crucial in making Australia a stimulating and interesting place to be.

The strong rates of immigration that Australia has enjoyed are also one of the reasons it has become a more important player on the international stage. In the 1950s, the population of the UK was five times that of Australia, but the much higher rate of growth means that Australia is now approaching half the population size of the UK. Australia has similarly gone from one-seventh the size of Germany to a third.

An island nation with no land neighbour and great distance to major population centres will tend to develop an insular and parochial culture. To the extent that Australia has avoided this, it is because of three things: immigration, overseas students and the propensity of Australians to travel overseas. At any one time, one in 20 Australians is living overseas. These million-plus expatriate Australians are scattered from New York to London to Hong Kong and Singapore. It is no longer necessary to leave Australia forever to prove yourself on the world stage, so the things expat Australians pick up are now absorbed back into domestic culture much more quickly. International travel has also become quicker and easier: the number of international trips taken by Australians in 2018 was six times greater than in 1980. The social, economic, artistic, technological and cultural benefits of this travel for Australia can't be overestimated.

Permanent immigration, though, remains the strongest way that the best of world culture and experience—from food and coffee to fashion and technology—gets transmitted into Australia. By the time transportation of convicts finally ceased, 157,000 people had been brought to the country. Compared to the 715,000 free settlers who immigrated during the gold rush and the 200,000 before that, the impact of convict history should not be overstated. Of course, the children of emancipated convicts swelled the population, but this was dwarfed by the number of new free immigrants arriving between 1851 and 1914. Between 1945 and 1965 there were more than two million immigrants, and it is estimated that about 60 per cent of the increase in population in the second half of the 20th century came from immigration. People have come from every country in the world; Australia is often tagged as the world's most successful multicultural nation.

Lowy Institute polling shows that half of Australians believe (correctly) that immigration is positive for the economy, and that the level of immigration is "about right". The most recent Scanlan Survey of Social Cohesion in Australia found that 94 per cent of Australians thought someone born outside Australia "is just as likely to be a good citizen than someone born here," 88 per cent said "multiculturalism has been good for Australia," 86 per cent agreed or strongly agreed that "immigrants are good for the Australian economy," and about 80 per cent thought that "accepting migrants from a broad range of countries makes Australia stronger". This reflects the real lived experience of modern Australia, as a similar proportion reported that they had people in their "close circle of friends from a different national, ethnic or religious background".

These are remarkable statistics in a world where suspicion of outsiders is rife (only Canadians are as likely as Australians to see immigrants as "making our country stronger because of their work and talents"). And while there is still a significant minority who see migrants as "taking jobs" or crowding cities, the majority understand, explicitly or implicitly, the evidence of the many studies showing that immigration, particularly skilled immigration, increases innovation and business formation and helps a country to export more; it also creates a younger, more productive population. Even 60 years ago, Horne was noting that overseas-born people were twice as well represented in the *Who's Who* of the 1960s than the native-born and made up two-thirds of the researchers at the Commonwealth Scientific and Industrial Research Organisation (CSIRO). It remains true that there are a very disproportionate number of immigrants among Australian doctors, nurses, company founders and researchers. More than 60 per cent of Australian engineers were born overseas; the country would have no chance of building infrastructure or making things without bringing in this talent.

This is, of course, not just true for Australia. A few years ago, I was on an Australian business mission to Israel to evaluate how that country had created such a successful tech industry. The thing that stood out most clearly was the influx of talent from the old Soviet Union that kickstarted the "start-up nation". Similarly, half of the 100 fastest-growing companies in the UK have an immigrant founder (including nine of the 14 "unicorn" start-ups worth more than a billion dollars), and so do half the companies in Silicon Valley, from the founders of Google and Tesla down. Similarly, nothing has contributed more to Australia's economy than the "brain gain" from (both short- and long-term) movement of people born overseas.

Yet despite the overwhelming benefits, immigration remains a sensitive issue politically and has recently come back into the headlines. The reasons are the same as those in other parts of the world. Firstly, that Australia, like many countries, has failed to build enough houses to match the increased population. Secondly, the rise in illegal immigration and increasing refugee claims by people immigrating for economic reasons. People living different lives in different parts of the globe also used to be largely unaware of how others live, but international plane trips went from a luxury of the top one per cent to being commonplace in every continent. Social media and Google connect almost everyone in the globe to others far away in a way that was unimaginable even a decade ago. People living under authoritarian governments, in war-torn countries or in poverty, can now see the affluent, free lives of those who live in Australia and countries like it. It is not surprising that so many refugees and migrants try to find their way to places like western Europe and Australia, and increasingly they will not wait for the door to be opened before they escape badly run and poor countries to find new lives in developed democracies.

The immigration debate

The Israeli historian Yuval Noah Harari has written that debates around immigration encompass three different questions. Will we allow immigrants in? What are the immigrants' obligations to adopt the core values and norms of the host country? Do the immigrants, or at least their children, eventually become full and equal members of the host country? The debate around each of these questions can easily become polarised—with one camp appalled that anyone with opposing views could be so heartless, while the other camp can't believe that anyone would be so naïve.

It is notable that almost all Australians accept that immigrants who have legally come to Australia and adopted the country's values should then be regarded as fully equal. This is not the case in many countries. In much of Asia, Africa, the Middle East and even Europe, you can be a second- or even third-generation immigrant doing all the "right things" and still not be "one of us", either because the notion of national identity is based on race or because there is a two-tier notion of belonging to the country (as is the case even in Europe and the US for undocumented "dreamers" and others). It speaks to Australia's successful experience with immigration, as well as its egalitarian values, that only a very small fringe would suggest that, once assimilated, migrants aren't as Australian as anyone else.

Australian debates therefore take place around the first two parts of the immigration bargain: who gets to come, and what are their obligations when they get here? Some say that allowing immigrants in is a duty, rather than a favour, and there's a moral requirement for those fortunate enough to be born in Australia to give all other less fortunate humans an opportunity at a decent life. The more widely held view is that a nation can't grow faster that the infrastructure and housing to support it and must be, at least to some extent, a cohesive group of people with shared values and mutual rights and obligations. Letting other people into the tribe to share the benefits of belonging is something for which people should be grateful, and it should not be simply expected. The people of a host country have an absolute right to choose who comes on any basis that they decide, usually based on the contribution the newcomer will make.

There are people in Australia who hold strongly to one or other of these positions, but policies have been, as often in Australia, a balance. Believing neither extreme ("we have to let everyone in" and "we can't let in people unless they're like us") has proven to be wise. Australian immigration policies mostly allow entry to immigrants carefully selected for the contribution they can bring the country, but also include a proportion of refugees on humanitarian grounds (provided they enter the country legally).

The third leg of the debate is what sort of obligations immigrants have to their new country. If they are coming to Australia, should they already speak, or at least try hard to learn, English, which is the common language that allows everyone to communicate and understand each other? Do they need to adopt Australian values—religious tolerance, feminism, egalitarianism—that may not be the values of their old country? Should they actively try to make friends outside of the community of other people from the same country of origin?

These are important issues to discuss. Australians already have a wide spectrum of values, opinions and ways of doing things, and continuing to build on this diversity makes for a more interesting and fun place. On the other hand, some values are sufficiently fundamental that it isn't possible to have a coherent community and maintain liberal democracy if a more-than-material portion of the population doesn't share them. The vast bulk of Australian immigrants have enthusiastically adopted these core values, although a small minority have not adjusted to the peaceful disagreement and legal processes that underpin Australian society. There is a strong argument for some degree of civic education to be reintroduced as part of the immigration programme, of the sort that existed when I first landed at the Endeavour Hostel. This would not only make migrants more likely to succeed, it would also reassure other people that the process is being "managed" for successful integration.

Cohesion in a multicultural society

With more than half the population having at least one parent born overseas, and with the extremely diverse range of countries of origin, you might expect social segregation or tension, as occurs in so many other countries with mixed cultures. But not in Australia. Migrant communities in Australia do not cluster into particular suburbs as much as they do in other countries, and are more likely to be skilled, have higher paid jobs than average, and to contribute more than they take from the fiscal position. They are less likely to be in prison, and their education results tend to be better than average.

One reason multiculturalism has worked better in Australia than other countries may be the easy-going culture and lifestyle, though there have also been conscious efforts to promote the positive aspects of multiculturalism (particularly in food and the arts) alongside a dedicated public broadcaster, the Special Broadcasting Service (SBS), that showcases international news, movies and television in multiple languages. There is another important factor which other countries are increasingly trying to emulate: Australian public policy has been relatively good at demonstrating to people that their government is "in control" of migration. We have seen in many parts of the world that the strongest backlash against migrants occurs where the average person decides that the government has "lost control" of the borders.

One element of this is that, more than half a century ago, Australia developed a "points-based" formula to select migrants (tweaking it regularly as particular skills and attributes become more desired). As a result, Australia predominantly receives migrants who are well-qualified, English-speaking and capable of positively contributing to the country. The only other country with a comparable focus on migrant selection is Canada, which has also enjoyed relatively harmonious multicultural relationships. By contrast, immigration to the UK and France has traditionally been via automatic-residency grants to particular geographies (notably their former colonies and then EU member states), with far less attempt, until quite recently, to select for skills or eagerness and capability to integrate. Integration in many parts of the UK and France has therefore been much slower, and community tensions have sometimes spilled over into violence. The reliance of countries like Germany and the US on low-skill "guest workers" without a clear path to permanency and integration has also created a different outcome to Australia's approach of emphasising skills, language proficiency and rapidly becoming "local".

While support for immigration remains high, Australians also have a sense of a "paradise found" that is a long way from the troubles of the world, and they want to put bolts on the door and require that the next wave of migrants be allowed in only selectively and slowly. Australians also hold, given their relative isolation and unusually peaceful history, that nobody should bring the troubles of their old country with them. There is no sympathy for argument, let alone violence, between ethnic groups who were at odds in their country of origin. Compared to other places that I have worked, there's a surprising lack of curiosity among most Australians towards the very interesting backgrounds of immigrants and their rich cultures. But the flipside of this lack of interest is an acceptance that those who have legally migrated to Australia are all now Australians. It looks forward to what will happen in this new "other end of the earth", rather than looking back at the enmities and injustices done in the "old world". Nations and peoples everywhere are happier when forward-looking; the outlook is grim for any country when the past casts too strong a shadow over the present.

A more controversial aspect of Australia's strong selectivity in the intake of migrants is that Australia has been particularly draconian in the ways it has stopped illegal migration, especially via boats. There was a spike in boat arrivals 25 years ago—although still small numbers compared to in Europe—and a debate raged about how to "stop the boats". Over a decade, a bipartisan consensus formed around harsh deterrent measures, including "offshore processing" of claims for asylum in Nauru and Papua New Guinea, and at times even the "turn back" of boats. These measures were controversial, and still attract opposition, but they did succeed in stopping illegal migration by boat. There has also been an upgrade of coastal surveillance and engagement with countries such as Indonesia to stop people smuggling from the north, and, at times, Temporary Protection Visas for asylum seekers that, until their claims have been assessed, provide a lower level of benefits than enjoyed by other Australians. Strict border controls now attract bipartisan support in

Australia, and whenever they have been weakened, and boat arrivals have ticked up again, the public reaction has forced a retightening. It can be argued that the comfort among Australian voters that illegal entry to the country is being "controlled" has allowed them to support a higher level of legal immigration (including one of the highest intakes of refugees through UN and other legal channels).

The draconian approach taken in Australia has been criticised by UN bodies but is seen by most Australians as a necessary evil to avoid the large numbers of illegal arrivals that have been seen in places such as the US and Italy and caused a wider societal and political backlash there. What's more, from the European Union to the Americas, variations of Australia's methods are now being implemented, or at least discussed, as leaders realise that they must prove to their people that they can control the flow of people—or else those governments will be replaced by far-right parties that promise to solve it.

Somewheres and Anywheres

The British author David Goodhart argues that modern societies have become polarised between what he calls the Anywheres (university-educated and geographically mobile people who think much like their foreign peers) and the Somewheres (people who live and die in a particular place and identify strongly with their local area). The identity of Anywheres is self-made, and often defined by groups of friends they meet at work or university (who are quite different to the community in which they grew up), while Somewheres derive their sense of identity from their local sports team and the particular region and towns in which they've grown up. Somewheres treasure the cohesiveness of a local community that the Anywheres are sometimes pleased to escape. It is easy to see how Anywheres and Somewheres will take a different view of immigrants—a welcome stimulation for cosmopolitan Anywheres, a threat to Somewheres who feel the primacy of their traditions and ways of life being challenged.

Fortunately for Australia, the separation of Anywheres and Somewheres is not as great as in some other countries. Around 40 per cent of Americans have never left the place in which they were born, and most British people outside London still identify very strongly with particular towns, regions and accents. By contrast, around 15 per cent of Australians change their address in a year (almost twice the global average), and a much larger proportion live in big cities where you can't help but meet a broad range of people. The Anywheres in Australia are also not as far-removed— relatively few people go to university outside their home city, and moving interstate for work reasons (and indeed incomes) is not nearly as skewed towards tertiary-educated people in Australia as elsewhere. Australians of all incomes are relatively mobile within Australia: about half of the population will move house in a five-year period, the highest proportion in the OECD and many times the mobility you see in countries such as Italy. When Australians move away, they tend to go overseas, and enough of them do so in their twenties and thirties that the gap between the over-travelled and the non-travellers is not nearly as wide as in the countries on which Goodhart focussed.

Australia steers a middle ground between the old notion of assimilation, which fell out of favour in the 1970s, and untrammelled multiculturalism, which can become divisive. A successful and vibrant country needs to be both diverse and coherent; a society that adapts and grows, but also one that doesn't splinter. A tolerant and free society can manage small illiberal minorities, but only up to a point.

The cosmopolitan members of society (the Anywheres) need to appreciate that globalism and immigration have limits imposed by the willingness of people to accept changes in their culture; the paradox being that maintaining an open society can sometimes entail managing the pace and way in which immigrants come in. But the Somewheres also need to appreciate that immigrants are vital not only to economic prosperity but also to the innovation and freshness that are part of the Australian character.

Making it work today

One of the impacts of Covid border closures was that immigration to Australia went to zero for a couple of years, though the initial impact was cushioned by the return of almost twice as many expatriates as the immigrants that didn't come. The return of Australian expats was a one-off, so the negative shock was postponed rather than avoided. By 2021, businesses were closing or postponing expansion because of an inability to get people into the business who had skills—whether software engineering, AI, or infrastructure and housebuilding related—that couldn't be found in Australia. When the Australian borders reopened, there was a boom in immigration, which has almost made up for the couple of lost years, but the size of the turnaround started to cause its own discomfort. When annual net arrivals exceeded a half a million people (and a lower proportion of them skilled migrants), draconian measures were introduced to reduce the numbers rapidly.

The cost of building, planning and environmental approvals, which haven't allowed for sufficient housing and infrastructure to be built, has capped the willingness of Australia to accept the number of people who could otherwise make a contribution. But reducing numbers should not be overdone or reckless.

If Australia had annual immigration of 270,000 a year, it would only be adding one person from elsewhere to every hundred people that are already here. It is reasonable that Australians want that person to come legally and to be the best suited to contribute to Australia from among the very many applying to come. Australians will also ask that she or he embraces fundamental Australian values and throws off the quarrels of the country from which they have come. But Australia would not work if it were to substantially slow the number of people coming in from all over the world. Immigrants make the nation richer, more dynamic and more interesting. Immigration itself is part of the Australian soul.

PART III
AUSTRALIAN QUALITIES

HEALTHY

Australia offers a potential model for lower-performing anglophone countries, such as the USA and UK, to follow to reduce both premature mortality and inequalities in life expectancy.

British Medical Journal, August 2024

Australian healthcare underpins an average life expectancy that is two years higher than in the UK and five years higher than the US, and it costs less than 10 per cent of GDP, compared to the 17 per cent of GDP spent in the US and 11 per cent in the UK. The Australian system is a hybrid that looks to balance both universal coverage and personal choice. The principle is that everyone should be able to get care at little or no cost, but those who can afford more and want to pay for more should be able to do that too, particularly as it results in better-paid doctors and more high-quality medical technologies for everyone.

I've experienced the downsides of both the overly centralised, one-provider universality of the NHS in the UK, and the expensive, privately driven system of Hong Kong. Australia, like the other highest-ranking systems, works through a carefully calibrated mix of public and private provision. Half of Australian hospitals are privately run, and they do a substantial proportion of certain key procedures, including about two thirds of elective procedures. More than half of Australians have private health insurance. The two things are connected, as having access to private hospitals makes it more attractive for people to pay for health insurance.

Australia's combination of universality plus a strong private system has emerged over a century of back-and-forth between those wanting to prioritise public healthcare and those who believed that a privately run system offers more efficient and flexible care. Someone who wants scans done, or wants IVF, can choose to have the service at little or no cost, funded by a levy on taxpayers of 2 per cent (rising to 3.5 per cent for high-income earners). Or you can choose to pay more for a premium service or to get that hip replacement done more quickly. Imagine two Australian sisters having babies. Both have private health insurance, but one elects to deliver in a public hospital where government funding pays for everything, from the obstetrician to epidurals. The other sister uses her private insurance to deliver at a private hospital with the obstetrician of her choice and a night in a nice hotel suite after delivery, at an out-of-pocket cost of a few thousand dollars.

Importantly, the one third of Australia's healthcare spend that comes from private sources allows doctors and nurses to be paid substantially better than in countries like the UK, particularly as they become more senior. For instance, registered nurses start on salaries that are 35 per cent higher in Australia than in the UK, and there are typically twice as many nurses per patient, shorter shifts and more generous overtime pay (the precise numbers vary between different states in Australia). Doctors enjoy a similarly higher starting salary, and both GPs and specialists can end up earning up to twice as much later in their careers—not least because GPs are paid on a fee-for-service basis and specialists can work in the private sector alongside their public hospital duties.

Medics also enjoy more flexible rotas, shorter days and more training opportunities, which adds to the inbuilt attraction of Australia's weather and lifestyle for many offshore professionals (albeit with a higher average cost of living).

Does it work?

The most authoritative recent cross-country comparison across rich developed countries ranked Australia as the leader in both "health care outcomes" and "equity". The Netherlands and Norway did slightly better on other measures ("access to care" and "care process") but also spend a higher share of their national income on healthcare than Australia does. The world-beating results of the Australian system are achieved with some frugality: Australia spends almost half as much per capita on healthcare than the US, for example.

Research by the King's Fund thinktank shows that the UK's health service has "higher avoidable mortality rates" than nearly all its peers. By contrast, Australia had the lowest rates on the list: 46 people per 100,000, compared to the UK's 69 people per 100,000. Like the similarly successful Singapore—which also provides universal access to healthcare while involving the private sector to offer care faster and better—the Australian system produces outcomes for patients that far exceed those in the NHS. Healthcare outcomes in these studies are rated according to different metrics: from how long you can expect to live after reaching the age of 60 (a further 25.6 years in Australia, which is the longest globally) to preventable mortality. For instance, only 59 per cent of people in England who are diagnosed with colon cancer live for five years or more, compared to 71 per cent of people in Australia who receive that diagnosis. And you could cite similar statistics if you were talking about infant mortality, maternal mortality or avoidance of "treatable and preventable" death in general.

An OECD study observed that a good indicator of quality of hospital care is the 30-day mortality rate following a heart attack. If you have a heart attack that sends you to hospital, then you are less likely to die within 30 days of your admission in Australia than in any of the European and North American countries surveyed. Australian women diagnosed with breast cancer have better survival rates than the average rates in northern America and western Europe, and the number of mothers dying in childbirth is also lower in Australia than anywhere except Germany.

A research team at Pennsylvania State University found not only that Australians enjoyed the highest life expectancy of any of the countries it analysed, but that most of these gains accrue after the age of 45, which suggests that it is mostly due to earlier diagnosis and better treatment of midlife risks such as cancer and heart disease. They also cited strong public health efforts to lower smoking, to use sunscreens to protect against skin cancer (a big issue in the Australian climate), and to take up vaccinations. They noted that Australia has a much lower life-expectancy gap between different regions and between rich and poor (in contrast to the UK, where men in the wealthiest areas lived nearly a decade longer than those in poor regions).

Australia also has less income-related disparity than other countries in things such as access to care, care process and administrative efficiency. We know, however, from the extensive work on Closing the Gap in Australia that healthcare outcomes in the most remote, and often indigenous, communities remain well behind those enjoyed by Australians in larger cities and towns.

How does it work?

If the Australian system works better for almost all of its citizens, then how is the Australian Way different when it comes to healthcare? As we have seen, the most obvious difference to many developed countries is Australia's extensive and integrated mix of public and private provision. The Medicare system means that government underpins a basic level of free care for every permanent resident, financed from general tax revenue and a specific "Medicare levy" that provides free public hospital care and free—or heavily subsidised—pharmaceuticals, diagnostics and other healthcare services. The little green Medicare card that Australians carry is universal, compulsory, funded by taxpayers, and has a single payer in the federal government.

The private hospitals provide additional capacity that the government doesn't need to pay for, subsidise the income of specialists, and take pressure off the public system. Meanwhile, the privately insured get access to private hospitals, dental care, and services from physiotherapy and optometry to podiatry and massages. There is a mix of "carrots and sticks" to make the private insurance market work, including both a rebate provided by government and a tax penalty on high-income households that don't take it up. Discounts are provided for younger people, and regulation of premiums imposed, to ensure that the overall insurance pool isn't skewed too much towards those with greater health needs.

This is markedly different to the US, where most healthcare is private and linked to your employment. I worked with a company whose CEO in the US received a diagnosis of a rare blood cancer which was not covered by that company's healthcare plan, but it had been covered by the company he left a month before the diagnosis and would also have been covered under Medicare if he were a year older. These sorts of capricious outcomes, and the large number of people completely outside the net, help to explain why lifespans are so much shorter in America. But they are also shorter in the UK where the NHS enjoys a virtual monopoly on most healthcare provision and where less than 10 per cent of people have private insurance.

The mix of free public health and private funding in Australia is also reflected in the successful Singapore system, albeit that the latter also has a compulsory saving and public insurance element which makes it structurally distinctive. It is probably no coincidence that the countries of Scandinavia, France and Japan, whose healthcare outcomes are closer to those of Australia, also have some form of mixed public and private healthcare provision.

Primary care and diagnostics

At a large summit of leading health policymakers organised by the Australian British Chamber of Commerce in 2021, one thing that struck me from all the comparative analysis of the two countries was that the Australian system has a greater focus on primary care and diagnostics. What particularly resonated was that general practitioners are more effective as gatekeepers to triage people into specialist care in Australia.

As in the UK, visiting a GP in Australia is either free or almost free for everyone—but, importantly, Australian doctors get paid per 15-minute increment of time that they spend seeing patients. This means that there is an incentive for doctors to see more patients, and, in more densely populated areas, there are 24/7 medical centres that make it easy for people with health issues to be seen by a doctor, even if their regular doctor is unavailable for its outside usual business hours. By contrast, even in the centre of London, I have found it very difficult to get an appointment with an NHS GP unless you have a personal connection with them. This is because GPs in the UK are paid based on how many patients are "registered" to them and on 55 different "practice targets", meaning that the incentive is for doctors to "sign up" patients but not to actually see them (this applies to all doctors affiliated to the NHS, but excludes private doctors for the especially wealthy). Late last year it was reported that 2.6 million UK patients waited more than four weeks to see a GP.

The fact that it is easier to find a GP in Australia than the UK has very real consequences. An earlier diagnosis can often be the difference between successful treatment and failure, when conditions are caught too late to effectively deal with them.

Australia also has significantly more MRI and CT scanners, relative to population, than most countries (around five times as many per person than the NHS). Radiologists have established large businesses in Australia that are focussed on diagnostic imaging, and they invest in the medical devices to support this. The government reimburses most scans so that diagnostics are mostly free to patients, but radiology businesses are also able to do cutting-edge work on a paid basis that allows Australian radiologists to be paid substantially more than their counterparts in the UK, which in turn enables greater investment in scanning equipment relative to the UK where investment in diagnostics competes with other NHS services for attention.

The combination of more GP visits and more diagnostics can arguably lead to some "over-servicing"—when people use medical services they could have done without—but the benefits exceed the cost; people get checked out more quickly and either get referred to the form of treatment that they need or go home reassured and do not waste the resources of expensive public hospitals. The greater efficiencies of the overall system also allow a bigger part of the public budget to be spent on doctors, nurses, and hospital beds, all of which Australia has more than most other countries compared to population size.

Other factors

Another important institution in the Australian healthcare system is the Pharmaceutical Benefits Scheme, under which an independent advisory board of doctors, academics and patient advocates recommends drugs for government subsidy based on their "bang for buck" in improving healthcare outcomes. This also provides a mechanism to push back on overpriced drugs and to balance the needs of different groups of people.

The relative healthiness of healthcare in Australia has also enabled a much greater investment in mental health and disability care than is seen in most other countries. An ambitious National Disability and Insurance Scheme has been launched to provide the world's best standard care for disabilities, although the initial design was poor. The Australian pragmatic adaptability will eventually fix this, but it's another example of the failure of large centrally planned "moonshot projects" in Australia to have the same level of success as more careful and evolutionary ones.

Another feature of the Australian healthcare system is the strong ecosystem of medical research and entrepreneurialism, especially in medical technologies. Australian companies have developed the cochlear hearing implant, sleep apnoea devices, blood plasma technologies, cutting-edge IVF fertility treatments and many other international healthcare businesses. This relative strength, in a country with a small population size, reflects the degree of government funding for medical research (safety-obsessed Australians prioritise medical spending), but also the ability of doctors to operate in both public and private spheres and the overall level of private funding for the healthcare sector.

Keeping it going

Of course, the Australian healthcare system is far from perfect. Nobody in the world feels completely happy with their own. People are living longer lives, and new drugs and treatments emerge every week that can address conditions which weren't dealt with before. Living longer also means an older average age in the population, with more years of chronic conditions that previous generations didn't display. The new treatments are also increasingly expensive, and our expectations grow at at least the same rate, so practically every healthcare system sees demand outstripping funding.

The growing gap between healthcare needs (let alone wants) and the funding of healthcare is an issue in Australia, as elsewhere. Not enough doctors are being trained and the culture in medicine increasingly pushes people to become specialists rather than GPs. The original Medicare design was intended to encourage doctors to fully "bulk bill" the government for a scheduled amount, rather than charge patients a market rate and have them claim a refund. But the amounts reimbursed in this way for non-concessional patients have fallen behind what's charged, and so around 25 per cent of GP services now attract some form of copayment from patients, as do about one-third of diagnostic scans. The increasing proportion of doctors' visits for conditions such as diabetes and obesity, as well as mental health issues, have also strained clinics.

There is also substantial waste and lack of coordination in the blurred accountabilities and duplicated roles of the federal government (which mostly funds healthcare) and the states (which provide almost all the actual healthcare delivery). While federation results in some messiness around how healthcare is delivered, it does also enable a certain level of comparison and benchmarking of best practices between states. If New South Wales is delivering more hospital beds and better health outcomes than Queensland, then there is at least some signal to providers about how they can improve.

There are fights between private hospitals and insurers about which of them bears the pain of rising costs (not least because the government caps insurance premiums, meaning that both are squeezed when costs rise), and the private insurance system is also always vulnerable to the classic adverse selection problem (people who are young and healthy are less likely to take up private cover, which then leaves the average person in the insurance pool older and sicker). The government has used both carrots and sticks to encourage a broad range of people into private health cover, recognising the importance of this part of the system to delivering higher levels of care. Premiums are lower for those who sign up before the age of 30, and the tax rebate for having private insurance is not far off the cost of buying a policy. Having been falling among people in their twenties before 2020, private insurance coverage has grown rapidly to be at its highest-ever level now.

While there will always be questions about how to maintain a world-leading system, Australia does rise to most of the challenges of 21st-century healthcare, with many advantages in its focus on primary care and diagnostics and its hybrid public-private system. And there is scope for more productivity and reducing complexity between federal and state health departments to free up even more resources to invest in new treatments and address the needs of rural communities that are currently under-served.

WEALTHY

> *Unlike most of its region, Australia was left unscathed by the Asian crash of 1997. Unlike most of the developed world, it shrugged off the global financial crisis and unlike most commodity-exporting countries, it weathered the resources bust too. No other rich country has ever managed to grow so steadily for so long. By that measure, at least, Australia boasts the world's most successful economy.*
>
> The Economist, October 2018

As the delegates gathered for the first of the two constitutional conventions that determined how the colonies would come together as a country in 1901, they were buoyed by the knowledge that a united Australia would be the richest country in the world if measured by wealth per person. Convicts had given way to a wave of free immigrants in the middle of the 19th century, and foreign investment streamed into the colonies. At the same time, the repeal of the Corn Laws in Britain launched half a century of unprecedented free trade and world peace. Australia, replete with sheep and gold, and possessing a liberal trading ethic, took full advantage of the opportunity.

By the time Donald Horne wrote the *The Lucky Country* in the 1960s, though, Australia was three quarters of the way through a slump in relative economic success that took the country down from first to 14th in the world. It was a slow and almost imperceptible decline over 80 years, attributable to several well-meaning but flawed decisions made in the early years of the 20th century. To get everyone over the line to create a national government, the newly federated states papered over differences between protectionists and free-traders and moved towards consensus on protecting Australian companies from global competition by applying tariffs on imports, as well as shielding Australian workers from competition through the White Australia policy and a centralised wage-fixing conciliation and arbitration process.

Horne conveys the impact of this world in which "to many Australian businessmen the way to make money is to grab some ideas from overseas, rush them into operation, however inefficiently, and then rely on the Tariff Board for protection. The central occupation of manufacturing is often to kill overseas competition with high tariffs." There is much of Horne's criticism of Australian big-business culture that still rings true (a lack of interest in R&D, board conservatism and parochialism, too many businesses coasting on government contracts), but few Australian businesses now lean on government to survive; most now compete confidently and profitably in global markets, including some of the world's leaders in areas from shopping centre development to infrastructure finance to medical technologies. In fact, technology companies are now one of the largest and fastest-growing sectors of the Australian economy, and the subsidies provided to these companies (in the form of R&D credits) don't rely on either protection from competition or governments trying to pick individual "winners" for their effect.

Though the weaning of Australia from the sins of the early 20th century happened in stages throughout the second half of the century (including a 25 per cent tariff cut as part of the reforms of the early 1970s), the conventional wisdom is correct when it is said that Australia really turned the corner in the 1980s. As late as 1980, Singapore's founding prime minister, Lee Kuan Yew, was warning that if Australia went on as it was, then it would become the "poor white trash of Asia". The reforms that started with the floating of the Australian dollar and accelerated through the 1980s and even into the 1990s are well documented and have put Australia back on top as the wealthiest country in the world, as measured by the median wealth of people.

Indeed, out of the 193 countries recognised by the United Nations, Australia is only the 55 largest in population but ranks 12th for the size of its economy and ninth for GDP per person (the average wealth is below the median wealth because wealth in Australia is more evenly distributed than in the eight countries that have higher averages but more concentration at the top). There was an inflection point when Australia lost its way at the start of the 20th century, and a time when it was rediscovered in the 1980s and 1990s. Australia then experienced a longer continuous spell of recession-free economic growth (almost 30 years) than any other OECD country and withstood the Covid economic slowdown better than other developed nations.

Australians are often complacent about this economic success, thinking that it will continue regardless. They sometimes even undervalue the whole idea of growth. It is easy to disparage material comforts as unexciting and unimportant, and true that many other things (family or sport and culture) underpin the well-lived life. But it is equally true that a strong economy underpins the investments we make in everything else we value. The security of the country, a family's standard of living and resilience, the healthcare and social welfare systems—all these things require a strong economy. Australia has been able to lead the world in making an unprecedented level of investment in goods such as disability care and mental health only because the country generates enough economic growth to fund it.

When economic success does get acknowledged, it is usually put down to a temporary dose of blind luck (China's rapacious demand for Australia's iron ore being the current case in point). The assumption is that the Australian economy is simply resource-rich and able to surf on the wave of offshore innovation. Not true. The last 30 years have certainly seen a long China-driven boom in commodity prices, but it has been a rollercoaster along the way. Resource exports were 11 per cent of GDP in 2011 and then 5 per cent in 2015, and yet economic growth held steady, while other major countries with big resources exports, such as Brazil, South Africa, even Canada, went into recession. The "coasting on the coattails of resources" thesis doesn't adequately explain 30 years without recession.

It also stands in contrast to the evidence in numerous international studies that, counter-intuitively, those countries with more resources usually have *lower* economic growth than those that are less well endowed. This has been dubbed the "resources curse", and compared with the difficulties that commonly affect lottery winners struggling to manage the side effects of sudden and unpredictable wealth. Resource wealth is typically either captured by a small group of people or appropriated by government for the benefit of wasteful rent-seekers. Norway, with its sovereign wealth fund, is one of the only other examples of not wasting commodity-driven income. Australians aren't rich just (or even mainly) because of the bounty of resources in the ground.

The true reason for Australia's sustained economic growth is its longstanding but underestimated flexibility, discipline, and adaptability—plus the newfound resilience built in throughout the 1980s and 1990s. The reforms of the 1980s (and to a lesser extent since then) fundamentally transformed what Horne recognised in the

1960s was holding back the country. In the characteristically blunt words of Paul Keating at Bob Hawke's memorial service, "Australia's creativity had been locked down by a stultifyingly paternal policy regime—the idea that government knew best, and that Australia was best protected and nurtured as a closed economy." In the same way as it did for China in the decades after 1979, an opening-out to the world and the freeing of markets allowed a once-rigid Australia to become adaptive and capable of higher growth rates than before.

There are challenges. Surveys show a lot of younger people don't trust the market economy and find socialism more appealing. One reason for this is that anyone under 40 has no memory of the sclerosis that existed in societies before the economic reforms of the 1980s—the Winter of Discontent in the UK and the pre-reform rigidity and deficiencies of Australia in the 1970s—and economic history is not well taught in schools and universities. Another reason is that there have been some appalling abuses that have given business a bad name, from the crony capitalism of firms using money and lobbyists to rig markets and create anticompetitive monopolies (especially in the US) to multinational tax avoidance and the bad behaviour outlined by Australia's Banking Royal Commission. If business does not act in a way that is worthy of people's trust, then it is no surprise that people turn against capitalism. The consequences for prosperity are serious.

I had an early lesson in this when I travelled through the old Soviet Union in the first few months after the fall of the Berlin Wall. The communists were still in control, but it was becoming clearer that the system had not worked and most people in the Eastern Bloc were desperate to enjoy the things we took for granted in the west. I had lots of offers for my Levi jeans, and everywhere I went there were long queues for things to buy. The sales ranges were often quirky because the central planners had decided to produce more of something than people wanted to buy and less of something else: that year, cucumbers were in over-supply, but milk and eggs were scarce. The longest line was outside the newly opened McDonald's in Moscow, where I queued for half an hour while being offered a chance to avoid the wait by buying "black market" McDonald's that was being passed out the back of the restaurant for foreigners at ten times the price. That's how it works without clear and transparent competitive markets to match what people want to buy with what they want to sell.

When I got to Warsaw in Poland, the people were a bit happier and there was more food in the shops. As control from Moscow receded, people had eagerly started to trade with each other. Finally, I crossed into West Berlin from the eastern side, and it was like going, Dorothy-style, from the sepia tones of Kansas to the Technicolor ones of Oz. From a bleak land of scarcity to a rich and modern city, from tinny Trabants to new Mercedes. As with North and South Korea (another border I later had the chance to visit), the gap between East and West Germany provided the perfect natural experiment to test a market-driven economy against a socialist one in what was basically the same land and culture. My experiences drove home the importance of teaching children about Germany and Korea, and about the different phases of Australia's own history, including the time when the country embraced protectionism and cronyism, leading to stagnation, and when the country opened itself up.

More than 20 years later, when I was studying how China had grown from poverty to be many times the size of Australia (while having my own on-the-ground tutorial through hundreds of trips to a dozen Chinese provinces), it became clear that the same thing drove China's "economic miracle". First the government allowed a few farmers in the collective to sell any extra food they produced. Those farms suddenly produced much more, and the programme was extended further. Then the government allowed small, privately owned businesses to be created in a special economic zone in Shenzhen, which also led to dramatic growth. Most of China's leaders were engineers by training in those days, so they set up more pilot projects to test the use of markets in different parts of the economy, and extended the ones that worked, until the whole country had markets working to some degree or another.

In the past few years, the state has relapsed into trying to "manage" the markets more tightly (with negative consequences that will continue to play out over time), but in the meantime China has achieved a velocity of growth and innovation that has become at least partly self-sustaining. Ironically, many people around the world have imagined China's growth to show that there is some new growth recipe of "state-driven capitalism", when the truth is that the growth of China for about 30 years was the great historical example of Adam Smith's "invisible hand"—of markets allocating resources more productively than a central authority had done before or ever could. China's growth since its loosening-up has not been qualitatively different in its drivers to other "Asian tiger" markets, it has just happened on a remarkably larger scale in a country with ten to 500 times as many people.

Using markets when they work should not be regarded as "neoliberal". It is true that more flexible labour markets and a floating dollar are important as shock absorbers that allow Australia to adapt. Keeping public debt low, having a mostly attractive regime for foreign investment and encouraging skilled immigration have been crucial for Australian success. But so too have universal healthcare through Medicare, compulsory superannuation savings to redress the previous "savings gap" in Australia and allowing university students to pay for their education only much later when they earn enough to do so. Having the OECD's highest minimum wages has not prevented the Australian unemployment rate from declining to 3 per cent. People who are more easily able to change jobs, move their house and keep educating themselves and their children will be much better able to move rapidly from areas of the economy that are slumping to those that are growing.

Superannuation

The superannuation system established in the 1980s has been particularly successful. Australians are required to put a substantial part of their wages (12 per cent from 2025) into a personal superannuation account that is locked up until they retire. Importantly, the account is a defined contribution fund, where pension payments are based on earnings (with concessional tax arrangements) and individuals can decide which fund manager(s) they want to invest for them, or they can invest directly. This means that the $3.9 trillion now in Australian superannuation accounts is poured into the stock market, infrastructure and other investments, and creates a massive savings pool, in contrast to the single-company defined-benefit schemes that dominate the UK, for example, which have resulted in over-investment in low-risk, low-return bonds and under-investment in local shares and alternative assets. The proportion of UK pension funds invested in the local stock market has fallen from more than half to about 3 per cent, while Australian superannuation funds invest almost a quarter of their funds in the local stock market and provide almost 40 per cent of the capital invested in the Australian stock exchange.

Australia's mandatory, employer-funded scheme puts more money into pensions but also provides more individual agency than the UK system does. The ease of moving or consolidating your superannuation accounts when you change jobs or aren't happy with the returns (portability) means that people accumulate larger sums than in the UK and are more focused on the returns that they are getting. The substantial scale of so-called "industry funds" (mutual structures under the control of union and employer groups) has enabled them to keep costs relatively low and invest in longer-term alternative assets such as infrastructure, property and private equity that have enjoyed strong returns. However, the proportion of these unlisted assets in the total mix has become sufficiently large that the integrity of how they are being valued is starting to attract more scrutiny, particularly when the industry funds are not currently subject to the same level of governance as other providers of superannuation funds.

The fact that pension-fund trustees and managers are required to focus on long-term returns under a "sole purpose test", alongside the regular statements that everybody receives to say how well their pot is performing, pushes investments towards a broader range of growth assets than in other markets. Poor-performing funds are named and shamed, switching is practical, and many more knowledgeable "professional investors" make their own investment decisions via self-managed superannuation funds. All of these things improve the long-term returns achieved. As well as providing substantial money for retirement (with the biggest current challenge being to get people to spend the money on themselves rather than pass it on to their heirs), the superannuation pot has supported a large and sophisticated financial sector that underpins investment in Australia and abroad.

The complexity myth

There was much gnashing of teeth in 2022 when the Harvard Growth Lab's *Atlas of Economic Complexity* ranked Australia as worse than its alphabetical fellows Albania and Argentina. This atlas marked Australia down for both the diversity and complexity of its exports. Its claim is that countries making more sophisticated products—rather than just "dumb" resources—and competing in more areas in their exports will thereby experience greater growth. Australia does badly in these measures because resources, tourism and education represent such a large proportion of its exports, and manufactured products are less prevalent.

In truth, it is the Harvard atlas that is simplistic, rather than the Australian economy. Firstly, the notion of "resources" as a "dumb" export does not recognise the high-tech nature of the modern mining industry, from autonomous train-loading to automated underground mining systems. It also doesn't pick up the sheer range of minerals (from lithium to uranium to platinum) that Australia produces, and how flexibly and efficiently investment can toggle between each new mineral and finance their development. Australia sells resources, tourism and education (not properly picked up in the Harvard Atlas) because the country is particularly competitive at doing so, and the biggest consumers of these things are proximate. That's what the economist David Ricardo called "comparative advantage", and Australia remains a great example of its power to fuel prosperity.

The Harvard Atlas definition of "productive knowledge" also doesn't account for the workforce. McKinsey has estimated that almost half of Australian jobs are "interaction jobs" that require high-order reasoning, judgement and the ability to manage non-routine tasks. Australia's skilled labour is above global averages and performs even more strongly than Japan (which ranks first in Harvard Atlas's economic complexity measure) when it comes to "complex problem solving". More than two-thirds of people in the Australian mining sector have advanced level degrees or diplomas. As one commentator pointed out, the Harvard Atlas is like judging the productive capability of kitchens in a restaurant by comparing menus, rather than by comparing the recipes, food and people in the kitchens.

There is nothing wrong with an Australian government highlighting emerging industries where they think Australia has potential, as they've done with health and life sciences, cyber and defence, space, clean energy and food and agricultural technologies. But it will take discipline to promote these only with the policies that we know do work (such as creating "precincts" and "centres of excellence" that link into educational institutions to develop critical mass, and giving visas to talented people from around the world who have those skills) and not with policies that don't work (like company-specific subsidies for the more articulate lobbyists in what bureaucrats deem to be "future industries").

Australians often don't even recognise their own comparative economic efficiencies, as they aren't things that manufacturing-centric economists naturally think about. Australia has an almost unique system of "dividend imputation" by which the tax paid by a company is "imputed" to whomever gets dividends from the company and reduces their tax (avoiding the double taxation of dividends from profits on which tax has already been paid, as happens in other countries). This encourages companies not only to pay their taxes but also to distribute any cash for which they don't have a compelling investment need. The allocation of capital among companies is more efficient as a result and the overall returns (including those dividends) to shareholders in Australia show it. The imputation system means that Australia's effective corporate tax rates on domestic companies are not as high as the headline numbers of 30 per cent (for large companies) and 25 per cent (for small companies). Higher corporate tax rates *do* affect the attractiveness of foreign investment, but stricter and slower Foreign Investment Review Board processes and glacial planning approvals currently scare away more foreign investment than corporate tax does. Increasing barriers to foreign direct investment (FDI) have seen inflows to Australia halve in the last decade, as a proportion of GDP. But even after this drop, in 2023, Australia still attracted more than twice as much FDI relative to GDP as the average amount for the similarly developed G7 countries.

The Australian dollar is the world's fifth most traded (and therefore liquid) currency. Australian capital markets raise new equity with 2 per cent fees (which is a half to a third of the cost in the US) and recapitalise companies through innovative structures such as accelerated rights offerings that reconcile equal treatment for shareholders with speed and transparency. Real estate agents take, on average, less than 2 per cent commission on house sales too, which is also about one third of the transaction cost for a US house sale. Almost all houses in Australia are sold by competitive auction, and detailed house-by-house valuation comparisons and online search are ubiquitous, whereas in most parts of the world there is an opaque and less market-based approach to pricing homes (outside Australia, auctions are rare, apart from big apartment projects). These aren't the things that jump to the mind of economists, let alone others, when we think about efficiency, but they underpin long-term productivity and partly offset the lack of productivity in other areas.

Australia also has one of the few AAA credit ratings in the world, and a unique set of free trade agreements with the US, China, Japan, the UK and India, giving Australian businesses preferential access to more than 80 per cent of the world. Australian attitudes to free trade have more in common with the dynamic economies of Asia than with other more fearful and self-defeating protectionist countries in what is identified as the west. Australia's robust anti-monopoly regime has preserved competition more successfully than the US system, despite (or because) a smaller market more naturally tending towards oligopoly, and a succession of strong competition regulators, have pushed back on excessive concentration. Australian venture capital funding for start-up companies exceeded $25 billion in total over the past five years, having been insignificant a decade prior, and that domestic investment in technology is on top of an increasing amount of attention from Silicon Valley.

The story of Australia's revival in the 1980s and 1990s has been told before, but it is worth retelling; knowing what was done right underpins a national narrative that can keep success going. The successful return to growth and high employment within a year of Covid added a fourth story of economic resilience to the three cited in the quote from *The Economist* at the start of this chapter. But Australians will need to be very vigilant not to give away these hard-won gains. Productivity growth averaged 2 per cent a year in the 1980s and 1990s, then fell to 1 per cent, and in recent years there has been no increase in productivity at all (though a similar pattern has been seen in other developed economies, and Australia's productivity performance is only slightly worse than its peers).

Instead of a slide backwards, Australia needs continuous improvement—what the Japanese call *kaizen*—to keep tweaking the settings and to stay adaptable as the world changes. At different times in Australia's history, both major political parties have shown the ability to drive this sort of incremental change are encourage resilience. It is not a matter of having grand plans for "solving" everything. Perhaps the only truly successful moonshot was the eponymous American mission in the 1960s to put a man on the moon (where the technologies existed, but just needed funding and political will to be harnessed). Analysis of cost-overruns on projects shows that the bigger and more bespoke the project, the more the spending spills out uncontrollably. Small, off-the-shelf procurement always provides better "bang for buck", but it doesn't look as good in an advertisement or political announcement. Most attempts at moonshots just end up costing a lot of money for indifferent results; think big, new IT systems, submarine fleets, or the Great Leap Forward.

Success far more often comes from the accumulation of smaller innovations from multiple parties that compete against each other (think of Covid vaccines and Silicon Valley)—or, in government, from the accumulation of many well-thought-through policies— often copied from what has already worked overseas. During my time at the financial group Macquarie, the income earned outside of Australia went up more than tenfold. This wasn't because of a grand plan or attempted moonshot, but because hundreds of small groups were building thousands of small businesses one step at a time under a small but tight set of risk controls. In Asia, we made many focussed decisions every day about whom to hire, about the sectors and countries where we could find some edge over competitors, winning clients one-by-one and removing obstacles for the team. Small incremental improvements, of which more work than don't, will add up over time to big things.

That, too, is a microcosm of how countries succeed. Less attention-grabbing than the risk-averse, large, listed companies in Australia are thousands of low-profile but highly focussed businesses driven by founders and teams that see and pursue opportunities, often global in scope from the start. They need to be supported and not held back.

Other lessons also stand out from reviewing the periods in Australia's history when a "miracle economy" has been achieved and those when the country has stalled or gone backwards. The first is that the good periods have seen stability of leadership and some degree of bipartisanship in the national interest. This does not mean that policy debates stop. On the contrary, the contestability of ideas is an absolute strength, and it is almost unique that even in wartime Australia continued to have an opposition to challenge the government (unlike, for example, in the UK). But it does mean "playing the ball and not the person", and that once a policy emerges as superior to the alternative it should be supported on principle and not blocked for short-term personal advantage. There will always be a temptation to frustrate opponents, and the media wants fisticuffs, but those politicians who truly care about and represent the national interest will "give credit where credit is due", or at least fight on the high moral ground rather than go for the "easy kill". Part of good government is good opposition. The gold standard is the way in which the Liberal opposition of the 1980s supported most of the Hawke/Keating reforms that underpinned the next 30 years of prosperity.

The then prime minister's party has only controlled the senate in Australia for three of the past 40 years. For much of the time, the ability to veto and block government legislation has been used constructively to amend and selectively challenge in a way that creates better legislation. But there are periods when it has been used in an almost kneejerk fashion to bring the policymaking procedure to a stalemate. The impact of negative opposition goes well beyond the specific reforms that don't get through parliament: it will discourage any further attempts at reform, to coarsen the public debate, polarise the media, and make voters more cynical about the whole democratic process. It is no exaggeration to say that oppositions have as much power as governments to do good or harm to the country.

The successful tax reforms of the 1980s and 1990s also show the importance of a second principle: balanced reform. The 1985 reforms resulted in new taxes on capital gains and fringe benefits, but these funded a substantial cut in the top marginal rate of tax. Even the sceptics could see it was reform rather than just a grab for money.

The 1980s brought successive waves of deregulation—from the floating of the dollar to removing tariffs, then finally to making wage-setting less centralised. But alongside these critical measures to open up the economy there came universal healthcare (in the form of Medicare), interest-free loans to ensure affordable university education, and the superannuation system. The government made changes that promoted efficiency and economic growth, supported by those on the opposite side of politics, but balanced them carefully with well-chosen policies to reassure people that their security wasn't being neglected. There has not been so much of this approach in recent times, and both parties would benefit from looking at balanced reform proposals, to match microeconomic reform (making Australia more competitive and open) with social reform (that clearly protects those who lose out in the short or longer term).

The third lesson of creating a "miracle economy" is that the environment in which decisions are made and the extent of advocacy and "education" is very important. Enduring change came when Hawke or Howard talked clearly to people, long and hard, about why change was required, and when bodies such as the Productivity Commission were able to independently assess changes and give a considered imprimatur. Changes have failed when reforms were rushed through without adequate education of the people affected, or where they too narrowly reflected the interests of one side. The government developed the case for tax reform in the 1980s via a summit of all the key stakeholders and after years of talk and negotiations. Other reforms slowly won support from the Reserve Bank, the Treasury and important media commentators before Keating and Hawke sold them articulately to the public. Introducing a consumption tax (the GST) failed twice, in 1984 and 1991, but the arguments for its necessity had been well made, and Howard and Costello had the courage to keep pushing and to make it happen, finally, in 1999. Political boldness is sometimes required, but it needs to build and to surf the wave of public understanding rather than try to move against it.

The existence of an independent Productivity Commission, able to advocate for evidence-based policy in areas where sectional interests would usually prevail, is a crucial strength of the Australian system and a huge contributor to Australia's prosperity. The slower improvement in economic performance in the 21st century reflects a diminishing appetite of government to listen to it.

It is often argued that it is too hard to promote worthwhile reform in Australia today. This comes both from protest movements, who take to the streets in frustration that the machinery of democracy doesn't appear to be delivering racial equality or effectively countering climate change, and from businesses who see an unwillingness to make worthwhile changes to make Australia more prosperous and competitive. Both would say that social media and the 24-hour media cycle have made it impossible to sustain a mature argument about what's required, and that the tendency for the senate to include minority parties makes it hard to pass legislation. Reform may be hard, but it is certainly not impossible. The developments of the 1980s and 1990s made the average Australian richer than the average citizen of every other country in the world. Another well-articulated, methodical programme for continuous improvement could make sure that Australians continue to lead the world in median wealth and prosperity.

WISE

Our future growth relies on competitiveness and innovation, skills and productivity, and these in turn rely on the education of our people ... through hard work and education, we can deliver a strong economy and opportunity for all.

JULIA GILLARD, former prime minister

The success of Australia was built on education. There was a rollout of free and universal schooling in 1872, one of the first places in the world that this occurred. University education has gone from covering less than three per cent of the population in the 1950s to the point that almost half of graduating high school students are now going on to tertiary education.

Most of the things that have driven Australia's success have their root in its people being well-educated and globally aware. It is therefore a concern to see the fall in standards in the last few decades, particularly in primary and secondary schooling. Because it has been a slow decline, Australians have been like the frog boiling in water, not understanding how bad it has got since the deterioration each year is slow.

Former prime ministers, Kevin Rudd and Julia Gillard, introduced the Naplan (National Assessment Program-Literacy and

Numeracy) in 2008 to identify where greater work and resources are required and to provide more transparency. Think tanks such as the Centre for Independent Studies and the Grattan Institute have consistently researched and advocated for evidence-based teaching. Slowly, the necessary changes are starting to happen to revive what has, in the past, been one of Australia's most important strengths.

Australian universities

Australia doesn't have a Harvard or a Stanford, an Oxford or a Cambridge, nor the concentration of national universities you see in Tokyo, Seoul and Paris. What Australia does have is six universities that rank in the top 100 globally, and 11 (spread across every state) that rank in the top 200. This typically Australian egalitarianism in universities is partly a function of history (most universities were founded and initially funded at state level), but also of the overwhelming tendency of students to study in the same state, and usually city, where they grew up. More than 80 per cent of students live at home compared to less than 20 per cent in the UK. There is not the culture of moving and boarding for college that there is in the US, nor the magnet of one or two universities attracting the best students from across the nation, as in most European and Asian countries. The eight most research-heavy universities (dubbed the G8) in Australia have a similar share of research to the Oxbridge ones, but each of the eight attracts top students from their catchment area—so none dominate. Australian universities are also big, with many of them having more domestic students than Cambridge or Oxford despite a population half the size of the UK.

Australia's first universities came early in the history of British settlement and were an expression of the soon-to-be-a-country's egalitarian values. They were among the first in the world to admit female students, religion was never a barrier to admission, and bursaries were available from the outset to bright students who were not able to afford tuition fees. For the past 50 years, the federal government has not imposed upfront fees; it will lend students their full tuition. This does not need to be paid back unless and until you are earning more than $50,000 a year.

Entry to Australian universities has historically been meritocratic, as it is in China or Singapore, using state-wide exams, anonymously marked and scaled to reflect relative difficulties of courses, with places allocated "'blind", based on the resulting score. They therefore better train the people most capable of benefiting from higher education, rather than losing the most well-equipped students to those with well-connected parents, athletic abilities, a particular racial background or the ability to smooth-talk their way through an interview. The fact that admission has historically been more strictly based on aptitude than anywhere else outside of Asia promotes the egalitarian nature of Australian universities. They are predominantly government-run and do not have the biases and inefficiencies of legacy admissions—aka, nepotism—or subjective "interview and portfolio" approaches to choosing students.

This has meant that, more so in Australia than in most of Europe and North America, getting into a particular university course is blind to class and colour. By training doctors, lawyers, economists and engineers according to their objective academic scores rather than more subjective criteria, a country is able to maximise the impact of its human talent. There has been dilution of these principles in recent years as some universities "adjust" admission requirements to accommodate a burgeoning number of "special considerations" in an attempt to satisfy particular agendas, usually to the detriment of the most disadvantaged students who are either less savvy in "gaming the system" or later drop out of courses for which they were unprepared. The objective Australian Tertiary Admission Ranking is still used in three-quarters of cases, though, and it is generally still true that a smart but poor girl or boy in Australia has a better prospect of getting into a top course at a top university than they would in almost any other country.

Australia is also the third most popular destination for university students to study abroad (behind only the US and UK), with Chinese and Indian students being particularly keen to study down under. The disproportionately large international education exports by Australia aren't just an economic force in their own right (the country's fourth largest export), they also underpin the research budgets of the universities. About one-third of the $12 billion spent on research in Australian universities each year is funded by the federal government, with a similar portion funded from the proceeds of educating foreign students. When done well, it also sets up a strong, continuing relationship between these students and Australia—with concomitant increases in business collaborations and direct investment. The contribution of international students, as well as from graduates via the tax system when they are able to do so, means that Australia invests a relatively high 2 per cent of GDP on tertiary education overall, with about one-third coming from the private sector and the rest from government.

More than 30 per cent of foreign students in Australia have come from China, attracted not only by the reputation of the universities, but also the relative safety and good weather. Australian higher education institutions have greatly benefited from the influx of Chinese students since the late 1980s, subsidising research, campus infrastructure and domestic student places. There was a lost opportunity, though, as most universities made little effort to integrate foreign students with the broader student body, and downplayed English-language proficiency. Having large numbers of Chinese students in Australia should be an opportunity for domestic students to understand a major trading partner and for Chinese students to appreciate the system in which they're living. But neither happens if Chinese students stick entirely to their own groups and read only Chinese-language newspapers that have, even in Australia, essentially come under the effective control of the Communist party.

More recently, there have been concerns about Chinese government activity on campuses, including intimidation of students. Australia was one of the first countries to tighten security around research collaborations to avoid leakage of sensitive AI, advanced materials and quantum computing research that could have military applications. Australian universities have also put a big effort into diversifying the international student cohort.

Despite the success of education as one Australia's largest exports outside of agriculture and minerals, the sector has been savaged recently as the federal government started refusing visas wholesale, to force immigration numbers down dramatically. There are legitimate concerns about the impact of big overseas student numbers on the quality of some courses. But the speed and severity of the push against international education has been a blunt instrument that has driven out good providers, damaged the economy and hurt Australia's reputation.

Australian schools

About 70 per cent of Australian primary school students (and 60 per cent of those in high school) are educated in free, government-run state schools. Government schools are controlled directly by each state, and many seemingly modest suburban schools have very proud histories of producing students who have gone to be Nobel Prize winners, High Court justices, and major contributors to society in other ways. A small number of selective schools in the state system typically dominate the top ranks of academic achievement in Year 12 and have become a particularly good route for smart immigrant children to enter the public service and professional ranks.

The other 40 per cent of Australian high-school students are educated in privately managed schools, most of which began with a religious denomination and of which Catholic schools still represent a very large proportion. This is a much higher percentage than in other countries; only 7 per cent of British, 7.5 per cent of Canadian, about 10 per cent of US and German students and 17 per cent of those in France are in private schools. The proportion in Australia has grown over time as more parents have been prepared to pay for the results of greater autonomy of private school principals and their often-tighter disciplinary environment, or because they believe these schools promote values that are important to them.

Government money (both state and federal) provides 100 per cent of funding for government schools, and a portion of the annual funding for the independent and Catholic schools, with parents of students at those schools making up the difference (as well as providing more than 90 per cent of the capital expenditure at non-government schools). There are sometimes concerns expressed about the better facilities and teacher pay that private schools can afford, although the relatively large injection of private funds into schooling in Australia is estimated to save taxpayers around $5 billion a year compared to what would be required if all students were in fully funded government schools.

Losing the advantage
The Australian school system used to be a great strength; it is part of the reason that an immigrant child growing up in Mount Isa, as I did, could have the opportunities that I have enjoyed in life. But,

despite a previously strong track record and substantial increases in funding, Australia has been losing its advantage in primary and high schools over the past couple of decades. Outcomes have slid, both in absolute terms and relative to other countries. In the past 20 years, Australia's performance in reading has declined by the equivalent of nine months of schooling, in science by 11 months, and in maths by 14 months. Not only have Australian students (both at the top and bottom end) fallen well behind places such as Singapore (by about a year and a half in reading and science and three years in maths), but Australia has also been overtaken by places such as the UK, Canada and New Zealand, who all used to lag. The fact that maths is the area in which Australians are falling most far behind is particularly alarming when the tech-hungry world is putting a higher and higher premium on this ability.

The annual Program for International Student Assessment (Pisa) charts the plummeting scores of Australian students, even as the government poured more money into schools. Australia went from 19th in the world for mathematics in 2012 to 23rd ten years later, and from 13th to 19th in reading. Over the same period, England overtook Australia for the first time in the survey, improving from 26th in mathematics to 21st, and up in reading from 23rd to 16th, even as austerity policies were cutting funding substantially. The difference was the English system's focus on teacher training, standards and accountability.

The decline in Australian educational standards, in spite of more money being spent, appears to have been mostly driven by a decline in the quality of teacher training since the 1970s, as well as a vogue for so-called "student-centred" learning methods that have been shown not to work. The curriculum grew crowded with all sorts of extra subjects, and government-sponsored reviews hyped up "revolutions" in classrooms to "prepare for new ways of working". The focus on the core skills of literacy and numeracy was lost, and principals and education bureaucrats let standards slide. Maths is not even compulsory in the last couple of years of school; worse still, more than a quarter of maths classes are taught by people without a maths background themselves. There has been an explosion of "group-learning" (perhaps because it is easier to mark one assignment than four of them), and bureaucrats have told schools to "teach" things like social skills, creativity and motivation. But there is little evidence that Australians are any worse at working in groups or thinking laterally than students from anywhere else in the world. On the contrary, as this book has shown, Australians are exceedingly creative. Where Australia is failing, according to the evidence, is in the basic grounding that underpins all endeavours: knowing how to read, write and do maths.

The OECD also reported that Australian teachers felt the least prepared among developed countries to deal with discipline issues, just as disruption in the classroom became the major issue stopping students from learning. The "disciplinary climate" in Australian schools was assessed as the fifth worst in the 37 countries of the OECD. Australian's lack of regard for hierarchy has many attractive consequences, but it has not helped to create healthy classrooms. Students, and their parents, don't have the respect for teachers that is found in higher-performing systems such as Finland and Singapore.

Can the Australian Way return?
There are belated signs that several of the state education departments are now responding and implementing the three things that all the evidence recommends: teacher training, discipline in the classroom and a rigorous curriculum. Teacher colleges are being encouraged to focus on practical, useful and evidence-based content, rather than untested academic theories, and efforts are

being made to get higher-performers into teaching as a profession (including copying successful overseas programmes to recruit teachers in mid-life and having high-achieving graduates do teaching for a short period in difficult schools before going on to other careers). There have also been some attempts to pay more to highly effective and more experienced teachers, although teaching unions remain opposed to this sort of differentiation. A top-rank teacher achieves the same results in a half year that take a low-ranked teacher a full year. Nothing positively changes a person's life as much as a good teacher. Like most people, I can remember that handful of teachers that changed mine.

The most recent Pisa results have shown some improvement, though not among lower-performing schools, where teachers are still not given practical training, support in maintaining discipline, nor high expectations. The negative impacts of not having evidence-based rigour in teaching are worst for disadvantaged students, and the national Naplan survey of results shows the increasing gap between kids from rich families in the centres of cities compared to poor kids in rural areas. The federal government is finally starting to tie funding increases to good policy, but many state education departments (who have to implement the improvements in teaching) are resistant to change; progress remains excruciatingly slow.

Pragmatic, problem-solving Australians will eventually do what's required: reward and respect the best teachers much more and enforce classroom behaviour so that they can teach; make it easier for principals to hire and fire teachers; have evidence-based curricula and regular professional development and peer reviews (as in any other respected professions) to hone quality and spread the lessons about what works; raise the bar for entry to teacher colleges; include more practical classroom skills in teaching degrees; and make it easier for mid-career professionals in other fields to devote part of their lives to helping the next generation.

Being able to read, write and do sums is the basis of all other knowledge. Literacy is the foundation not only of a career but of basic citizenship; whether you want to be good at history, FinTech, Shakespeare or oncology, or simply to participate in a liberal democracy, you must first be able to read what others know, and then articulate it. Being financially literate (and thereby running a business, saving effectively for retirement and looking after your family budget) requires first that you can do basic maths. There is no way to know for certain how people will work and live in the future, so we shouldn't let ill-defined notions of a changing world steer us away from the timeless essence of education: literacy, numeracy and an immersion in the best thinking of the past.

DIVERSE

It is to Australia's great credit that we are a mongrel nation. None of that Aryan or ethnic purity for us. We benefit from hybrid vigour. Every race and religion—as mixed up as the flora in our multi-horticultural society.

PHILLIP ADAMS, Australian writer and radio presenter

Earlier chapters of this book have examined the Australian personality and character, and the institutions and beliefs distinct to Australia. Of course, among 27 million people, there will be many different stories, and not everyone will share every characteristic of the Australian norm. There are elitists, humourless people and ideologues in Australia, as everywhere else. They just don't represent the dominant culture. The culture of a place or people comprises things that are shared broadly and that are more or less prevalent than in other places; Australia's culture is distinct, but it exists within the context of a migrant-rich and geographically spread society that allows space for individuals to do their own thing.

States and cities

The lack of a dominant city in Australia has meant that the intellectual resources and financial capital of the country are unusually dispersed compared to other countries. Canberra is the political and bureaucratic capital, but has little business, and directly provides few services. Sydney, Melbourne and now Greater Brisbane are the population centres and traditional hubs of business, while Western Australia dominates the crucial resource industry.

Donald Horne's *The Lucky Country* included a roll call of major cities which remains recognisable today. Sydney with its sprawl of suburban villages linked by a shared self-image of beaches, boats and harbour—a glossy city, benchmarking itself against the global cities rather than domestic peers. Melbourne is more European in style, with both a British-style establishment and left-wing activism, a religious obsession with Australian Rules football and a greater emphasis on cafes, culture and conformity than Sydney. Melbourne is competitive, zealously promoting its unique events and attractions, whereas only occasionally does self-satisfied Sydney rouse itself from sunbaking to do some serious self-improvement. A cliché is that in Melbourne people ask you about your school and your football team, in Sydney your job and where you live. Sydney overtook Melbourne in population just after federation, but Melbourne has closed the gap again.

Then there is Brisbane—which in 2032 will become the third Australian city to host an Olympic Games—growing fast enough that, together with its Sunshine Coast and Gold Coast communities to the north and south, it is projected to become a third five-million-person population centre before 2040. Brisbane is the only capital city of a state to make up less than half the population of the state itself. The Gold Coast and Sunshine Coast are rapidly growing in a way that echoes the growth of Florida in the US, and then it takes several days to drive to the most northerly point of Queensland (covering territory which would happily become a separate state).

In South Australia, founded by free settlers, there is Adelaide mixing every kind of festival with a willingness to experiment that palely echoes the time around federation when the city enjoyed a burst of reform (female suffrage, the secret ballot, Torrens Title to democratise property ownership) that almost amounted to an Adelaide Enlightenment.

Perth is still, as Horne noted, the most isolated city of its size in the world, a long way from Sydney or Canberra, and is still "relaxed, hospitable, a world of fishing, backyard beer parties" and distrustful of those "over East". The strength of the natural resources industries in Western Australia, as well as the area's closer proximity to Asia, have also made Perth more attuned to Asia, and more forward-looking and risk-taking than most of the rest of the country.

Hobart, in Tasmania, has developed the Mona art gallery—that is, the Museum of Old and New Art—and a New Zealand-style ecotourism industry that have made it a popular destination. Canberra still feels more like a town than a city despite being the centre of administrative power. It is a higher-income and more tertiary-educated place relative to other parts of Australia, a world of government buildings and garden suburbs, with a stream of supplicants filling planes from every part of Australia to lobby for the good graces of the federal government. It's perhaps unsurprising that Australia undersells itself among the great powers of the world, considering the national capital is a suburban plan carved out of an Australian bush landscape.

The differences between states have always been there, but they seemed less and less relevant in the 75 years that followed the Commonwealth taking control of the purse strings during the Second World War. It was Covid that reminded Australians of how the differences between states at the time of federation have not gone away; most people, outside of New South Wales at least, have a strong sense of state identity that can be as powerful as their sense of being Australian in times of stress.

While the different attitudes of states need to be recognised, and the archetypes of each of the cities are interesting, it is also true that there is much uniformity in the Australian character. You might try to pick out someone's locality from their accent, but you would often be wrong. There is certainly far less diversity between rural and urban Australia, north and south, than there is between northern California and southern Alabama, between Glasgow and the home counties of England, or between the Dōngběi region of northeast China around Beijing and the people of the southern coastal areas of China.

Gender

When Horne wrote *The Lucky Country*, there were barely any women in parliament or on the judiciary, and it is unlikely that a single female director was appointed to one of Australia's 300 largest listed companies. Since then, one or more women have served as prime minister, chief justice of the High Court, governor-general, and premier of every state and territory except South Australia. There have been 15 women who have served as deputy leaders of a state or the Commonwealth, and more than half of the federal senators in Australia are female. Women now comprise 43 per cent of the leaders of diplomatic missions overseas; one in every three directors of Australia's 300 largest listed companies is female, and so are around 40 per cent of the new directors being appointed. Outstanding female leaders are currently in charge of the Australian central bank, the Productivity Commission and my old firm, Macquarie.

There may have been substantial progress made in recent years, but it remains a work-in-progress—with very few female chief executives across major companies and serious under-representation in many professions. Perhaps the all-important area of sports will lead the way: there has been a strong growth in the profile of female athletes (who accounted for most of Australia's medals in the 2024 Paris Olympics), increasing coverage of the female leagues of major sports codes, and just as many young girls as young men now play rugby and AFL. It is nonetheless still true, as it was when Horne noted it, that Australian barbeques and dinner parties segregate by gender more readily than in other western countries. And Australia ranked only 43rd in the World Economic Forum's most recent global gender gap report (well behind North America and most of Europe).

Disadvantage

The level of median wealth and income may be higher in Australia than in other places, but this certainly does not mean that there is not a substantial number of people whose lives are very tough. Australia has, like every other country, pockets of real disadvantage—and these are often hidden. They range from isolated indigenous communities with crushing drug, alcohol and sexual abuse issues to homeless people suffering mental illness to "broken" suburbs where disadvantage has become endemic. I'd seen the issues experienced in communities such as Mount Isa as a child, and then, many years later, through the Smith Family charity, I was confronted with whole streets of a suburb in Sydney where no family unit was intact, none of the (single) parents worked, and nobody had ever been to a university. The Smith Family programme attempted to break the cycle: proper breakfast so kids could concentrate in school; introductions to mentors; extra money for clothes and books. These initiatives, and their public sector equivalents, are crucial, but the issues underlying this sort of social disadvantage are complex and often involve difficult trade-offs between respect for individual choice and the limited resources available to people in these situations.

Australia's egalitarian and safety-conscious values prompt action to help disadvantaged citizens. At the same time, Australians' individualism and aversion to long-term plans mean that good intentions don't always translate into lasting change. People in poverty can be out of sight, out of mind in most prosperous countries, let alone Australia—and their problems don't have the same political cut-through as those that impact the middle classes.

Fragmentation

As the Catholic/Protestant sectarianism of the early 20th century faded away, Australia became the epitome of a country in which individuals can follow their own path and thrive regardless of their ethnicity, religion or other identities. But this is not to say that intolerance has been eradicated. There have always been some Australians unwilling to give equal space or respect to those who look, speak or worship differently—and recently, with the rise of identity politics, this impulse to differentiate has also emerged among progressives. The extremes of right and left have become united in framing—and judging—people according to their differences of race, religion, gender and sexual identity, rather than striving for a society that is blind to these qualities. Social media has stirred the pot still further.

While often in the news, identity politics appears to have less impact on everyday life in Australia than it does in America—not least, one suspects, because it does not come naturally to sceptical, pragmatic and individualistic Australians. And yet the persistent influence of America in Australia, and the entrenched position of critical theory in universities, means that the "culture wars" will continue to simmer. This is reflected in Edelman's 2023 Trust Barometer, which now rates Australia as "moderately polarised"—though still more cohesive than both the US (which is regarded as "severely polarised") and the UK and much of Europe ("in danger of severe polarisation").

Australia is also rated higher than both the US and UK for the level of trust that people have in NGOs, business, government and the media—although it ought to be noted that trust in government has slipped recently and that more Australians now regard the media as a "source of false and misleading information" rather than a "reliable source of trustworthy information".

Australia is well served, overall, by the diversity of opinions and political viewpoints in its media, but the decline in trust in media suggests that people seek more insight and factual analysis. Many of the stories of the day are clickbait-y and focus on scandals, scares and internal party micro-dynamics. This may be what consumers of the news seek out themselves, yet, perversely, giving people what they want can, in this instance, leave them feeling less satisfied over time. The growing success of longer-form podcasts and higher-brow global newspapers and magazines in Australia speaks to a latent desire for greater depth in the way that politics, economics, business and various other subjects are covered. Both politicians and the media may help themselves by tempering the cynicism that makes positive change more difficult.

Real positive change does happen, often through the detailed studies and consultations conducted by senate committees, royal commissions, the Productivity Commission and others. Their important work often goes unreported, but they are the true essence of Australian parliamentary government. A successfully diverse country needs politicians who sometimes show restraint, alongside a responsible media that provides balance by showing achievements as well as screw-ups. This may help Australia to avoid the slide into even lower levels of trust and fellow feeling that the US and many European countries have already gone down.

DEMOCRATIC

> *No one pretends that democracy is perfect or all-wise.*
> *Indeed, it has been said that democracy is the worst form of*
> *Government except for all the other forms that have been*
> *tried from time to time . . .*
> WINSTON CHURCHILL

After university, like so many Australians, I packed a backpack and spent three months travelling around Europe. As well as the usual places in western Europe, I went up as far as Norway and through what was then the USSR, coming back from Russia through what were its satellite states and across the newly punctured Berlin Wall into West Germany. Following Eastern Europe's sudden emergence into daylight, the wonders of a free, open, and democratic society seemed obvious to almost everyone.

But the memories of those days have faded, and now cynicism about government is high, fuelled in part by social media algorithms, polarisation in the media and, more recently, subversive uses of AI. Each of these challenge open societies like Australia, but they also reinforce each other and are further fuelled by deliberate disinformation from vested interests at home and adversaries abroad. There are, nonetheless, some signs that Australian values and institutions are relatively well positioned to counter the impact.

Democracy and balance

It is often lamented that most Australians aren't engaged with politics; they tune in around election time and cast their votes for whoever is the least-worst to run the country for another three years, paying little attention to the detailed policy debate. But if there is a lack of day-to-day chat about politics outside those who are professionally involved in it, that arguably shows strength rather than weakness in the system.

When almost two million people in Hong Kong took to the streets in 2019, it was because the relationship with Beijing was fundamentally changing, and they feared the loss of their everyday freedoms. By contrast, Australians just go on doing the things they want to do. Ukrainians, Israelis, and Taiwanese talk a lot about politics because the decisions they make about their representatives can lead to war or peace. Most Australians can comfortably tune out of a debate that will lead to one of two relatively sensible centrist parties running the show within the parameters of a sound constitution and legal system. Brexit highlighted weaknesses in the UK's constitutional framework and social cohesion, and thereby prompted ongoing upheaval. Australia's republican and Indigenous Voice referenda debates passed quickly; the questions asked and the rules for the public's decisions were fully clear—and the people's decisions accepted, even by those who disagreed with them.

A lack of interest in politics among most people is only a problem if it comes from a lack of respect for government. Australians, paradoxically, respect and obey government while at the same time being deeply sceptical of the actual individuals in power. The country went straight from British governors (charged with developing the colony broadly and therefore broadly aligned with average citizens rather than any local aristocracy) to what was then the world's broadest democratic franchise. Perhaps history and circumstance have inadvertently grounded Australia in the observed truth that, when you get it right, the process behind the law-making makes more difference to the success of a country than which individuals occupy particular positions.

It may be an irony of democracy that people are inherently more sceptical and demanding of the representatives they choose than those who are imposed in nondemocratic systems. There are, nevertheless, limits to how much distrust can be absorbed without damage to the cultural fabric and without descending into the populism that has recently scarred other countries. Fortunately, there are things that can be done to minimise the public's distrust of democratic politics. The most obvious is a government that solves problems and governs well. Over the medium term, no amount of pork barrelling or spin will make up for not delivering on the basic needs of the country. Populism thrives when the political classes don't deliver on what a sizeable portion of the people think is most important to them.

Fortunately, the evidence on how to deliver is clear, and the Australian system aligns pretty well with it: a representative form of democratic government with sufficient independent institutions around it, alongside technocrats who have the time and space to solve long-term problems while also being accountable to elected representatives. Australia has so far been able to strike the right balance between the people arguing for less of that "noisy and disruptive" democratic combat and those for whom "too much democracy is never enough".

There is a balance in an effective democracy between the elected representatives and the permanent administrators, between accountability and expertise. It has become fashionable to suggest that the balance needs to shift more to real-time polling of attitudes and away from allegedly out-of-touch experts. This is despite all the evidence suggesting that technocratic governments (for example, Singapore) are often better at granular problem-solving and at delivering people-centred results than governments subject to more direct democracy. Weakening the administrative side of government has hurt several countries in Europe and North America; thoughtful reflection and administrative competence are crucial. Australia has been fortunate to have a strong civil service, with particularly talented people in the Treasury, the Reserve Bank and institutions such as the Productivity Commission taking a long-term view, mitigating the inevitable learning-curved, career-focussed and short-term perspective that comes with elected politicians.

It is easy to fall into the trap of thinking that the solution to people being dissatisfied is to give them direct democracy—more referenda and plebiscites, more snap online polls, more hour-by-hour second-guessing of decisions. But most people are getting on with their lives and don't have the time nor the inclination to thoughtfully review the evidence around a particular issue. Australia has been a pioneer of so-called "deliberative democracy" that brings together randomly selected citizens to analyse and evaluate policies on particularly difficult or controversial issues and give people a better understanding of the trade-offs involved. Digital and AI solutions have been used in places like Taiwan to better listen to communities; Australia, true to the spirit that pioneered female participation in democracy and secret ballots, can innovate in these areas. But just because we now have the technology to instantly sum up all the "likes" for different policies does not mean that we should; the solutions to problems look simpler from far away, and look easiest to solve when you understand them the least.

The alternative model

The Chinese, Russian and fundamentalist Islamic critiques of liberal democracy are all variations of the same ones that have echoed through every generation since the counter-Enlightenment of the 18th century: individual aspirations should not come before the social harmony of a nation, tribe or family; that a strong, clear leader is better than messy argument between democratic leaders; and that comfortable feelings of "belonging" matter more than impersonal materialism.

Australia has seldom been tempted by these ideas (partly because of prosperity and partly because it's a nation founded on values rather than race or religion), but it is not immune. The Covid experience demonstrated Australian pragmatism and the ability to adapt and correct errors quickly, but it also showed examples of heavy-handed government action and overreach, with little pushback from a frightened public. A creeping curtailment of liberties can easily occur when people are scared—whether of terrorists, refugees, foreign spies, or an invisible virus. Testing each new apparent security measure is important to make sure it is proportionate and not eroding liberties. Just after the outbreak of the Second World War, the then Australian prime minister, Robert Menzies, introduced legislation that gave the government extensive wartime powers, but he still made a point of not undermining two-party, parliamentary government nor the free press, noting that, "The greatest tragedy that could overcome a country would be for it to fight a successful war in defence of liberty and to lose its own liberty in the process."

The geography of Australia may also have helped to positively shape the country. Liberal democracy correlates most strongly with average income levels, but it has also taken strongest root in countries like Australia (and Britain, America, New Zealand) that have few or no land borders; whereas it has taken longer to cultivate in places with multiple or ill-defined and hard-to-defend borders, where insecurity trumps the desire for personal liberty. Australia is not only the lucky country that came of age and wrote a constitution just as the influence of liberal ideas was at its peak, it also had the barriers of the natural world to allow democracy to marinate without challenge and disruption from surrounding countries.

In addition to the strategic security offered by its geographical position, Australia has also been very fortunate to have sat within the US-led world order, which from 1945 to recent times made most countries and peoples feel more secure. Under the umbrella of the US and the institutions it set up, many countries have been able to trade freely and organise themselves to best look after their own citizens. It is no coincidence that the number of democracies fell in the 1930s as America withdrew from the world, and then increased rapidly under the postwar settlement. The recent travails of American-style democracy have led to another drop.

There will be no permanent victory of liberal democracy or its more authoritarian alternative. The tension between the two has its roots in a very fundamental human paradox—that we want both to be free and to be looked after. In most places and for most of history the latter instinct prevailed—it was better to leave the running of the tribe to the strongest person and trust that they would organise and deliver victory in an uncertain world. It was only as countries became internally and externally secure enough that liberal democracy was able to take root. The better angels of our nature come to the fore when the devil of fear is suppressed. Although even angels sometimes feel as though the grass is greener elsewhere—and will be tempted accordingly.

Indeed, when I was running an Asian business and travelling weekly into various parts of China, there were plenty of Australian (let alone local) businesspeople who would praise the Chinese-style of government for its focus on the longer term, without elections to drive things off-course. This is naive. When you see the country up close, the strengths of China have nothing to do with its political system. Rather, it is the attention paid to education and respect for teachers, the meritocratic selection of civil servants, the emphasis on living standards, and the pragmatic desire to implement what works. These are Chinese cultural attributes that have worked just as well—indeed *better*—in places such as Singapore, Taiwan and Hong Kong, as well as among the successful Chinese diaspora. An authoritarian environment is not necessary.

As one China scholar has put it: the Communist party likes to credit itself with "lifting millions out of poverty", but it is truer to say that those millions lifted the party. Entrepreneurial, hardworking and smart Chinese people built amazing businesses and created wealth on a scale never seen before. Key technocrats and leaders, such as Premier Zhu Rongji, deserve credit for the way they allowed this to happen in the 40 golden years after 1979, but their main accomplishment was to improve education and infrastructure, open China to international trade and investment, and then to get out of the way of the ordinary Chinese people, whose energy fuelled China's growth (assisted, of course, by globalisation, which saw other countries open up to Chinese exports and investment flows).

Undemocratic governments don't self-correct; when they go off-piste, they do so very badly. They also don't have mechanisms for the regular and peaceful transfer of power (Deng Xiaoping set up term limits in China as an alternative to elections to peacefully transfer power, but this lasted less than a decade after he died). By contrast, democracies always seem to be in crisis but are actually very stable in the longer term. Non-democratic countries appear deceptively stable, until suddenly they're not.

The future

Australia gets the balance of democratic accountability and apolitical expertise better than most countries, but in a more contested and complex world it will need to better articulate the fundamentals of representative democracy. Citizens elect people as representatives to properly consider the issues and solve problems. Anyone can lobby them on any issue they feel strongly about and/or know something about, and ultimately the majority can and will change who represents them if they don't like the current lot.

Arguably, the ways to make government work better in Australia are evolutionary—such as fixed four-year parliamentary terms at a national level, instead of the current term of up to three years, under which governments get only a year, at best, to pursue a new agenda before a frenzy of speculation about the next election intervenes. Government in Australia could also be improved by greater transparency: there is insufficient release of government-collected data, and the "conflict of interest" rules contain loopholes that allow former ministers to take on inappropriate roles too soon after their terms end. Australia already ranked very low for corruption in every global survey but has recently added a National Anti-Corruption Commission to the existing state-level bodies to provide more scrutiny of political and bureaucratic decision-making.

It helps that a proportion of the money for Australian election campaigns is provided through public funding (based on prior share of vote), which lessens the reliance on private donors. Unions and union-aligned pension funds more than match donations from businesses, and the small number of billionaires who have made large donations have not made any material impact to the results. Australian politicians are not particularly well paid, but the relatively low cost of campaigns gives them, overall, greater freedom from external financial pressures than politicians have in most comparable systems. What's more, Australia's rules for disclosure of political donations are strong by global standards—though the speed of these disclosures should be improved.

Vigilance remains necessary, even with the relative resilience that Australia's institutions provide: "hard" rules can be stretched to breaking point if the "soft" conventions of decent behaviour are ignored too many times. Good faith, rational debate and courtesy may seem like quaint virtues, but they are what has allowed civil society to develop. Some willingness to suspend partisanship is essential to the proper functioning of democracy.

Technology and social media

Australia has been one of the first countries to try to regulate social media companies, partly in the belief that aspects of their business models create long-term threats to democracy. This reflects the heavily risk- and safety-focussed strands of the Australian character (as discussed in Chapter Two) as well as an egalitarian confidence that relative size is no reason to shy away from a battle. Three areas have drawn particular attention: the impact of social media on the provision of news; attempts to legislate against "misinformation"; and restrictions on children having access to social platforms.

The first piece of legislation of note was the News Media Bargaining Code in 2020, which required tech companies such as Meta (the parent of Facebook) and Alphabet (Google) to pay money to traditional media organisations whose headlines frequently appeared on their platforms. The amounts to be paid were to be commercially negotiated, but with the proviso that the government could force a compulsory arbitration if there was no agreement. Facebook initially pulled news off its Australian sites but inadvertently included important public service information about bushfires and Covid, leading to a public backlash and ended up agreeing the deals which, together with deals done by Alphabet, are estimated to have injected about $200 million a year into mainstream media organisations (the agreements reached are not public). The legislation is up for review in 2025, and Meta has threatened to drop news content while the Australian Government says it will legislate for financial penalties where social media businesses pull news content from Australian users, so further conflict is likely.

Another piece of legislation was passed in late 2024 to ban social media for children under the age of 16. While very popular with the public and not in itself illiberal (since open and liberal societies have always provided protections for children until they are ready for, say, alcohol or other challenges of adulthood), the mechanics remain to be sorted out. For instance, there is no clear way for ages to be verified, with the government putting the onus on the social media companies to do it in a way that does not involve taking government-approved ID data. The rush to pass the ban did not allow adequate exploration of more targeted ways to address the harm done by advertising-driven algorithms, such as not allowing social platforms to retain the page-history data that is crucial for propagating addictive content. Nor has enough thought been given to the likelihood that children will use virtual private networks (VPNs) to appear as though they are based outside Australia. Nonetheless, this move has already prompted more work from tech companies to address the negative effects of their products on children. Australian public schools (and most private ones) have also sensibly taken phones out of classrooms in recognition of the distraction and discipline problems they cause, as well as the psychological issues. The UK is yet to enforce a national mobile phone ban in schools.

The third major attempt to address the harms of social media was a "misinformation" bill that ended up being blocked by the

Australian senate. The opposition believed, correctly, that legislation is not the answer to untruths on the internet. It is tempting to look for alternative solutions beyond that of an educated populace applying sceptical reasoning, but none are attractive. Those alternatives all involve some bureaucracy, whether in the public or private sphere, deciding what can and cannot be posted, potentially making the cure worse than the disease. It is, of course, important for existing laws to be enforced against incitements to violence, defamation and other crimes. There may even be a role for "health warnings' to tell a reader whether a post is disputed and to direct them to alternative sites for balance or clarification. But blocking content—or people—entirely will only encourage conspiracy theories and the other pathologies that emerge whenever ideas are immune from challenge. Blocking certain views is also a recipe for getting things wrong; for every ten counter-narratives about Covid that were false or fake there was one that was true. Societies need to provision for those times when the consensus is wrong, as it inevitably will be. Natural Australian scepticism and the power of a free and educated population are the best counters to bad ideas, prejudice and lies. They have always been necessary, but now are essential as the volume of disinformation gets turned up

It may be true, as one commentator has observed, that "the currency of the internet [has] changed from the paragraph to the sentence, from the blog to the tweet, from the word to the image," and this makes complex political debates harder. But a person can enjoy TikTok videos and still have an informed view on tax policy and it is usually grossly overstated how many people engaged in complex ideas before the internet. The investment needed is more of the same sort of education that has always been required: how to reason, how to interrogate an idea, how to contextualise information. Government does have a role to play in ensuring that the source of online information is transparent, and that material generated by deep fake AIs and malicious foreign states is taken down; the right of free speech is for citizens and does not extend to bots or to foreign adversaries. But, beyond that, misinformation is a human problem, not a technology problem; it is something to be dealt with by educating children to have the literacy and numeracy to properly assess what they read and hear.

Other negative impacts of social media are also hard to legislate against. For instance, the algorithms favour posts that create strong emotional reactions, which will often drive people towards echo chambers that reinforce what they already think. But this is not entirely new; social media is simply an amplifier rather of echo chambers that already exist. Australians who get their news from the *Guardian*, *Sydney Morning Herald*, *The Age*, Crikey or the ABC will have one worldview reinforced, just as surely as someone who reads the *Australian*, *Telegraph*, *Herald Sun*, *Spectator* or watches Sky News after dark will have quite another reinforced. Creating thoughtful and balanced citizens is a broad societal responsibility and challenge, not something that we can legislate for any individual company or industry to do.

The danger of echo chambers distorting democratic debate is, of course, not the only issue. There are also the unrealistic expectations created by heavily filtered photos and people posting their "best lives", all of which is bolstered by what the algorithms do and do not push into people's feeds. Becoming immersed in this distorted reality can result in mental health problems, particularly in those who already face difficulties, and can also be a powerful distraction from more constructive pursuits. Once again, however, Australia is in a better position to counter these challenges than many other cultures. Sceptical Aussies, with their piss-taking sense of humour, see through filtered posts more quickly than most. Meanwhile, Australia has an unusually strong societal focus on mental health and a relatively widespread outdoors, sporty culture that pulls people into real-world interactions more frequently than in other countries. Pushing people into regular contact with a broad range of people in the real world is the best disinfectant for online echo chambers.

Technology is neutral—it's the values and culture of a country that determine how it gets used. New innovations such as facial recognition and AI will enable authoritarian regimes to strengthen their hold on power, but they also allow groups such as Bellingcat, the open-source investigators, to tie individual Russian operatives to their crimes in Salisbury and other places. It is better to stop seeking to "un-invent" technologies (which is impossible, in any case) or ban their use, but instead to have clear rules around what purposes these technologies can be put to. For instance, we can't stop our movements being tracked on our phones, but we can prescribe that the data isn't used by anyone who doesn't need it and that it is not abused. Social media also has many positive features, from connectivity to entertainment, and its problems are mostly just new variants of problems we already know how to combat. During the first round of trying to deal with social media and other new technologies, Australia has been proactive, though it has likely made mistakes too—but we can be confident that the country's values and institutions are up to this long-term challenge.

PART IV

AUSTRALIA'S PLACE IN THE WORLD

ISLAND NATION

No choice we can make as a nation lies between our history and our geography ... they are immutable. The only choice we can make as a nation is about our future.

PAUL KEATING, former prime minister

The physical geography of a country shapes its culture and strategic choices. Australia's most obviously unique geographic feature is being a single country (indeed, a single continent) on an island. It's a big island; when my family moved to Mount Isa, we did 24 hours of driving to the north and then another ten hours to the west to get to that Queensland town from Sydney. Australia is by far the largest country that has no land border with any other nation. By contrast, China has 14 land borders, and almost every country in Europe, Africa and the Americas has at least two other nations separated by only a mountain or a river. While the borders of Europe, Africa and the Americas have been constantly reshaped many times through war, the Australian continent has been almost entirely undisturbed by outsiders for tens of thousands of years (with the coming of Europeans in the late 18th century being the single exception).

The first settlers migrated south from New Guinea when sea levels were lower and were then isolated for more than 50,000 years after the sea rose and cut Australia off from the north. The population was split into hundreds of groups across the whole of Australia, but their small numbers, their nomadic habits and the sheer size of the country meant that different groups, developing their own languages, didn't have major wars over territory. When Europeans landed, there was a very real possibility that different parts of Australia could have ended up under the control of rival colonial powers, a situation that would likely have led in time to wars between rival states within Australia. But, instead, all the settlements across the country ended up being subsidiaries of the British empire (which was also the largest and most enduring in the region) and came together as one country via an act of parliament rather than in armed combat.

However, even this deep-sea buffer and isolation from war on the home front has not eliminated all insecurities. Donald Horne's contemporaries thought of Australia as an overwhelmingly European population sitting "on the other side of the world" from Europe and feared being "cut off" in a country that even today is a full 24-hours flight time away from the ancestral countries of most of Australia's population and where political leaders have traditionally looked for allies. The fear of being subsumed by non-Europeans from the north has eased over recent decades as Australia's own population becomes slowly more Asian (at least in major cities) and Australians become more confident in their own identity (including the indigenous part of their history). But the "fear of abandonment" remains a streak in Australian politics and society.

The sense of Australia as physically isolated from kindred spirits has a history of creating fear and emasculating confidence. The White Australia policy of the early 20th century was mostly about economic protectionism, reflecting the power of workers at the time to keep low-cost labour out of the country, but it also clearly had overtones of racial prejudice and antipathy towards unfamiliar cultures. Fortunately, prejudices of this kind are increasingly confined to the fringes. But, having found a quiet spot away from the fight, many Australians want to be careful who gets let into the sandbox. There was a palpable sense of Fortress Australia during Covid—and reopening to the world became a slow and painful process for many people, despite the necessity of doing it.

The sense of Australia as distant and smaller is also not helped by how European mapmakers put their own continent at the centre of the world. Australia is typically shown at the bottom right-hand corner of the Earth, and as much smaller than its true relative size. Would a drawn-to-scale Australia, the size of the US and the size of the whole of Europe, sitting in the middle of the map, have a different psychological impact on Australians and others?

The fear of invasion

Invading a country that is as isolated and spread out as Australia is not easy. It was not easy even in 1942, when Australia was as wide-open as ever before or since, and sufficiently scared by the Japanese air attack on Darwin to make an historic appeal to America for protection. While many people believed that Australia was a target for invasion (and perhaps it could have become one eventually, if the war had gone differently), Japanese army and naval records make it clear that an invasion was never seriously considered at the time. Australia was deemed too far away, the coastline too long and the population too scattered for any realistic occupation.

With the exception of frontier violence involving indigenous dispossession, Australia has experienced an unusually peaceful history and could arguably have among the least experience of conflict of any country in the world. In modern times, unlike almost every other country in the world, Australians have never fought in a war that resulted in a loss or gain of its own territory, and the present nation of Australia has never been occupied by another country. Non-indigenous Australians have known conflict only as something that happens on distant shores.

Australia's desire to be part of global institutions such as the UN is for prudent and perhaps even abstract notions of security and idealism, rather than the visceral reaction that led war-torn European countries to support the UN and then to form the EU. There is little intrinsic interest in foreign affairs among most people; instead, there is a desire to avoid the sort of realpolitik that other countries have had to engage in while Australians have peacefully got richer and enjoyed their quality of life. Television news bulletins cover the current conflicts in Ukraine and Gaza but are otherwise mostly silent on what's going on beyond Australia's shores. There is more airing of conflicts between Australian states, cities and the two houses of federal parliament than of those between other nations.

Not only is Australia fully "girt by sea" (as its anthem proclaims), but this island nation is also far away from most major population centres and, except for the island chain of the Torres Strait, is not even close to another land mass. Everything north of Singapore is more than seven hours' flying time away, which is beyond the refuelling range of all current fighter jets. It was only by taking almost all the territory to Australia's north that the Japanese were even able to put aircraft over Darwin in 1942. Military power is much harder to project over water than land, much harder with distance, and with other countries in the middle.

This may not sound intuitively right. Isn't Australia weakened by its vast undefended coastline and small, diffuse population? Such fears underpinned the post-war migration boom and Australia's following the US into multiple wars across the 20th century, partly from ideals of "mateship" but also in the hope that Americans might return the favour one day. But the fear of invasion is exaggerated, and changes in the world of warfare have made Australia more, rather than less, able to defend itself.

For starters, anyone who wants to occupy Australia needs to commit enough troops to hold and secure a massive amount of territory, as well as to trek from their most likely landing points in the north of Australia for days, probably weeks, to population centres. With modern GPS and surveillance technology, they would also be tracked all the way and easy to pick off as they struggled the 3,200 kilometres from the Northern Territory to Sydney through inhospitable country with no rivers and limited roads.

More importantly, they'd first have to get to Australia, which is not easy. Not only is Australia an island that is an extremely long way from anywhere else, but to the north there is nothing but other islands for tens of thousands of kilometres. Indonesia sprawls across the oceans to the north and is a major barrier that any hostile power needs to get past before it could reach the seas to the north of Australia. To the south there is New Zealand and the Antarctic, and to the east and west the sea goes on so far that it reaches Africa and the Americas. Provided Australia can withstand a blockade (food is not an issue, but oil and pharmaceuticals are), then it is very well insulated.

Since the Second World War, the advantage in sea battle has skewed more towards the defender. It is much easier to deny the sea to someone else than to control it. Submarines, drones and aircraft now have precision weapons that can easily locate and destroy any ship big enough to carry the troop numbers necessary for an invasion. Australian defence forces do need to invest in the right kit and to locate it in the right place, which is not always what has happened. But if the type of adaptability and effectiveness shown in industries such as mining and finance were to be applied to defence, there is no reason Australia cannot be made as secure as anywhere in the world at a level of spending that is affordable.

A small population has also become less of an issue in modern war, particularly on sea and in the air, which is where Australia would be defended. The key to having sufficient submarines and planes to counter any aggressor is money rather than people. Deterrence can be achieved through long-range missiles in the far north, and a country with a quarter of the world's uranium reserves is quite capable of nuclear deterrence, too, if it were really concerned about an attack.

If Indonesia is a buffer to any threat to Australia, then could that country itself become a threat? It's theoretically not impossible that some theocracy inimical to Australia might one day come to power, though this seems extremely unlikely at a time when Indonesia is democratic, pluralist and outwardly focussed. In any event, the same observations about Australia's excellent geography and ability to deny the sea and the air would apply as much to Indonesia as to anyone else.

But Indonesia is also a reminder of the most important point: the need for military defences only arises when all other means of resolving disputes have been exhausted. Australia needs to have a sensible and credible capability to defend the air and sea to the north, but war will forever be entirely hypothetical unless there is a colossal failure of diplomacy. It is increasingly understood that the stability and goodwill of Indonesia, Papua New Guinea and the other Pacific island states is the key determinant of Australia's security. A constructive and friendly relationship with those countries will always need to be at the top of national priorities.

For the time being, then, the major threats to Australia are likely to continue to be cyber and economic in nature, not military. These need to be countered accordingly. Never does the old adage about generals "always fighting the last" war ring truer than when cyberattacks and drones are countered by a plan to build tanks and recruit infantry.

The psychology of perceived distance

The sense of being "far away" also leads Australians (and others) to consistently underestimate Australia's weight in the world. Australia is, it has been said, "a substantial middle power that thinks it's a small power". Australia's economy is almost the size of the Russian economy (and its GDP per capita is six times greater), but Aussies don't swagger like Putin. The wealth of the average middle Australian is twice that of the average middle American (and the Aussie also has free healthcare and longer holidays), yet Australians hang on every twist of American politics as though it offers inspiration. Australia's GDP per capita is almost a third higher than that of the UK, but in top-level business and political meetings Australians banter about cricket and rugby as if there's nothing to teach the Brits off the sports field.

The isolation of Australia isn't just felt on the home side. A common refrain in meetings over several decades in Europe is that "I'd love to visit, but Australia is just so far away". Distance is up there with fear of snakes and spiders as a reason not to visit. An era of more video calls might mitigate the issue but won't make it go away. Until supersonic flight allows a lot of people to fly from London to Sydney in five or six hours, Australia will have to work hard to get attention in Europe and parts of North America commensurate with its actual size and contribution. Barack Obama's post-presidential biography is 768 pages long, but Australia doesn't get a single mention.

Climate and population

Another feature of Australia's geography is the unpredictability of the weather. Australia is not only the driest continent on Earth, but also the one with the least naturally fertile soil. Australia is very unusual in having the majority of its weather driven by the El Niño and El Niña temperature oscillations, rather than the regular annual cycle of seasons. The upshot is that Australia experiences savage drought for several years—and then, almost from nowhere, torrential rain.

Jared Diamond, in his cross-cultural study *Guns, Germs & Steel* has suggested that this unique climate is why the First Australians mostly adopted a flexible, nomadic, hunter-gatherer paradigm rather than creating farms and fixed settlements which would be vulnerable to erratic weather. The indigenous approach was adaptive to the unique Australian environment: having multiple sources of food instead of a particular cultivated crop, investing little in possessions, and moving regularly as conditions became better or worse in particular localities. It is only with the coming of modern fertilisers, transport and markets that fixed food production and farms became viable in Australia. Farming is still not easy, though, and climate change is going to make it harder still.

Australia's approach

Australia's foreign policy expresses the national personality and culture described earlier in this book. There is a strong belief in "following the rules", and in the notion that countries should enjoy "safety". There is a feisty willingness to defend democratic ideals and self-determination (sometimes to the disquiet of neighbouring countries, whose instinct is to keep their heads down), but this is combined with a sceptical pragmatism that lets other countries get on with their own business.

Australia will continue to be proactive in diplomacy and security. It needs to fix its falling education standards, a cumbersome and centralised approach to defence procurement and its economic complacency. But a lack of self-confidence leads to bad decisions in foreign policy. As the region to the north becomes more contested, it is right for Australia to be alert but not alarmed.

THE CHINA CHALLENGE

I think we should always strive to have a peaceful coexistence with China, an agreed co-operation, accepting our ideological differences ... For the foreseeable future we are going to have a more assertive Chinese leadership [but] perhaps not indefinitely.

JOHN HOWARD, former prime minister

It was 8.08pm on the 8th day of the 8th month of 2008. At that auspicious minute, the 91,000 people in Beijing's Birds Nest Stadium watched the first spectacular act of the Olympic Opening Ceremony. Australia's prime minister joined the presidents of the US and Russia and leaders of a hundred other countries to admire Zhang Yimou's choreography. I was one of many Australians in the stadium that steamy August day: people in sports, business, media, government and the arts. My week leading up to the Opening Ceremony included a celebration of Macquarie Group's first ten years in China and a function to toast the friendship and collaboration between Australia and China in swimming and diving at that time.

Beijing was an invigorating place to be in 2008. China was almost 30 years into the reform era that started by opening markets from 1979—first allowing people in the countryside to sell outside of agricultural collectives, then allowing private enterprises to operate in small towns, and, finally, letting market forces into large sectors and capital markets. The Communist party was still in charge but was happy in those days to trust clever technocrats, often engineers mostly trained in the US, and to "cross the river by feeling the stones" in an iterative process of reform. China was consequently growing by double-digit percentages every year, and the newly created wealth and middle-class consumers were as obvious as all the shiny new infrastructure. Entry to the World Trade Organisation had forced further reform internally in China, making trade with Australia and other countries take off.

There was not only a material sense of momentum. Restaurants and bars flourished, and foreign-educated Chinese flocked home to set up businesses and import ideas and cultures they had picked up overseas. Investigative newspapers were starting to shine a light on corruption and other issues (at least in provinces outside of where they were based). The 798 Art district in Beijing had emerged, and there was more and more freedom of expression on the internet, provided people didn't directly challenge national leaders or push particularly sensitive issues. There was a sense in 2008 that, while red lines were always there, the average Chinese person was slowly getting a larger and larger space in which to live the kind of life they wanted to live. My Chinese friends and colleagues were happy.

Not only was President Bush at the Olympics, but the US had real influence in China at that time. Senior people in government and business in China wanted to preserve distinct "Chinese characteristics", but they admired the strength and success of America, and there was an active debate about how far to emulate American ways. The US shares the "bigness" that is central to Chinese understanding of itself, and so it seemed to offer lessons for a country seeking a more prosperous and open future. While in Asia for his Olympic trip, the US president also led 12 countries in the region into negotiations for a Trans-Pacific Partnership to cement trade, investment and co-operation among market economies in Asia (China could only look on with envy, since its state subsidies kept it on the outside of this pact).

Beijing in 2024 is very different to the Beijing of 2008. The limited freedoms of the press and universities have been wound back, censorship has tightened, and internal security and surveillance have ramped up. The liberalising economic reforms and cautious foreign policy of China's leader in the 1980s, Deng Xiaoping, have been put aside. Meanwhile, ideological imperatives and a personality cult around the leader have returned—but in modern technology-enabled forms that Mao couldn't have conceived. Some economic reform continues, but the government has pivoted to openly favouring state-owned enterprises over private companies, entrepreneurs have been brought down, and the technocrats in government are much more driven by party politics. This has already slowed China's growth, and will do so even more over time, as well as making it harder for foreign businesses who will increasingly have to deal with politically driven agendas rather than more commercially minded businesses. The Chinese tech industry that thrived in Hangzhou and Shenzhen, away from Beijing control, has been bound more tightly to the party, and innovators such as Jack Ma, the co-founder of Alibaba Group, pushed out. Private companies lose top graduates to the mandarin bureaucracy, as smart youngsters see which way the wind is blowing. Investment is being driven towards those technologies with applications for internal security and the military, rather than into business models with the opportunity to create profits by meeting consumer needs. Consumer confidence has gone from among the world's highest to among the lowest.

America is no longer a role model in China, either. The financial meltdown of 2009 made Chinese decisionmakers query whether the US really did know what it was doing, and the costly and inconclusive ends to wars in Iraq and Afghanistan tarnished the idea that Washington rules the world. Political and social dramas in America have since further strengthened the hand of those in Beijing who argue that the US model is not the one to follow. In 2016, under President Trump, the US even walked away from the Trans-Pacific Partnership it had started, leaving Japan and Australia to conclude the trade and investment pact with the remaining 11 countries that the US had originally assembled. The US and China increasingly aggravate, rather than fascinate each other.

Several years after the Beijing Olympics, as Xi Jinping was first taking control of the party, I was headhunted to run some global operations of a Hong Kong-based company owned by one of China's largest listed conglomerates. During the four years I was there, the Chinese shareholder asserted more and more control, turning a previously commercially minded business into something deeply state-driven. Every decision, whether it was related to credit, hiring or remuneration, became deeply political. There was a growing distrust of foreigners, the party cell in the organisation became more influential, and staff began to compete against each other to be seen as the most loyal to the head office in Beijing, rather than be the most competent. This was obviously just a microcosm of the broader change that was underway in Hong Kong more broadly over that time. After I left, any vestiges of autonomy in the media, the legislature and the legal system of the "special administrative region"' started to be dismantled too—and those out of step with the party were sidelined, or worse.

Some think the promise of opening-up was always an illusion. The west, they say, was too trusting; the Communist party was always going to take back control and reverse reforms. Others note that China has had cycles of opening-up and then closing-in throughout its history (most famously from the voyages of Zheng

He to the complete closure of the country in the mid Ming dynasty, but also frequently through the 20th century and within the post-1979 reform era).

Either way, China has enough smart, educated and hard-working people, along with sufficient momentum from the reforms of the 30 years of opening-up, that it will continue to be an economic powerhouse, even under the new management. Even those who don't agree with the new direction of the party in government are still proud that the country is reclaiming its historic stature as a leading world power and grant the central government a lot of latitude. Australia and the world, then, need to deal with the China that exists today—one that is increasingly assertive and party-driven.

Australia has always been at the front of the pack when it comes to China: one of the first countries to give diplomatic recognition, in 1972, and one of the first to recognise the country's more recent turn and to put in place effective protections. Many countries can learn much from the Australian experience of modern China. As recently as 2018, more than half of Australians said they trusted China to act responsibly in the world; now only 17 per cent say the same. But trade and economic engagement do the talking, and, in this respect, China has only continued to grow more influential. Three decades of growth have not only lifted hundreds of millions of people out of poverty and made China the largest player in most global trade, but they have also made Australians and others more prosperous. During my first few years living in Hong Kong in the lead up to the Beijing Olympics, most Australians started to focus on China for the first time. The country that was "too small to notice" quickly became "too large to ignore". New markets were created, ranging from wine, baby milk and vitamins to architecture, education and engineering services. About a third of Australia's exports now go to China.

Almost all Australians agree that the current Chinese government is authoritarian and that the Chinese system is not one under which they would want to live. The Chinese people themselves will need to decide, in time, whether they want to evolve their system as they get richer, but it's telling how many Chinese people want their children to be brought up in countries such as Australia, and how few people now migrate permanently to China. Historians tell us that countries tend to become democracies when their per capita GDP reaches about US$10,000, a point China passed a few years ago. It would not be surprising if China resists this tendency for longer than others, but the appetite for greater representation among those Chinese people whose per capita incomes are well beyond US$10,000 (notably in Hong Kong and Taiwan) suggests that there is no intrinsic ethnic or cultural reason that the normal rules won't eventually apply, even if that moment is still a generation away.

In the meantime, Australians are tempted by two big China myths. The first is that China's domination is inevitable, and that Australia has no choice but to concede to the future hegemon of the region as the US withdraws. The second myth is that conflict between China and the US is inevitable, and there is no choice but to row behind the latter superpower, not only going all the way with the most hawkish Americans but pushing them to go even harder.

However, the typically pragmatic response of most Australians is one that rejects both myths. The current Australian foreign minister has summarised it as "co-operating where we can, disagreeing where we must". It's an approach that calls out coercion when it occurs and protects Australian interests, but that also seeks common ground where it is in the national interest.

What does Australia have to fear?

To read some commentators, you would think China is an unstoppable power with the desire and capacity to crush Australia. This narrative not only misunderstands Australia's strengths and sells its capacities short, but it also overstates the ways in which China can realistically cause harm and the extent of its interest in doing so. If you want to counter a threat, then it is best to be very clear about what that threat is. If you cannot articulate precisely what you are afraid of, then the things you do probably won't counter the threat—and could even make things worse. Unfortunately, the conversation about China is at its blurriest when it comes to this most important question.

China is, as one of Australia's former ambassadors has described it, a country "constrained by its geography, its history, and most of all by its resource endowments". China has 14 different land borders, many with countries that are hostile to it or with which it has unresolved territorial disputes. Its soft power (the ability to influence without coercion) is low, and surveys suggest this power is falling in most of Asia and other developed countries. Then there are major "internal stability" issues—from Xinjiang to Tibet, from Taiwan to Hong Kong—which preoccupy the Communist party's focus, plus all the tensions that are inherent in any country without a clear line of succession nor institutional checks and balances. On top of all these geographic and strategic issues, China relies almost entirely on foreign suppliers for its energy and resources. About three quarters of China's oil is imported, mostly through thin choke points in the Malacca Straits. Australia alone is the source of two thirds of the iron ore and half the coking coal that China needs to make steel (which, in turn, goes into everything from housing to aircraft carriers).

Faced with such a challenging deck of cards to play, China's threats to Australia are only in very specific areas, all which can be countered without needing to overreact. The most coercive things that China has tried to do in Australia have been addressed by the government in the past few years. There are now tight rules about foreign interference in Australian elections; an overdue ban on foreign-sourced donations to political parties; greater scrutiny of universities to ensure that collaborative research with Chinese entities is not being used for military purposes; and much stronger investment in cybersecurity. Some of these measures have been criticised by China's ruling party, but they are all appropriate.

As for any military threat, the main debate among Australian strategists is whether to focus on "defending the island" (easier to do, as noted in previous chapters) or whether to be integrated into a US-led "forward defence" strategy that includes the possibility of fighting far north of Australia. Since the start of China's "wolf warrior diplomacy"—a more aggressive policy that began in 2017—the second strategy has become ascendant. China has built up islands in the South China Sea, which can be used to give it better access to open waters and prompted a fear that certain shipping lanes could be cut off to Australian trade (although China would likely let through ships bringing iron ore, baby milk, and wheat they want to buy, so the worry is more that Australian trade to Japan, Korea and Taiwan could be blockaded).

But when it comes to trade and investment, the case for intervention is much less clear, and Australia will need to keep guarding against any self-inflicted damage. The business-related things China does with Australia include investing in companies and buying Australian goods (be they minerals or food) and services (particularly education and tourism). Investment from China into Australia has fallen from a peak of over $20 billion in 2008 to less than $1 billion in 2023. The total stock of investment from China in Australia (from the very first investments in the mid-1980s to now) makes up less than three per cent of total foreign investment, far smaller than it looms in the popular imagination. Foreign investment in Australia continues to be dominated by the US, UK, Europe and Japan.

Australia's Foreign Investment Review Board has always knocked back investments that were suspect on national security and other grounds, but this scrutiny has recently become much more intense, with even very small and non-sensitive investment (whether from China or elsewhere) being treated to long delays in approvals, with numerous other government agencies getting involved. In the last decade, Australia has gone from being one of the countries most open to foreign investment to the fifth most restrictive in the OECD. Some tightening was arguably necessary, but there's a danger it has gone too far. It is important to make it harder for foreigners to get inside critical infrastructure and data, but slowing or stopping money from coming into the country is not necessarily a particularly effective way to do it. Measures that keep IP ownership local and secure facilities and data make more sense than blunt but vague rules about who holds the share certificates.

The most obvious conclusion from looking at the hundreds of major deals that have taken place over the years is that Australians have had by far the better part of the bargain. Australia is an efficient and transparent market, and locals have a shrewd sense of what their businesses and assets are worth and are tough negotiators. Foreign investors usually pay either fair value or too much. The only bargains are Australian businesses with big offshore divisions; Aussie investors don't give anything away when it's a business they understand, but many of them undervalue businesses operating outside Australia. Chinese investment in Australia has not only made fortunes for Australians; the brief flurry of overly expensive purchases from 2006 to 2012 also left China *even more* reliant on Australian iron ore and coal.

It is not unusual for countries to keep their economic and political relationships separate, and there are many examples of Australia selling wheat and other products to countries with which it had no political relationship at the time, including to China during peak Maoism. Though it is fair to say that Australia will need to be particularly clear about the difference between economics and politics at a time when both China and America are, for different reasons, likely to blur the two.

China and the United States

Australia's interests are very much aligned with those of the US in wanting an open and free Asia-Pacific which is not dominated by a single country. But the US now also sees China as a superpower competitor that it wants to decouple from, while Australia (and its region) still benefits from more Chinese growth.

While the wiser heads continue to take a balanced view of China as both an opportunity and a potential threat, there's a powerful and vocal group across government, the military and the media who want Australia to join America in a crusade to "contain" China. They reach for clumsy historical analogies—Cold War, appeasement, and the like—and lecture that Australia needs to stop hugging the panda and join the US in slaying a dragon. There is increasing awareness of the Thucydides Trap, the more-common-than-not history of war between an existing great power and an emerging power that threatens to displace it.

If there is a real risk that the two countries most important to Australia will veer into armed conflict with each other, then Australia will need to decide whether to be a voice of caution or of escalation. The room for manoeuvre will be limited by Australia having often outsourced defence to America, made poor procurement decisions and under-provided for its own security.

A core-interests playbook

How does Australia relate to a country that is increasingly powerful and important, but is at the same time inclined, by history and by the ideology of its bosses, to be prickly? It's obviously a difficult path to take, and each situation needs to be considered in context. But I would put forward two general principles, based on 15 years of negotiating in China. Firstly, be clear about your core interests and red lines, but flexible and constructive about co-operating in other things. Secondly, talk less, smile more—and save most of the hard talk for private communications.

China understands core interests (it is certainly very firm about its own), and Australia needs to understand its own red lines and be clear and unambiguous about what is acceptable and what is not. Having parties associated with the Chinese government interfere in elections or buy off Australian politicians is not acceptable; neither are cyberattacks on Australian businesses or forcing Chinese companies to suspend trading relations as a "bullying" technique for achieving other objectives. Australian citizens should not be threatened (in Australia) or detained without cause (in China), regardless of their ethnicity.

On the other hand, Australians generally acknowledge the need to be flexible and constructive when Australia's core national interests are not threatened. Australia cannot just reflexively follow the (increasingly strict) US lead on China. It is better to be a constructive force, helping America and China to find a path of managed competition, a way that acknowledges their inevitable rivalry but maintains enough guardrails to stop outright kinetic warfare.

Cultural differences between Australia and China will also become more important as conversations continue to complexify beyond simple questions of what price to charge for a box of minerals. For instance, it is apparent to anyone spending time in China that Chinese people put a lot of emphasis on "feelings" and "relationships", while Australians tend to focus, more contractually, on rules, treaties and the levelness (or otherwise) of the playing field. When China is displeased with another country, the most common complaint is that the other country has "hurt the feelings of the Chinese people". This sounds strange to Australian ears. Australians would complain someone has "broken the rules" or used force when they should have settled things another way. For countries like Australia to engage constructively, then it is important to understand the different way China thinks—the emphasis on hierarchy and harmony, and even the subtle differences reflected in language. Chinese grammar is relatively straightforward, but the language uses multiple tones, each one affecting the meaning of words that sound or write similarly. Language therefore expresses feeling and intent better than it conveys legal precision; Chinese is great for poetry, but not for contracts.

The Communist party's rhetoric has also shifted in the 20 years since I first started going to China—from one of "seeking truth from facts" (an engineer's mindset that welcomes improvement) back to a focus on Leninist notions of "struggle" and "contradiction" that feed a continual paranoia about external threats. Any order built around a cult of personality, and without a robust civil society and legitimate means of dissent, is a fragile and unpredictable one.

Which China?

It is also important to define exactly what we mean when we talk about China. Their national government is not entirely the same as the Communist party (though there is much less difference now than when I was working there) and there are federal, provincial and municipal levels of governance that each act and think in different ways; the more local branches of government are typically more accommodating when it comes to allowing businesses and people to go abroad and to attract investment to their region. There are also big differences between the warriors and bureaucrats of northern China and the commercial traders and bon vivants of the south, and between the interior of the country and the more outward-facing coast. Australia's thinking about China—let alone its policy—needs to better recognise these nuances and be more tailored to specific circumstances, rather than assuming that China, or even the Chinese government, is a monolith.

This is relevant because there are certain issues—such as territorial disputes, promoting Chinese influence in international institutions, and promoting a strong China—where the Chinese people and their government will think as one. But there are other issues—such as internet freedoms, freedom of movement, private property rights, and protection of private businesses—where they will not. We should also not forget that the real power in China is the middle class, a force that didn't exist two decades ago. The legitimacy of the party is built on people believing that the lives of their children will be better than their own, with the party's tools for achieving this goal being economic growth and nationalism. When we talk of "containing" China, of "trade wars", and of China as "the other", then the middle class fall in lockstep with the party. When we talk of an open internet, a China engaged with the world as an equal, of values of transparency and individual opportunity, then we are constructive. Australia demonstrates through its own success that these values deliver for the people.

People of Chinese descent in Australia comprise up to 10 per cent of the population in the urban centres of major cities. They are particularly heterogeneous, and not always on the same page as the "official" Chinese position on certain issues. Chinese-Australians range from Cantonese and Taiwanese speakers, who may be quite disconnected from the Beijing orthodoxy, to strong supporters of

Beijing in the Chinese-language media and the business establishment. Australians have to be more discerning about the differences between the two.

The party is ubiquitous in a one-party state, and nobody who has business or social ties in China will have been able to avoid being associated in some way with it, even if only indirectly. Australia is increasingly vigilant against real situations of spying, but applying guilt-by-association would quickly lead to economic damage and the unfair stigmatisation of Chinese-Australians who are some of the country's greatest assets in the 21st century. A very healthy dose of Aussie scepticism will be needed in the next decade as an antidote to the hysteria that is likely to be generated by certain commentators acting in bad faith.

The decision about whether China opens up again or closes even tighter will be one for the Chinese people—and especially the mass middle class—to make. It would be arrogant and presumptuous to think that any country, let alone Australia, can influence what they will decide. But we know that the behaviour of the rest of the world will make a difference and that Australia, at the cutting edge (for good and bad) of China's rise, can influence how other key countries act. If all interactions are confrontational and challenge China's stature and right to grow, then it will be easy for the Communist party to carry the people along with their nationalist agenda. But if the appeal is instead to freedom of global commerce and travel, to an open internet, to global standards of protection against the arbitrary power of officials, then China's people are likely to respond positively. Australia will have a significant role to play in the evolution of these narratives.

Underestimating power

The potential of Australia's diplomacy and soft power is underdeveloped but also hugely underestimated. Working in China, I saw first-hand how the 2009 financial crisis destroyed faith in US-style financial markets among Chinese policymakers and active participants. "We were following your example, but you actually didn't know what you were doing," they said, and the loss of credibility in financial markets also affected faith in other markets. Chinese hardliners seize on every misstep and mess in America to discredit those in China who want to carve a path towards greater legal certainty and political influence for the broader population. Australia has little say in the sort of example America sets, but Australians should always hope and encourage its friends across the Pacific to recommit to those qualities and abilities that made America such an inspiration to the world, including to a generation of China's finest young minds.

America's greatest soft power came from creating a world order that gave market access and cheaper financing to the world—which has also resulted in its own superior growth. Whereas authoritarians struggle in the longer term: local governments hide debt from the centre; health authorities in provinces avoid reporting issues that might bring down wrath upon them; and entrepreneurs spend as much time safeguarding their wealth by hiding or exporting it as they spend looking for new investments.

A lack of confidence in Australia's own strengths distorts the relationship with China. Not only does Australia share the strengths of America's open markets and society, its institutions and values work even better. Australia showed in the four years after China's boycott of Australian exports that it would not kowtow when the Communist party is coercive or unreasonable, but it has also almost always avoided being self-defeating as a result of an exaggerated fear of China. Most Australians are wary of the motives of those who want the country to strike a more belligerent pose, to choose America over China in all situations and to sacrifice economic strength for ideological purity. Are they truly advancing the Australian interest, ask sceptical Australians, or are they simply lashing out at the unfamiliar?

Australia can approach China in a way that is not naive, not supplicant but also not confrontational, built on a real understanding of its culture, history and circumstances. Australia is very distant from China, and the Chinese have a multitude of very pressing concerns that limit the ways that they can plausibly threaten Australia. The threats should not be overstated, and the strengths of the Australian system should not be underestimated.

AMERICAN UMBRELLA?

> *Dependence on American power does not seem to arouse in Australia the bitterness it arouses in other parts of the world ... Australians are used to being insignificant and relying on the power of others. They have lived in a state of such protected comfort and innocence for so long that one of their noticeable weaknesses is to have taken the power of Britain and then America so much for granted that they often ignore the realities of power and do not take it into their calculation.*
>
> DONALD HORNE, *The Lucky Country*

As the Second World War ended, the winners gathered to redesign the world to ensure such a war wouldn't happen again. The losers of the war were economically destroyed, countries such as the UK and France weren't in much better shape despite being on the winning side, and the newly decolonised countries of Asia and Africa were mostly even weaker afterwards than their already underdeveloped pre-war status.

So it was that the US, accounting for more than half the world's GDP at the end of the war, and with 80 per cent of the world's hard currency reserves, dominated the way that world order was redesigned. There would be no more colonies, even for those on the winning side. Created were a United Nations with every country represented (based in New York), the IMF and World Bank, the WTO to ensure free and fair trade and the Bretton Woods agreement for financial market stability. For countries that weren't setting themselves up in opposition to the US, there were also military alliances: Nato for allies in Europe, alliances in Asia with Japan, South Korea and later with Australia and New Zealand. It was a stunningly broad and enlightened investment in global cooperation and a rules-based order. As a happy side effect for American policymakers, it would also help dozens of countries to become both markets and suppliers for the US.

Australia was one of the first places to be "saved by America" (at least in its own mind), and had no colonial baggage to lose, so Australians were always one of the most enthusiastic about the post-1945 world order. Australia is the only country to have fought alongside America in every one of its major conflicts since 1914. It has done so in both righteous wars and mistaken wars, victories and defeats. Australians trust that America will do the same for them, if and when it becomes necessary, and the country has become increasingly tied to the Pentagon for most of its weapon systems.

The US-driven world order that emerged in the decades after 1945 worked better than any world order before. The world has experienced eight decades of unprecedented relative peace and prosperity. Almost every country has grown its economy, the lifespan and health of its people and the richness of its engagement with the rest of the world. It has become less fashionable to see America as making the world "safe for democracy" through its military dominance, but it is true that—under the umbrella of a superpower that prioritised freedom of trade and navigation and that imposed liberal constitutions on major defeated powers—countries were safe enough to prioritise freedom over security. With no need to live in fear of hostile powers, countries from Germany and Japan to Korea and Singapore could get on with democratic market-based systems that made them (and the US) prosperous and safe.

But the architects of this system are now dead, and the US has slipped from accounting for more than half of the world's GDP to less than a quarter—not because it hasn't grown and isn't strong, but because others have grown too and were coming off such a low base. At the same time, the challenges to the world order have become stronger. Many are from small and rogue nations, and can be dealt with; but, in the last couple of decades, there have been more and more challenges from emerging powers who, often very understandably, take issue with the notion that global institutions should be dominated by countries who were the most powerful in 1950. And then, most surprising of all, the US itself started to upset the order that it was so instrumental in setting up.

The US challenge to its own world order has not come entirely out of the blue. The number of global intergovernmental agencies grew from 37 to more than 400 in the 1990s alone. Global entities created by states can take on a life of their own and start driving agendas with which their founders are uncomfortable. America doesn't have the patience for the politics involved in choosing leaders for many bodies, and in recent decades has inadvertently let China and other powers, who have played a longer and more patient game, to take control of some of them. It is also unsurprising that a country whose GDP no longer looms so far above all others would be less eager to subsidise others who benefit from the system. By contrast, the Australian government has decided to double down on the UN and other truly significant global entities—making sure that it has real influence in those—while pulling back from those that are less immediately relevant to Australian interests.

It must be reiterated that America is not fading away. Far from it. The US remains the leader—economically, militarily and in the size of the shadow that its culture casts across the world. But it's also true that you can't run the show in quite the same way when you're 25 per cent of the world's GDP (or only 16 per cent on a purchasing power parity measure) than when you're more than half.

The US has reacted in three different ways to its decline in relative (not absolute) power. The first is denial. Since 2010, the US has resisted proposed changes to voting systems at global institutions that would better reflect the new power dynamics in the world. This has led to resentment and the creation of new structures outside the post-war world order by countries such as China, India and Brazil. If there's no role in existing bodies for rising powers that's commensurate with their new significance, then you get the Asian Development Bank, Belt and Road, BRICS and regional security alliances in Asia, Eastern Europe and Latin America.

A second way the US has reacted—particularly in the age of Trump's "America First"—is to do less globally and focus only on issues which require urgent attention in their own national interest. It's easy to see the appeal of this approach to many Americans, as it's simple, unilateral, quick and its longer-term consequences are harder to see. Besides, the US economy is still bigger than any other, so it can often win the immediate battle in bilateral disputes. This, however, is shortsighted and there is no substitute for the laborious and sometimes complicated process of building and maintaining alliances, making long-term plans and coordinating positions.

The third way the US has reacted is through strengthening the latticework of its alliances. America's share of world economic power rises to more than a third with Europe and Japan—and more if countries such as Australia, South Korea and others are added. There's enough commonality of interest between the US and much of the world that they will usually collectively still have the majority.

Australia obviously has a particularly big stake in how this all plays out. Its preference will always be for America to go the third way, rather than the first two; encouraging the US to work within the current world order and counter its decline in relative power through a more intelligent and constructive use of alliances. But, of course, an enlightened foreign policy also requires, increasingly, that Australia work independently to preserve and enhance the world order. This will sometimes mean supporting existing institutions such as the World Trade and Health Organisations that may be under attack from friends such as the US but that are essential for smaller countries.

And sometimes it will even mean pushing for new global institutions (as Australia did successfully with Apec and the G20), some of which might not have the US in them (for example, the Comprehensive and Progressive Agreement for Trans-Pacific Partnership [CPTPP], which has been enormously successful despite the US, its original sponsor, having pulled out at the last minute). Countries like Australia cannot rely on the US alone and will need to demonstrate far more courage and imagination in the future to make sure the rules-based world order continues.

Australian views

There are three strands of opinion about the US in Australia. The first is summarised by then prime minister Harold Holt's "All the way with LBJ!" exhortation during the time of the Vietnam War. This view, particularly strong among national-security mandarins and thinktanks on the right of politics, sees Australia's fate as inextricably linked to America's and downplays any difference between Australian and US culture and interests. In this view, keeping America ascendant in the Asia-Pacific is an existential priority for Australia and must dominate all other considerations.

A second view, held by a much smaller constituency, is best articulated by another former prime minister, Paul Keating, who argues that Australia should "seek security in Asia rather than from Asia," and that it is unrealistic to suppose that America will retain superior power, or even interest, in the region. On this view, the sooner Australia accommodates itself to a China-dominated region the better. They downplay the threat posed by China to Australia and don't see American power in the world as being inherently more virtuous than that of any other superpower.

The third view is held by the majority of Australians and is the one that has guided most of the country's foreign policy. This view does prefer the US to China while, at the same time not putting all its eggs in one basket—and approaching individual issues on their merits where possible. Lowy Institute polling of the Australian population clearly shows the contours of this approach. Despite rising tensions, seven out of ten Australians still say that is it possible to have good relations with both the US and China at the same time. Australians strongly support hosting US military facilities in Australia, but more than half would want Australia to stay neutral in a military conflict between China and the US. About half see the overall relationship with the US as more important than China, while the other half see the Chinese relationship as more important.

The general preference for US hegemony is partly because of shared values such as democracy, free speech and the separation of powers (although these are usually manifested in quite different ways), but even more so because of demonstrated behaviour. The US established a global institutional environment that enables smaller countries to thrive; it works to keep sea lanes free in Asia; and it pushes back against bigger countries trying to coerce their neighbours. By contrast, China has in the last decade, under its current leadership, demonstrated a propensity to push its weight around—economically and militarily—which understandably makes the prospect of a China-dominated region unappealing.

Though this clear majority of Australians strongly support the American alliance and want to make preparations to resist China's worst instincts, they are also reluctant to join in with those in America who simply want to decouple from China entirely—or, worse, actively damage its economy in order to stay on top. The greater mass of Australians want Chinese people to become more prosperous and want to cooperate wherever it makes sense. The test is not whether something is "pro-China" or "pro-America", but whether it breaches Australia's sovereignty to trade freely and make its own decisions.

The US in Asia

The American era has been an historical exception rather than the rule, but we often forget the extent of its exceptionalism. Without a strong multilateral system as an alternative to a single top dog, the world falls naturally—and messily—into spheres of influence around a handful of great powers. The "balance of power" dynamic that largely kept the peace in Europe throughout the 18th century may well be a model for keeping the peace in Asia in years to come, but it is "value neutral" and requires that we maintain a working relationship with people whose systems and cultures we do not share—and may not like.

The response in Australia to this changing world has been to huddle ever closer to the US, the successor to Britain as the "great and powerful friend". This is arguably a legitimate response to a more dangerous world—seeking a bigger brother—and history suggests that it can work. Australia will, however, need to be careful not to put all its eggs in the basket of America, which would make national decision-making less sovereign and subject to the goodwill of the dominant partner. Even in 1942 it took the attack on American territory at Pearl Harbor to get America to mobilise its war machine, and there is no certainty that Japanese threats to Australia would otherwise have attracted intervention. The will for the US to take on an even bigger task with relatively less strength in the future cannot be guaranteed. The notion that America will always come to Australia's rescue is a hope rather than a certainty.

It is also, though, common to underestimate the amount of agency in Australian foreign policy. The ANZUS Treaty in 1951 came from Australian pushing to get American involvement entrenched in the region, and then in 1957 Australia became the first nation to sign a trade agreement with Japan. Australia was also one of the first to recognise China (both literally and metaphorically) when the latter started to re-emerge in the seventies, and to push for organisations like Apec and the G20, which helped to incorporate China into the rules-based international order, as well as giving Australia a far greater seat at the table in global decision making than the old international architecture. Australia has always sought a closer relationship with Asean, and has more than 30 bilateral policing, defence and security agreements in Asia and the Pacific. When the US pulled out of the Trans-Pacific Partnership, it was Australia and Japan that led the trade agreement to get signed by the other parties anyway, and Australia has been proactive, rather than a follower, when it comes to the Quad (bringing Japan, India and the US together with Australia) and the Aukus alliance (between Australia, the UK and the US), as the Chinese Communist party became more aggressive in its words and actions in recent years. There is often the simplistic view Australia is sheltering under the cloak of bigger players that misrepresents how active Australia has been in adapting to changes to the region and creating, rather than just responding, to the strategic environment.

To create networks of cooperation and security among the middle powers (particularly, but not only, those in the Asia-Pacific region) is complementary to the US alliance, rather than being an either/or. Being part of a middle-power multilateralism with regional allies is not an alternative to an alliance with America; it makes Australia a more valuable partner—even if sometimes one with its own views—as well as hedging against those times that Big Brother won't be there to save the day.

The Cold War provided a common enemy for liberal democracies to reinforce each other, and a motivation for America to take on the responsibility of protecting the global order. It allowed the impulse for individuals to improve their economic and social freedoms to prevail over the lesser angels of human nature. The countries under the sway of the USSR were initially excluded, but then they also won the benefits of this freedom after 1989. An American retreat from liberal democratic values (both internally and in how America projects itself globally) would tip the balance the wrong way in many parts of the globe. Australia can't change this, but it can be a wise and supportive friend to the US to encourage it to do what's in its own interests, as well as of friendly nations. Australia is also building coalitions with others to support liberal democratic values while still supporting America where it's ready to lead the fight. There will be more trade deals and other situations where Australia needs to move without the US, and other situations where it will welcome US leadership.

In Australia, as in America, in the public debate there is often a narrow focus on military competition. But this is only one aspect of a competition that will ultimately be decided (as was the Cold War) by who has the most efficient and powerful economy and innovative technological system. Australia's degree of independence in the face of Chinese efforts to control the region will depend less on defence than it will depend on Australia's economic strength and resilience, how it influences UN organisations that set global standards, what decisions are made by Indonesia and other Asean countries about how independent of China they wish to be, and how effectively private companies and individuals protect their computers, servers, and phones. America may get things wrong, and China can keep funding a lot of hard power from the fruits of its previous 40 years of reform and opening up, but the US remains the strongest power in the world.

ASCENDANT ASIA

Australia must have a new idea of itself. We have to strike out in a new direction, in a new way, armed with our own self-regard, our own confidence and fully appreciating our own uniqueness.

PAUL KEATING, former prime minister

When I talk to Europeans about investing in Australia, or even basing themselves in Australia, the proximity to Asia always resonates with them—being so much closer to those rapidly growing markets means that Australia can act as a "stepping stone" to a lot of potential customers and business. Besides, Asian countries are all roughly in the same time zones as Australia—which is no small matter when it comes to doing video calls between offices or shuttling up and down without jet lag. That "proximity" can be deceptive, however: Europeans are always surprised when I tell them that Beijing is closer to London than to Sydney, and a relatively small number of native-born Australians have significant knowledge of Asian language and culture. Indeed, the study of Asian languages is falling in Australian schools.

Fortunately, though, more than 12 per cent of Australians now identify as Asian-Australian, and it is projected that there will soon be almost half a million Australians working in Asia. Enough immigrants have come from Asia that Mandarin, Cantonese, Vietnamese, Punjabi and Hindi make up half of the ten most widely spoken foreign languages in Australia. The flow of people between Australia and Asian countries, in both directions, is an ace in the 21st century, and just as important as material resources in making Australia strong.

The significance of the Asian diaspora in Australia has not yet been properly captured in the corridors of power; there are only a few senior politicians or bureaucrats of Asian descent or who have even spent time living in Asia, and, according to a recent survey, only seven per cent of board directors of Australian companies were deemed to have experience that would make them "Asia-capable". But many Asian-Australians have become successful entrepreneurs. Their children are now starting to enter the most senior levels of the professions and (more slowly) the boardrooms and C-suites of Australian companies.

The future of the world is Asia-centred simply because more than half the world's people live in Asia, and because those things that, for a few hundred years, made Asia less of a force than its population would imply have either already disappeared or are on their way out. It was only from about the year 1500 that Asian countries fell behind: slow to adopt technology, divided up and occupied by colonial powers, and then divided again by the Cold War blocs. But technology in Asia—bought, stolen or invented—is now in many cases the equal of European and American tech, and the nations of Asia have been steadily integrating with each other—to the point that, since 2000, Asian countries have traded more within the region than with the rest of the world. This trend will accelerate. Asia is writing free-trade agreements with enthusiasm, even as America and Europe retreat from them.

The collective economies of Asia have grown from less than 20 per cent of the world economy in 1980 to more than 40 per cent now. Every projection has them catching up to their share of population (that is, more than half of world GDP) within the next 20 years. Meanwhile, the US (which was half of the world's entire economy in the 1950s) has gone to less than a quarter, and Europe (as a whole) to around a fifth. Asia is therefore overtaking the combination of Europe and the US in economic importance. And it is not just a China and India story, either. Southeast Asia is already bigger than the economies of France and the UK and is on track to be the fourth-largest economy behind the US, China and India by 2040. Growth has occurred at two to three times the rate of the rest of the world and is being driven by trade and by young and digitally savvy populations. Australia has, incidentally, remained at about one per cent of the world economy, so its relative economic influence has barely changed. The rise of Asia matters for everyone, but it particularly matters for a country that is closer to Asia than it is to any other continent.

As I discovered when I moved to Asia to run a business, there is enormous diversity across the region. In building teams and businesses from India to Japan, from Korea to Indonesia, I quickly found that there was no single culture or formula for success. The multiplicity of languages, religions and historical enmities in Asia is greater than it is in Europe. Stages of development and business cultures also vary considerably, even between countries such as the Philippines, Singapore, Indonesia and Malaysia, which are physically close to each other. While China absorbed a lot of my time—as it did for most businesses and governments—the bulk of Asia, by population and area, is not China.

We can think about Australia's relationship with these countries in three broad categories. The first ring of countries closest to Australia is made up of Papua New Guinea, Timor-Leste, New Zealand and 15 other countries in the Pacific islands. This is Australia's real neighbourhood, in the sense that most countries would use the term. Australia is a large power relative to these countries and has the responsibility and influence that this brings. There is a natural common market, and a mutual interest in economic development. These countries are also on major trade routes and close enough that planes launched from there can reach Australia, so they must never become hostile to Australia and be allied with an aggressor. Australia provides lots of aid and security support to countries in the Pacific, but those countries are more interested in infrastructure investment, climate change and economic development. Australia is now increasingly taking the lead on these issues, in a belated recognition that it must be the partner of choice for the Pacific, otherwise China's long-term and strategic wooing of Pacific elites could pose a threat.

Australia's relationship with New Zealand is close, but still not as close as it might be for two countries so similar in history, institutions and strategic environment, and whose national identities were formed together as Anzacs, who fielded joint teams for the Olympics in the early 20th century, and who could indeed have been one country if the constitutional conventions had gone differently. In the 1980s, agreements were reached for trade and people to move more freely between the two countries, but this process of integration seems now to have stalled, and foreign policies sometimes diverge.

The second ring of countries to the north is the Asean region. This ten-member grouping of middle-sized countries such as Indonesia and Thailand includes 671 million people and stretches from the near north of Australia to the southern border of China. It is a pivotal part of the world, growing in prosperity and conflicted about the superpower rivalry of China and the US. Asean has its own challenges moulding consensus among disparate nations (of which Myanmar is the most glaring example), but in a world in which neither China nor the US can dominate Asia, the middle powers will become more and more important, and none as important as the Asean countries. They are currently split between countries leaning a little more towards America, those leaning a bit more towards China and those who aim, self-consciously, to be "balancers". Most countries in the region are less focused than Australians on the abstract question of "Who is right?" between the US and China; they want neither of them to upset the status quo.

Australia has a free trade agreement with Asean, defence ties with four of the Asean countries, and formalised a regular strategic dialogue a few years ago. It would like to be even closer (indeed, Australia has tried to join Asean on a couple of occasions since it was established in 1967, but has had to settle for being one of the countries in what's known as the Asean Plus dialogue) and has recently launched a public-private partnership to increase the level of trade and investment between Australia and Asean, which has lagged the diplomatic and strategic relationship. Australia has as many, or more, shared national interests with Asean as with Europe or North America, even if language and history make some Australians less comfortable than they should be to embrace that. Countries like Australia are sometimes frustrated that Asean works on consensus and is slow to come to decisions, but this underestimates the power of the grouping; it has been said that Asean is less about what it can do than what it can prevent.

Australia is relatively more idealistic and in the American camp than most Asean countries, who all, to varying degrees, are more comfortable with ambiguity and shared power in the region, and less inclined to jump to black-and-white conclusions about China's rise. Asean is a rapidly growing region, with arguably less structural and financial risk than China. The Asean countries are not all democracies, but most of them are, and most share with Australia a belief in a rules-based order for trade and security. Australians need to invest more in Asia and avoid own-goals in areas such as immigration, energy and foreign investment approvals that prevent those countries from investing much more in Australia, too.

Countries such as Vietnam, Thailand and Singapore have also learned a lot from dealing with China (in some cases for centuries) and can help Australia benefit from China's rise without kowtowing. With other countries lining up with the US or with China, the Asean collective becomes the swing vote that will help determine the extent to which Asia becomes a sphere of Chinese influence. Australia may be stepping up its economic engagement, but it will be an ongoing challenge to win and keep the hearts and minds of the key countries that hold the balance of power in the region.

To the north of Asean are Australia's major trading partners: China, Japan and South Korea, and then, to the west of them, the Indian subcontinent. Japan is one of the four pillars of Australian trade and investment, along with China, the US and the UK, and one of the best strategic partners. I have been a regular visitor for decades, including spending ten years on the Australia-Japan Business Cooperation Committee, and there is no place with better food, better snow or more regard for Australia. South Korea also remains a close friend and very complementary economic trading partner, most notably in recent years by matching Australia's critical minerals with its manufacturers.

While the Japanese and Korean relationships continue to strengthen on a long-established base, the relationship with India has rapidly accelerated from a much lower base, including the signing of a free(ish) trade agreement. Indian students and tourists have become a much larger part of the mix in the past five years, and the Indian subcontinent is now Australia's biggest source of immigrants. As well as the Quad relationship—which brings Australia and India together with the US and Japan—there are regular business delegations and bilateral visits between leaders. India remains a much smaller potential trading partner than China (both because of its size and its more domestic focus), and its democracy and legal system are more different to Australia than they appear superficially, but Australia is rightly making a lot of effort there.

There are three ways to learn wisdom, said Confucius: "First by reflection, which is noblest; second, by imitation, which is easiest; and third by experience, which is the bitterest." When it comes to dealing with China, Australia has mostly taken the bitter road to wisdom via experience. But there are many opportunities to be gained from reflection and imitation; listening and watching what Japan and Asean countries do can help Australia to better manage the China relationship. Unlike Australia, Japan and several Asean nations have real territorial disputes with China; planes and frigates clash regularly. They handle the China relationship through back channels—people no longer in executive government who can test solutions to problems and smooth misunderstandings. Business and government work together as a team to ensure that trade and investment is calibrated to help, rather than hinder, strategic objectives. Many Asian (and some European) countries will "talk softly" even while building up their capacity to defend themselves, and they "tend the garden" of the relationship by building trust, seedbed by seedbed, even while dealing with far more dangerous situations than those faced by Australia.

The inability of the US to engage properly with Asian countries in trade and investment—hamstrung as it is by domestic protectionism—is the major threat to US primacy in the region. Asean and other Asian powers like a strong US presence in the region, but when the US pushes for them to take a stronger stand against China, a common rejoinder is that "You give us a lecture, China gives us an airport." There is a sad irony in the fact that no country has done more to create the global trading system than the US, yet it is pulling back just at the wrong time.

The slowdown in China has not stopped Asean countries' growth, and India also continues to perform strongly. By 2040, Asia will be behind 40 per cent of global consumption. The region already hosts over half of the world's internet users due to rapid growth in digital penetration; a wave of digital innovation is being nurtured by huge amounts of venture capital and interest in research and development from the public sector; the governments of China, South Korea, Singapore and Japan have made AI and machine learning a strategic objective, and are now considered pioneers in those areas.

During the 13 years I was based in Hong Kong, I first flew between 15 offices across Asia (from India to Japan and down to Indonesia), then later added responsibility for offices in Europe, North America, and Australia. The biggest thing that struck me in this time was the contrast between the optimism, confidence and forward-looking nature of most people in Asia and the pessimism, inward-focus and anti-trade, anti-globalisation sentiment in much of the rest of the world.

Polling by the OECD supports these impressions. Trust in government leadership has been found to be highest in Asia, well above the OECD average. It's important to stress—particularly since many businesspeople who should know better do not—that this greater level of support for leadership in Asia is not a function of political systems. The world's largest elections are held in India and Indonesia, and almost all the region is composed of democracies where governments are called to account by opposition parties. They can and do change policy in response, even in those situations, like Singapore, where one party has long stayed in power.

Rather, the difference in confidence and optimism reflects the fact that in Asia each generation has been so obviously better off than the last, while progress for each generation in America and Europe is decreasingly easy to see. Even when there is progress in more developed countries, it can be harder to perceive because of the *relative* decline of the US and Europe (compared to Asia) and the prevailing narrative of "defending" long-held prosperity rather than "catching up" and attaining it for the first time.

Australia is fortunate to be in a very interesting position amid this intellectual and psychological divergence. It has a strong immigration intake from Asia; large and vibrant diasporas in both directions; and greater economic leverage with Asia because of the goods it sells and the services (especially education and tourism) that it provides. There is no reason why Australia can't continue to be different from America and Europe in the way it thinks about the future. Australians have objective reasons to be more optimistic, more forward-looking and more engaged in the new emerging world.

DIPLOMACY IN THE 21ST CENTURY

> *Australia does not have to choose between deeper partnerships or a broader range of partners. We can and must look to build both.*
>
> ANTHONY ALBANESE, Australian prime minister

Despite having spent most of my executive career in Asia, I currently do much of my work in the UK and other parts of Europe. Australia, too, has refreshed its ties with Europe while its engagement with Asia goes from strength to strength. This reflects a reality of the 21st century—that, in an online world that trades in services and shares cybersecurity challenges, geographic proximity is becoming less important. Threats and opportunities are now global in scope, and allies and adversaries can be found in any part of the world. What's more, the perceived success of different models of government could determine how certain "swing" countries develop their own governance; cooperation among open societies may lead to successes that aren't just desirable in themselves—but also inspirational to others.

The announcement in 2021 that Australia would be buying nuclear-powered submarines from the US before eventually making them in collaboration with the UK—as well as stepping up work on quantum computing and AI with both countries—drew out some strong opinions. For former Australian prime minister Paul Keating, it was a "throwback" to seeking "security from Asia," rather than "security in Asia". China was not happy, and some of Australia's Asean neighbours fretted that it might fuel an arms race in the region. But there was enthusiasm among other countries in the region—and among most Australians, who welcomed the opportunity to reinforce long-term relationships with countries with shared values.

The truth is that Australia needs to walk and chew gum at the same time. It simply has to keep ramping up its engagement with Asean, Japan and South Korea, and should also bolster its connections in the Pacific. There also needs to be continued cooperation and trade with China, where it is mutually beneficial and where China is willing. But Australia is also becoming ever more active in multilateral organisations and nurturing strong relationships with other like-minded nations who are further away geographically. The world is increasingly interconnected, and a country like Australia needs multiple friends and allies everywhere.

Britain

It is almost 250 years since the British parliament decided to establish a settlement in Sydney. Over that time, Australia has become more and more independent and more and more conscious that the continent was not *terra nullius* before the British arrived. For most of the past 60 years, the traditionally tight relationship with Britain seemed to be turning into a thing of the past, as Britain entered the European Union and Australia began to pivot towards Asia while doubling down on its alliance with the US. Today this is changing again, and Australia and Britain have become more closely engaged than the two countries have been for half a century.

Since I became chair of the Australian British Chamber of Commerce a few years ago, this sense of rediscovery has continued to grow in both Australia and the UK, as many forces drive a reconsideration of Australia's oldest foreign relationship. There has been more than enough written about Britain's exit from the EU, but one positive impact was a UK-Australia free trade agreement that has already substantially increased exports for both countries, as well as making it easier for young people from each country to work in the other. This was the first genuinely new free trade agreement that the UK signed with a G20 country after Brexit.

The last few chapters have also discussed the more fragmented and dangerous world in which Australia now resides. Coalitions of the like-minded are becoming more important; friends who care about free trade and liberal democratic values need to stick together when there is no longer an uncontested commitment to these things in the international commons.

The most interesting part of the Aukus pact between Australia, the UK and the US is not the plans for building nuclear submarines with the US and UK, but the agreement to share existing technology and develop new technology together—from AI to quantum computing and advanced manufacturing. (This so-called "pillar two" of Aukus will likely expand to other countries, such as Japan.) The US is the powerhouse, but Australia and the UK add almost 100 million more people, 17 more of the world's top 100 universities (bringing Aukus partners collectively up to more than half of the top hundred), vast critical mineral resources and some crucial niche technologies. Three countries that trust each other in sensitive areas will inevitably achieve breakthroughs that any one country on its own will not.

Today's mature relationship is different to what it was. Australia was very much a junior partner when Donald Horne was writing in the 1960s; Britain's empire was only recently dismantled, and

Australians still looked to the UK to make sense of her own politics. There were Australians nostalgic for empire and happy to sing *God Save the Queen* as the national anthem; while other Australians, reflecting a more Irish-Catholic and working-class heritage, defined themselves in opposition to British elites. Independent Australian passports were only issued for the first time 20 years prior to *The Lucky Country*. Legal appeals to Britain's Privy Council weren't abolished until 20 years after. Horne wrote prophetically in the 1960s that it might be good for Australia if Britain joined the European Economic Community (at that time, Charles de Gaulle was still blocking British entry) since, for Australia, "the psychological shock of being dumped might have hastened that dramatic reorientation, of admitting where in the world Australia really is and doing something about it." A decade later, Britain did join the EEC—and Australia *did* have to confront its circumstances, as Horne had predicted, and is now a much stronger country for having done so.

Australia now approaches the UK with an assuredness that it did not have when Horne was writing. A country as agile and prosperous as Australia has less need to trivialise itself with sporting banter and self-deprecating stereotypes. Australia has long borrowed ideas from Whitehall, but now the public policy (and sometimes even academic) traffic just as often flows in the other direction. Australia is typically seen as tough-minded and competent, and worth listening to on issues ranging from immigration to health. The adjective "Australian-style" was first applied in connection with Britain implementing a "points-based" immigration system, but it has since been applied to many other policies. Ministers in both national governments talk regularly.

While Australia and the UK now relate as peers, there is still much for the former to admire—and perhaps even emulate—about the latter. Despite some failures in the pandemic, the British invented a Covid vaccine and then rolled it out quicker than almost anywhere else. The UK remains the sixth-largest economy in the world, a permanent member of the United Nations Security Council, and one of the two nations with the greatest soft power. Britain has several of the world's top-ranked universities, and arguably the leading secondary school system of a major country. Much of the most eloquent and thoughtful writing in the English language is still to be found in British magazines and in a handful of its newspapers.

Nevertheless, there are still some in Australia who see alliance with Britain as an act of self-harming nostalgia, a failure to look towards the future and Asia. This blends with a perception that the UK is a country of white men and women, of monarchy and class differentiation, of residual imperial arrogance. Horne preferred that Australia move on from these ways. But Britain is no longer the place it was in the mid-1960s. It is more diverse, less class-conscious and reconciled to the Commonwealth as a club of connected nations rather than a construct of empire. Indeed, the Commonwealth now offers Australia and Britain (which is one of the world's largest foreign aid donors as a proportion of GDP) the chance to drive initiatives and build partnerships in developing countries.

It's also not accurate to see Australia's British heritage as being in opposition to Australia's indigenous heritage, as some people still do. One of the first pronouncements of the original governor of New South Wales, Arthur Phillip, was that "there will be no slavery in a free land" (20 years before it was abolished in Britain) and that those in the colony were to "live in amity and kindness" with the Eora people living in the Sydney area, so as to encourage "a High Opinion of their New Guests through kindness and gifts". There were, of course, many situations in Australian history where settlers didn't measure up to Phillip's ideal, and Australia's indigenous peoples suffered as a result. Yet the legal system inherited from Britain is also a source of redress for those impacted by racist policies.

A renewed focus on the UK is also completely consistent with deeper engagement in Asia. Australia is even more interesting and attractive to the UK for being entwined with its Asean, Pacific, and North Asian neighbours. The UK, too, has recently joined Asia-Pacific trade deals and is making greater efforts in the region as part of its post-Brexit foreign policy efforts. Joining the CPTPP was a particular win, as it makes the UK the first non-Japan country in the G7 to get itself into one of the largest and fastest-growing economic blocs.

The republic

The Lucky Country was one of the first mainstream books to advocate an Australian republic, which Horne saw as part of a "new and relevant sense of reorientation and self-definition, a final casting off." The reorientation and self-definition happened, partly forced upon Australia by the UK's move into the EU, but a republic hasn't yet. This is partly because it would make no difference to people's day-to-day lives or to the process of public policy, and because, for many pragmatic and sceptical Australians, the country's relationship with Britain's monarchy counts as something that only needs fixing when it is clearly broken. It is no longer true to suggest, as Horne did in the 1960s, that other countries regard Australia as "a half-sovereign state", especially in Asia. In my 13 years living in Asia, nobody ever suggested that links to the British monarchy make Australia less sovereign. The only friends of mine who find the situation especially weird are all British.

Sceptical-pragmatist Australians likely *will* vote for a republic at some point; the notion of inherited office sits badly with their egalitarian views. But they are in no hurry to make the change, and it will need to be a minimalist change, a severing of the governor-general's connection back to the king. A separate election for a new head of state, a president, is highly unlikely to attract enough support, as it will change the constitutional balance in ways that are hard to predict and will scare the conservative Australian voter, who, rightly, sees the present system as working better than a presidential system.

In any event, Australia becoming a republic would not really affect its relationship with the UK. Almost all Australians would happily remain a part of the Commonwealth (only 14 of the 56 Commonwealth countries still have the reigning British monarch as their head of state), and could still tune into the pageantry and drama of the royal family for entertainment, as the Americans do. The bond Australians enjoy with Britain depends not on a shared monarch but on shared values, character and institutions. It is based on us seeing the world in much the same way and having the same aspiration to create a good life for the ordinary person; a life that encompasses not only prosperity but a freedom to think and say what you want, to be your own person in a way that few other countries truly allow.

Europe

If Britain is Australia's "back to the future" partner, many of the same arguments apply to the other countries still in the EU. The EU itself is often mocked for its slow and unwieldy decision-making, but it remains a remarkable institution. Twenty-seven countries with different languages, cultures and a history of war within the lifetime of many Australians. Yet, when I first visited the European parliament as a director of the European Australian Business Council, I watched the representatives of these 27 disparate countries vote peacefully by pushing buttons on their tables. There were far-right representatives and radical Trotskyites, and every shade of political view in between, arguing legislation by ballot rather than on the streets.

The EU certainly has flaws, from protectionism to the failure of the euro currency area to anticipate and manage very different fiscal and debt positions between nations. However, many political and business leaders in Australia underestimate its ability to achieve things because it doesn't have a formal common foreign policy and because its decisions involve horse-trading. Individual nation states are only one level of legitimacy. A modern world requires layers of government that address local, national and international issues according to how they are best solved—and the notion of being both European and, say, French is not the contradiction it is sometimes made out to be.

Europe is collectively the second- or third-largest economy in the world (depending on how you adjust for currency or purchasing power), and the euro remains by far the best alternative to the US dollar as a global reserve currency. France is also one of the five permanent members of the UN Security Council and is a substantial economic, military and cultural power in its own right. It has two million citizens in the Pacific, shares a border with Australia in Antarctica to the south, and the first islands both east and west of Australia in the ocean are French (New Caledonia and Reunion). France is one of the five global powers in which Australians have the greatest trust (the other four are, according to a Lowy Institute poll, Japan, the UK, India and the US).

Australia sees eye to eye with Europe on many issues, with the differences often being matters of degree. I have noted in previous chapters how important Japan and the Asean nations are for Australia, but Europe is also essential to the coalitions that can progress the causes that are so important to Australia. These coalitions will often incorporate the US, sometimes China, and sometimes even both. But recent trends in UN voting patterns suggest that they will even more often incorporate Japan, Korea and (some or all of) Asean, and they should almost always incorporate the UK and Europe. Australia's foreign policy will need to be dexterous and broad in a world of much more complex relationships.

Diplomacy in the 21st century

A world in which both opportunities and threats are global is a world that requires lots of engagement, nuance and judgement. Australia's diplomats are well trained and do a good job, but diplomacy in the 21st century is a whole-of-country effort, not least because the citizens of a responsive democracy will want to be involved, and social media empowers them in that way. A couple of years ago, I was appointed chair of Advance Global Australians, a network supported by both government and the private sector that mobilises the Australian diaspora. At any one time, it's estimated that five per cent of the Australian population (more than a million people) are living and working abroad, and their success and influence in fields from academia to business, from media to philanthropy, is positively disproportionate to their numbers.

On 31st December every year, people all over the northern hemisphere enjoy the first New Year's Eve fireworks on their televisions—the Sydney Opera House and Harbour Bridge exploding in summer colours—and then a few weeks later they watch the world's best tennis players in the Melbourne sunshine (the most popular Grand Slam among the players), while thousands of students from all over the world start courses in Australian universities, colleges and defence training schools. From the time of the visionary Colombo Plan, which provided scholarships for rising leaders in Asia, many of these students have gone on to define their own countries, having been partly defined by their experiences in Australia.

Australia's strategic strength has been its ability to walk and chew gum at the same time: to align with the US and G7 countries on questions of values and to counter threats, while still engaging with countries that have very different political systems. This is not always easy: judgements need to be made about what to do in lockstep with Australia's friend, the US—and where to diverge. Fear of the unknown and an exaggerated sense of vulnerability could drive Australia to make the wrong decisions. The best defence is self-knowledge. Australians will need to recognise their strength as a nation—and work to maximise the scope for independent action within a strong patchwork of alliances.

PART V

THE LUCKY COUNTRY

MAKING IT LAST

I've found that when asked about current events, it's best to take the pessimistic side of the argument. It gives you more gravitas.

HENRY KISSINGER

Contrary to Kissinger's advice, this is an optimistic book. When it comes to Australia's relative prosperity, health and quality of life, the facts are too hard to ignore. It is also true, though, that there are some dark clouds on Australia's sunny horizon. Almost all of Australia's outperformance (on measures from median wealth to life expectancy) has flowed from reforms in the 1980s and 1990s that are now at least 25 years old. And after coasting for a period, Australia has, in the past five years, even walked back from important elements of the successful Australian Way. The results are unsurprising: a fall in productivity and growth, with inflation and housing prices staying stubbornly higher than in other countries.

Just as the rest of the world has started to focus on the unique elements that have led to Australian success, Australia itself seems to be throwing some of them out. The lack of focus on education standards has started to bite, and some insular attitudes and policies re-emerged during Covid. There has been a bipartisan retreat from skilled migration, foreign investment, flexibility and economic rigour. Parts of the economy where Australia has comparative advantage, such as natural resources and education, have been damaged, while opaque subsidies have gone into sectors where it doesn't.

Should the title of this book be *Why the Australian Way Worked* (past tense) rather than *Why the Australian Way Works*? Not yet. It's too early to conclude that the Australian Way has been lost; there is still time for Australia to rediscover its mojo. Australia's political institutions remain more responsive and adaptive than other countries, and a feisty media, independent institutions and senate inquiries mean that the issues are known and are at least being transparently debated. Australia can course-correct more easily than a country like China and get itself back on track, but the next few years will be decisive.

The ability to solve problems is crucial to the legitimacy of any system of governance. This applies to all problems, but Australia's economic prosperity, the energy transition and housing affordability will be particularly closely watched.

Economic backsliding

We've seen that the Australian economy has outperformed the world when it's been open to trade and investment, and when governments focussed on equipping people with skills and promoting competition but left individuals and businesses to make decisions about what to buy and where to invest. But every few decades there have been swings towards more paternalism: using tariffs and subsidies to shift resources away from what consumers and investors want to support and towards those things that politicians think *should* be supported. These generally occur when the wider western world has retreated from free trade—in the early years of the 20th century, for instance, and in the 1930s. The vogue for large-scale industry policy and protectionism in America and Europe, following China, has also reawakened these instincts in Australia. There are mixed signals as to how well Australia will resist these broader trends, improve productivity and maintain its current level of prosperity.

It makes no sense for Australia to try to manufacture things in which it has no comparative advantage, or to take resources away from what works in order to "pick winners" in what politicians deem to be the right industries. Australia will work if it continues to do what it has done successfully for years: invest in areas of comparative advantage, and otherwise use the technologies and products that are developed by those who can and do throw vast subsidies at them. Australians want to have high wages and comfortable lifestyles. They can achieve these things, but only if they let other countries make those things that require low labour costs and greater environmental impacts.

Australian politicians and bureaucrats find it as hard as anyone to resist trying to predict the future. The energy transition will provide particular temptations in the next few years. Australia has traditionally enjoyed low energy costs, which have offset higher wages and helped to keep Australian industries competitive, but the phasing out of fossil fuels will reduce that advantage—at least until renewables, battery storage and reliable baseload power have been rolled out in sufficient scale to reduce costs.

Australia has also stepped back from its traditional openness to foreign investment and skilled migration in the past five years, introducing tighter restrictions and making approval processes slower and more cumbersome. Some of this is an understandable reaction to national security concerns in sensitive sectors, as well as to housing pressures. But some of it has been overkill and reflects a more centralised and bureaucratic approach to deciding what money and people Australia wants and doesn't want.

The subsidies spent on supporting favoured companies and industries to date have been less than one per cent of GDP, much smaller than in China, America and Europe, and the restrictions on foreign investment have not choked it off (foreign investment as a proportion of GDP remains higher than in most developed countries). But the jury is still out as to whether Australia will maintain the economic approach of the past 30 years and the relative prosperity that has accompanied it.

Energy and climate

Someone in a foreign government once asked me why Australians were so focussed on climate change. Australia accounts for one per cent of the world's emissions, so it can't make much difference alone. Whether the world warms by more than two degrees will almost entirely depend on what happens in China, the US and India (across which about half of all emissions are generated). I explained that Australians are not only directly impacted by climate change (which could make large parts of the north of the country uninhabitable), but also want to be at the forefront of doing the right thing globally. Australians are the beneficiaries of and believers in a global rules-based order, and cooperation, fairness and rule-following are important parts of the Australian personality. Australians are also a people who feel connected to the land and environment, benefit from a "clean and green" brand and want a close relationship with Pacific countries for whom climate change is existential.

There was a moment, in 2009, when it seemed that Australia might lead the world in establishing a market-based emissions trading system to prompt reductions in carbon emissions. The "cap and trade" system developed at that time has since been adopted in numerous countries. Ironically, it was the notionally pro-environment Green party that blocked the scheme and forced the then-government into a more arbitrary "carbon tax" that set the scene for a decade-long fight over climate policy. The bitter arguments over energy policy during this period were in marked contrast to the relatively bipartisan approach to climate change in places such as the UK and Europe at the time.

Australia's federal and market-based system came to the rescue. State governments set ambitious targets for renewable energy, and businesses invested in solar and wind, particularly as costs came down and the technologies became more economically appealing. In the years from 2005 to 2020, Australia reduced carbon emissions by 20 per cent, even as emissions increased in many countries more loudly committed to action on climate change. Individuals also rushed into rooftop solar, with more than a third of Australian households now deriving power from solar panels on their roofs. Solar generation makes particular sense for Australia, which has the highest solar radiation per square metre of any continent, and where the University of NSW has been a global leader in developing solar panel technology (the technologies they developed in the 1980s were rolled out on massive scale by graduates who went back to China, but a second generation of more efficient solar cells is now emerging from that same university).

In the first phase of global efforts on climate change, the focus was on belief: people were either "believers" for whom the prevention of "the end of the world as we know it" is worth any sacrifice, or "deniers" who reject all scientific research as false or hyped-up and insist that any meaningful action to slow climate change is worthless. But the latest COP conferences are starting to focus on the real practicalities of change, ground in which the pragmatic Australian temperament will thrive. Businesses and unions—and, in fact, most of the population—have a typically Australian, sceptical, fact-based and balanced approach. They reject the sort of masochism that will materially damage prosperity in order to secure changes in emissions that will barely move the dial, but they see every reason to be ahead of the game, migrating the energy balance to clean energy wherever it can be done without threatening the affordability and availability of power.

While Canberra bickered, the rest of Australia was just getting on with emissions reductions. The proportion of Australian electricity production coming from renewables has gone from less than 10 per cent in 2010 to around 40 per cent now and will soon make up the majority of generation (even it doesn't get to the stated target of 82 per cent by 2030). Almost all of Australia's coal-fired power stations will close in the next 10 years. Australia may be reducing emissions intensity faster than others, but it also started with a "dirtier" power grid than others, so there is catching up to do. But Australian culture and institutions are getting results: the Clean Energy Financing Corporation has been a world leader in backing clean energy—and making a profit for the government out of it. Australian firms such as my old stable Macquarie are among the world's biggest investors in renewables. Companies such as Lendlease lead the world in green building technologies (now exported to others), while CSIRO and private sector organisations are doing cutting-edge research into everything from clean hydrogen to seaweed-infused cattle feed designed to prevent—let's say—*methane emissions* from cows.

The main things now slowing down renewables are: glacial planning and environmental approvals (particularly for new transmission lines); constraints on letting enough workers into the country to build the infrastructure; and the fact that wind and solar don't put energy into the grid as consistently as coal (sometimes the wind isn't blowing, sometimes the sun isn't shining). There will be a highwire act to bring on new investment (including in the 10,000km of new power cables required to transmit power from the new solar and wind farms) in time to avoid gaps or price surges while fossil fuel sources are being rapidly shut down. The large increase in energy consumption from the use of AI will make it even harder.

Energy and climate need not be turned into a culture war. The roadmap is now well understood, and decisions can fit into the great Australian culture of sceptical pragmatism. Australia will make continual improvements in how to generate, distribute and store energy. Some economists have even argued that Australia can become a global superpower in energy, carbon absorption and low-carbon industry. I have worked with lithium companies (both Australian and international) who have invested billions of dollars in mining Australian ore and processing it into battery-grade lithium hydroxide which can be used for electric cars and other batteries. Though these investments have now slowed, caught in the pincer between lower lithium prices and slow regulatory approvals and rising costs in Australia, it remains possible that clean-energy projects will assume an export importance to replace that of iron ore, just as iron ore took the place of wool and, before that, wool took the place of gold. It is also possible that, in time, Australians will embrace having the world's largest reserves of uranium and especially stable tectonic geology—and welcome becoming a major nuclear energy power.

But Australians don't know—or need to guess—what the next "golden ticket" is going to be in the future, because Australia's success won't be about a particular commodity. Instead, it will be about the ability of Australian businesses to execute large, long-term projects for trusted customers—which will in turn require advanced engineering skills, the ability to structure complex financing and contractual certainty via the Australian legal system.

Housing

Young Australians in big cities fret about the affordability of housing (to buy or to rent) even more than they do about the economy, climate or security. Falling interest rates over a decade, a lack of building and increasing availability of finance have pushed house prices in good areas up to levels that are beyond anyone who doesn't have a wealthy parent to subsidise them. Australia has been one of the slowest countries in the OECD when it comes to building homes. Prices have moved more quickly than the capacity of ordinary wage earners to keep up, and my kids' generation cannot lever themselves up from small flat to larger flat to house in the way that I did. Only half of 30- to 34-year-olds own their own home now, whereas 70 per cent of those born before the 1990s did at the same age. These issues are most acute in Sydney and Melbourne, where more than 40 per cent of the Australian population lives (compared with the less than 10 per cent that live in the two major cities of the US, China and Germany).

Housing affordability is also important because it fuels the concerns that young people have about inequality—and thereby undermines faith in the market system that has made Australians so well off. True to its egalitarian culture, Australia does not have a particularly high level of *income* inequality. Decent minimum wages and high tax rates for higher-income earners mean that after-tax incomes are less widely distributed than in most countries. But while Australia doesn't have an *income* inequality issue, it does have a growing issue with *wealth* inequality, mostly because of housing prices.

The greater-than-usual disparity of wealth in Australia has come from the combination of interest rates falling so dramatically over the past 20 years (which makes all assets more valuable, but especially helps those who had a lot to start with) and special tax breaks for property. Australia is the only country where you will be taxed almost half your income if you earn $200,000 doing a job, but you will be taxed zero if you inherit or sell a $20 million house. The accumulation of all this tax-free gain for richer families cuts against Australians' egalitarian instincts. But fixing it will also cut against the emotive Australian reverence for the home.

There are also things that can be done, if governments have the will, to encourage downsizing by older people who are "asset rich and cash poor". There are ways to deliver more equitable opportunities for first-home buyers who lack access to the Bank of Mum and Dad, such as introducing annual property levies (land taxes) in place of big upfront stamp duties or enabling access to superannuation to fund the asset that will, more than any other, allow security in retirement.

But the only sustainable way to make housing more affordable is to build more of it. The Productivity Commission has estimated that a 10 per cent increase in supply would reduce the cost of housing by 25 per cent. This requires more training and bringing into the country the people who can do the building; multiple homes where there are currently single homes and empty space; strategic transport links and infrastructure that make vacant land attractive for housing; and more public sector finance to fund construction. Recent cuts in skilled immigration can be reversed, and painters, roof tilers and brick workers added to the priority list.

Lack of housing supply is an issue in other countries, but it is actually easier to solve in Australia. Density is a fraction of that endured by other countries, so there is lots of room for more infill building. Local councils have been delegated the power to block new homes, but state governments can withdraw this delegation or overrule them in particular instances. Australia currently restricts the number of construction workers that come to the country to keep wages high for those already here; just having fewer barriers would mean more and cheaper houses. And a government with comparatively low debt, like Australia's, can more easily finance social housing or subsidise build-to-rent builds.

Initiatives such as "pattern building" and giving more powers to bigger councils or state bodies are starting to address the lack of development, making sure that new homes are close to jobs and that infrastructure isn't overstretched. Governments at both the federal and state levels are belatedly investing in building themselves, alongside the private sector. Well-designed fast trains to near-city areas (Melbourne–Geelong, Sydney–Central Coast–Newcastle, north and south of Brisbane, and even Canberra–Sydney) will allow more people to enjoy quality homes while still being close enough to workplaces and the facilities that only a big city can offer.

More density in Australian cities is not only good for allowing young Australians to have their own homes—it is a driver of economic success in the 21st century. Increasingly, it is competition between global cities, rather than between countries, that drives growth. Highly skilled and mobile people who work in technology, finance and medical research want to be in places that have a critical mass of other talented people and entrepreneurial businesses, places that also offer a lifestyle, stimulation and fun. From Athens to Rome, Venice to Amsterdam, London to New York, it has historically been cities that drive the world; they agglomerate talent and ideas and stimulate innovation and ingenuity.

Tolerating mediocrity

One of the reasons that *The Lucky Country* had such an impact on Australians in the 1960s was the way in which Horne's book skewered the conformity and mediocrity that he perceived, especially in the nation's elite. Six decades later, Australia's economy has gone from relative laggard to global poster child, and the white-picket fences have given way to a multicoloured tapestry. Yet, when rereading the book, I found it hard not to recognise the continuing truth of some of his criticisms.

It is, for example, still true that there is a strong impulse towards conformity and not rocking the boat. Tall poppies are not widely welcomed, other than on the sporting field, and even the richest and most powerful families profess themselves to be ordinary, down-to-earth Aussies—and sometimes even believe it. Indeed, the rich and powerful in Australia have so convinced themselves that they aren't any different from anyone else that philanthropic giving rises less with increasing wealth in Australia than elsewhere.

This assumption of sameness allows for the very casual and open manners of Australians. Foreign visitors always remark on the relaxed warmth, friendliness, direct speaking and robust humour of their hosts; there is among Australians an instinctive suspicion of too much politeness, a disdain for social pretence and a perverse pride in being underdressed for almost any occasion. Australian conformity doesn't spring from a fanatical desire for society to be a particular way, but from what Horne described as an "inability to imagine a life different from one's own".

It is only when this easy camaraderie rubs up against other cultures that it can backfire. More and more, Australians travel around the world, encounter other cultures and find, in the process, as Horne observed, that "since Australian friendliness often lacks knowledge of social forms and ceremonies, it can sometimes be taken for rudeness". Australians, open and direct, and assuming that all people are the same as they are, expect others to share their easy-going ways, and are disappointed when they do not.

When harnessed properly and with sensitivity to other cultures, the direct, no-bullshit, egalitarian approach can be powerful beyond Australian shores. The most successful global Australian companies have been driven by flat, open and informal cultures that leverage the Australian approach to drive a brutal honesty and accountability that is not always found in other organisations. When it is less well harnessed it can lead to trouble. Australian diplomatic missions around the world are constantly intervening on behalf of Australian tourists whose "pranks" don't always amuse the local police.

Australians are adaptable, but also underprepared for a more hierarchical and less forgiving world. When China gets angry, the Australian instinct is to try to reach over the fence and sort things out with a candid exchange of views. Naturally, this doesn't always work. But there are other approaches: investing in understanding your interlocuter as well as they research you; having at least some China-savvy people in positions of power; educating Australians about how other cultures and people think, so that leaders can distinguish a real threat from the merely unfamiliar; understanding how other countries have successfully dealt with the same challenges.

The gravitational force of levelling down in Australian culture may also go some way to explaining Horne's view that the Australian elite are disappointing in comparison to the ordinary Australian. I have had the good fortune to work with many of the country's leaders—in politics, business and other areas—and they are mostly impressive people. But it's also true that many leaders avoid sticking their necks out and prefer not to rock the boat. There are fewer penalties for mediocrity in an environment where appearing superior is fatal. If being in a particular profession for long enough without doing anything untoward is sufficient to rise to the top, then why swing for the fences?

Australia's failures are usually not due to it going completely off-piste, but because it settles for average. Perhaps the price of not making any big mistakes is a smallness of ambition and a willingness to muddle on through, rather than striving for the outstanding. Or perhaps Australia is simply waiting for another bout of imaginative leadership of the sort it enjoyed in the 1980s and 1990s, so that it can live up to its full potential.

STILL LUCKY, STILL WORKING

Australia is a lucky country run mainly by second-rate people who share its luck. It lives mostly on other people's ideas, and, though its ordinary people are adaptable, most of its leaders (in all fields) so lack curiosity about the events that surround them that they are often taken by surprise. A nation more concerned with styles of life than with achievement has managed to achieve what may be the most evenly prosperous society in the world. It has done this in a social climate largely inimical to originality and the desire for excellence (except in sport) and in which there is less and less acclamation of hard work. According to the rules, Australia has not deserved its good fortune.

DONALD HORNE, *The Lucky Country*

This is the most famous paragraph in *The Lucky Country*, and a characterisation of Australia that comes up time and again. The usual sniffy observation from commentators is to note that the words "lucky country" have been misconstrued as being a pat on the back when, in the context of the whole paragraph, they are actually an ironic criticism. However, the truth is that they are both.

Horne did deploy his phrase "the lucky country" with lashings of irony. He thought that the prime minister of the time, Robert

Menzies, had, after 15 years, been in power too long and run out of ideas. But he also noted that even his Australia, the Australia of 60 years ago, "has managed to achieve what may be the most evenly prosperous society in the world," and attributed this success to the adaptability of ordinary Australians in taking breakthroughs from elsewhere and applying them at home, and in avoiding the mistakes made in countries more prone to following grand visions. But he worried whether too much reliance on luck, last-minute adjustment and improvisation would take the country successfully through the two challenges that he foresaw in the 1960s: the rise of Asia and technological change. It is ironic (or perhaps instructive) that the same two issues remain top of mind for policymakers today. An issue that wasn't as pervasive in the 1960s has emerged in the slow downwards slide of educational standards. For a country that pioneered free, compulsory education for all in the late 1800s, and was founded partly in a quest for universal literacy, it is disturbing to see Australia's relative performance in reading, science and maths fall year by year. Foundational skills underpin all the other things that make a country strong and successful.

It's true that Horne tired of his phrase being used simply as a celebration of how good things are in Australia. His description of Australian elites is cutting, and it is hard to argue that the country hasn't been sometimes blindsided by outside events, be they technologies or changes in the world, that a more curious and globally aware polity would have seen coming.

However, he didn't give enough credit to the Australian institutions which the newly constituted nation had the fortune to inherit at just the right moment in history—and then significantly improved. Nor did he sufficiently recognise the strength of egalitarian, individual and adaptative values—relative to those of hierarchy, collective planning and grand visions—in building a successful society. The past 60 years have also brought a greater worldliness (through travel, immigration and broadband); an explosion of education (only one in 50 Australians had degrees when Horne was writing, now it's almost one in two among people under 35); and, more recently, technological growth (home-grown as well as imported); a stronger work ethic (on weekdays at least); and more globally competitive businesses and regulation.

The 60 years that have elapsed since Horne wrote have also shown the strength of incremental improvement and of democratic "trial and error". It is not necessary for a country to have a Lincoln, a Churchill or a Deng Xiaoping if it starts in a good position and has the right framework for measuring and reacting to what people want and need, as required.

Why nations succeed or fail

It has long been understood that national success depends almost entirely on strong and inclusive institutions. It depends much less on the individual brilliance of leaders at a particular point in time, and on culture, geography or resource endowment. But there has also been intuitive resistance to this idea as it cuts against the hero myths of our primal storytelling brains, even as the real-world evidence keeps piling up. There are so many examples of how different sets of institutions layered across the same geography and culture lead to dramatically different outcomes: the standard of living in North versus South Korea, East versus West Germany, the American versus the Mexican side of the Rio Grande, to name but a few.

Daron Acemoglu and James A Robinson's book *Why Nations Fail* cites Australia as a case study for how countries can succeed. They contrast the inclusive political institutions developed in Australia with places of equal mineral wealth and more attractive geographies who didn't get it right. Nineteenth-century mining in Africa often used slaves, and property and political rights were widely denied; Argentina (equal to Australia in wealth at the time of federation in 1901) allowed landowners and then Peronists to dominate; and countries from the Philippines to Russia have experienced long periods in which leaders extracted the value of the country's resources and very little was put back.

By contrast, Australia's miners gained rights in the Victorian gold rushes of the 1850s and 1860s, and, ever since that time, the wealth of (often foreign) corporate owners of resources has been more broadly shared in Australia than elsewhere—with suppliers, workers and taxpayers. Australia's retreat into a more parochial frame of mind by the time that Horne was writing cost the country in reduced prosperity, but the country was able in the 1980s and 1990s to reform its institutions and policies and get back on top.

The fact that institutions are paramount doesn't mean that leaders lack importance. Institutions need to be defended and improved over time, or else they deteriorate. Plenty of countries have gone backwards as they allow democratic practices to decay, turn a blind eye to illiberal behaviour in government or security services, or become inward-looking and protectionist. Continuing the success of Australia will mean continuing to build on the intricate platform of institutions the country has, to use them more ambitiously and to evolve them for new challenges.

Sharpening the saw

There are many more ways for things to fail than to go right, and new human energy is constantly needed to keep a system going. Because we don't intuitively recognise this most important law of nature, we tend to see every unsolved social problem as a sign that some person or group is to blame. In truth, it is the solving of the problem that should give us purpose. As Steven Pinker has pointed out, atoms don't spontaneously arrange themselves into shelter and clothing any more than the complex institutions of liberal democracy emerge and get maintained without a lot of work. The set of values and institutions that make Australia so successful require energy to maintain them, which is why I argue they need now to be articulated.

Too many people see the minutiae of parliamentary process, judicial independence and accountability in politics as quaint—or even as hindrances to "getting stuff done". But we have recently seen numerous examples around the world of how neglecting the norms and slowly chipping away at the integrity of institutions becomes a slippery slope. The liberal democracy that has delivered Australians the best quality of life in the world will deteriorate unless respect is shown for it, unless it is invested in and unless those who deviate from it are quickly and effectively called out.

Still lucky, still working

At the end of *The Lucky Country*, Horne quotes Bertrand Russell, who said, when he departed Australia in 1950, "I leave your shores with more hope for mankind than I had when I came among you." The philosopher saw Australia, even then, as pointing the way to a happier and more widely shared prosperity for ordinary citizens. The last few decades have done nothing to spoil this assessment; Australia's success is more evident now than it was 60 years ago.

A few years ago, I helped to write a report about how to attract more job-creating investment in Australia. People with money and talent told us what the (mostly tax- and visa-related) issues were that had made them relocate from Australia to Singapore or elsewhere. But they also told us what they liked and why Australia is a great place to invest: a growing population and world-leading quality of life; a stable and market-based democracy with the rule of law and efficient and honest administration; a globally oriented, immigrant-rich and well-educated talent pool; proximity to some of the fastest-growing countries in the world; an independent and internationally respected central bank and a relatively strong fiscal position. Australians are adaptable, technologically savvy and increasingly entrepreneurial.

A more belligerent communist leadership in China is challenging, but, even there, the cards Australia has been dealt are better than most—a natural trading relationship that benefits both countries, no historical territorial disputes, and many Chinese-Australians. The outcome will depend on how Australia plays these cards and how America and China play theirs, but Australia has been dealt a strong suit.

In this light, it is surprising to hear the negativity of Australia's political and media debate. Most countries have much bigger challenges than Australia, but in the Asia time zone, at least, they exhibit a greater belief in the possibility of a bright future and are given to thinking big. Australia's position is strong, and the potential even stronger, yet this is rarely articulated. It is an argument of this book that Australians can teach some things to the rest of the world, but also that they need to step back and understand their own story. If Australians don't recognise, preserve and trust in their own strengths, they will forfeit a formidable future.

Horne asked whether Australia could maintain its happiness, or whether being so lucky would dull its reflexes and weaken its ability to adapt. In the last decades of the 20th century, Australians passed the test, before losing momentum in the first quarter of the 21st. Will Australia retreat "back under the doona" or instead emerge with a renewed willingness to "have a go" and provide its people with a "fair go"?

Australia works. That is a truth not universally acknowledged—and especially not by Australians. To make it work even better,

Australians need to understand what has been done right as well as what has been done wrong—to appreciate what underpins Australia's economic and social success and reverse the decline in educational standards, then push forward with a spirit of incremental but continuous improvement that comes from the centre of politics. Australians need to avoid both the siren call of revolutionary change and the slothful appeal of the status quo. If Australians remain sceptical pragmatists and open to the world, then their country will be known as the lucky country for many generations to come.

NOTES AND FURTHER READING

There are lots of people who have made this book possible. Starting with my parents, Don and Eth, who made the decision to migrate to Australia with no money and no job in the hope that my brother and sister and I would have a better life here, and my children, Ashley and James, whom I hope will find in this book some inspiration for the future that they and their generation will create. My teachers, work colleagues, and many others have helped to inform whatever insight may be in here.

I'm very grateful for the support and time that many of Australia's leaders, from both sides of politics, were willing to give me as I researched and thought about how Australia works. From former prime ministers (particularly John Howard, Kevin Rudd and Malcolm Turnbull) to former state premiers and ministers (including Bob Carr, Lindsay Tanner, Nick Greiner, Warwick Smith and the late Simon Crean), everyone was engaged and thoughtful about the country that they all love and have served. I also thought it was important in a book that compares Australia to other countries to speak to those who have represented Australia in those places; I particularly acknowledge the current high commissioner to the UK, Stephen Smith, and his predecessor, George Brandis, and Australia's ambassador to the US, Kevin Rudd (again), and his two predecessors, Arthur Sinodinos and Joe Hockey. Business leaders who read parts of this book and provided valuable comments include my old colleagues Mark Johnson and Nicholas Moore, and Josephine Linden, Lucy Turnbull, Ticky Fullerton, Vicki Thomson, Sir Ed Byrne, Cat Douglas, Jessica Michaels and Kate McQuestin. Thanks also to Mike Walsh, Damian Walsh, Georgie Skipper, Michael Lannan, Dennis Cowdroy, Peter van Onselen, Amy Rose Sadubin and Jason Collins for their input.

Needless to say, not all of the people mentioned above will agree with everything I've said in this book! Nevertheless, I was surprised at how consistent all these leaders were in what they saw as Australia's strengths, weaknesses, challenges and opportunities, and without exception they would all agree that Australia has a unique and effective place in the world and a bright future.

Peter Hoskin and Mark Beard at Prospect Editions have guided the book through the journey from manuscript to bookshops with great energy and enthusiasm, and I'm grateful for their support. Aimee Yi did a brilliant job assisting me with research, fact-checking and the perspectives of an emerging Australian leader, and Fergus Edmondson with preparing to publish. I had the great fortune to meet Sir Clive Cowdery at a time when he was curious about Australia and what the UK could learn from it; his support and counsel has enormously enhanced the result.

When I first started writing this book, I thought it would be interesting to follow the same chapter headings and structure of Horne's *The Lucky Country*, as a comparison to the Australia of half a century ago. But it quickly became clear that this wouldn't work in the 2020s. For one thing, Horne had a chapter titled "The Age of Menzies" (referring to the long-serving prime minister of the time), as well as sections dealing with censorship, wowsers and the position of Catholics versus Protestants. These are now historical relics. Horne's chapters on "Men at Work" and "Men in Power" are not only dated in their gender references but also reflect the political and industry structure of the 1960s.

Horne's discussion of what I've called "Australia in the World" was comprised of two chapters headed "Between Britain and America" and "Living with Asia". Britain and America remain important, but in the 2020s it is necessary to also consider China more specifically, and to address the breakdown of the overall global rules-based order that was taken for granted 60 years ago. The "Asian Century" remains just as important as it was in the 1960s (even more so, in fact) and still gets its own chapter.

The rest of the chapters are still as relevant as they were when Horne was writing, even though my conclusions are sometimes different from the perspective of 60 years ago. I start by asking (as Horne did) "What is an Australian?" and examining the "The Australian Dream(s)". I have approached Australian identity, though, through the lens of the three pillars of modern Australia rather than Horne's sections on "Innocent Happiness" and "A Nation without a Mind". There was far less focus on indigenous Australia in the 1960s and less appreciation of the unique impact that came from turbocharging a state-of-the-art liberal democracy with strong multicultural immigration. These are important things to address in any book about modern Australia.

INTRODUCING AUSTRALIA

1. UBS, *Global Wealth Report 2024* ranks median wealth (Luxembourg has been ignored in this analysis due to its size and economic shape).
2. R Wilkie and J Ho in the British Medical Journal, August 2024, compared six high-income Anglophone countries for life expectancy and within-country geographic variation in life expectancy across US, UK, Australia, Canada, Ireland and New Zealand. Australia was the clear outperformer, leading peer countries by one to four years for women and one to five years for men by 2018. It is likely that the margins will have subsequently increased as a result of Covid.
3. Life Expectancy (website), Australian Bureau of Statistics, accessed 11th August 11 2024: https://www.abs.gov.au/statistics/people/population/life-expectancy/latest-release In most countries, people are living longer lives, but notable exceptions include the US, due to opioid and other conditions, and a number of countries in the Middle East and Africa.
4. According to Australian Bureau of Statistics, GDP growth one year after the pandemic showed that Australia's economy experienced a faster recovery than most OECD countries. See "International economic comparisons after a year of the pandemic" (website), Australian Bureau of Statistics, accessed 28th May 2023: https://www.abs.gov.au/articles/international-economic-comparisons-after-year-pandemic
5. S&P Global Rating reaffirmed its "AAA" long-term and "A+1" short-term unsolicited sovereign credit ratings in Australia. See "Research Update: Australia 'AAA/A-1+' Ratings Affirmed, Outlook Stable" (website), S&P Global Ratings, accessed 28th May 2023: https://www.spglobal.com/ratings/en/research/articles/230130-research-update-australia-aaa-a-1-ratings-affirmed-outlook-stable-12623870 Australia is one of only nine countries to be rated AAA by all three major credit rating agencies—see, Jim Chalmers, "Australia's AAA credit rating reaffirmed following MYEFO", media release, 13 February 2024: https://ministers.treasury.gov.au/ministers/jim-chalmers-2022/media-releases/australias-aaa-credit-rating-reaffirmed-following-myefo#:~:text=Australia 20per 20cent20is 20per 20cent20one 20per 20cent20of 20per 20cent20only,access 20per 20cent20funds 20per 20cent20at 20per 20cent20lower 20per 20cent20rates.
6. "GDP per capita" (website), Our World in Data, accessed 23rd August 2024: https://data.worldbank.org/indicator/NY.GDP.PCAP.CD
7. The Economist Intelligence Unit's Where-to-be-born Index (previously called the Quality-of-life Index) ranked Australia number two behind Switzerland out of the 80 countries surveyed, see "The lottery of life—where to be born in 2013" (website), *The Economist*: https://www.economist.com/news/2012/11/21/the-lottery-of-life The EIU used a multivariate regression of factors including security, freedom, climate, health, material well-being and life satisfaction. Other studies have also ranked Australia at or close to the top in the world.
8. Australia was ranked first for "Health Outcomes" and 'Equity" and third overall in Health Care by the Commonwealth Fund study of major countries in 2021. See "Mirror, Mirror 2021—Reflecting Poorly" (website), The Commonwealth

Fund, accessed 28th May 2023, https://interactives.commonwealthfund.org/2017/july/mirror-mirror/

9. D Horne, *The Lucky Country* (Penguin, 1964).
10. "World Bank Open Data" (website), World Bank Group, accessed 11th August 2024: https://data.worldbank.org
11. D Acemoglu and J Robinson, *Why Nations Fail*, Profile Books, 2013.
12. There are books that need to be noted as a qualifier to my comment about Australia being under-examined relative to its size and increasing geopolitical importance. For instance, N Bryant's *The Rise and Fall of Australia: How a great nation lost its way* (Bantam, 2015), which was written by the BBC's Australian correspondent, and G Megalogenis's *The Australian Moment: How we were made for these times* (Hamish Hamilton 2012).
13. J Kearsley, E Bagshaw and A Galloway, "'If you make China the enemy, China will be the enemy: Beijing's fresh threat to Australia", *Sydney Morning Herald*, 18th November 2020: https://www.smh.com.au/world/asia/if-you-make-china-the-enemy-china-will-be-the-enemy-beijing-s-fresh-threat-to-australia-20201118-p56fqs.html
14. A Cambridge study found that young people globally are more disillusioned with democracy than older age groups, see RS Foa, A Klassen, D Wenger, A Rand and M Slade, *Youth and Satisfaction with Democracy: Reversing the democratic disconnect?* (Centre for the Future of Democracy, UK, 2020): https://www.cam.ac.uk/system/files/youth_and_satisfaction_with_democracy.pdf Across the OECD countries, only 37 per cent of people aged 18-29 said they trust the national government, compared to 41 per cent of those aged 30-49, see G Gerthin, "Why Are Youth Dissatisfied with Democracy?", Freedom House, 14th September 2023: https://freedomhouse.org/article/why-are-youth-dissatisfied-democracy.
15. Throughout the period I was based in Hong Kong (most of 2004–2017), the hope that China would "become more like us" was very commonly held, particularly among Americans, although it was much less believed by those with a deeper understanding of China and its history. Japan had already provided a case study that modernity and wealth don't necessarily create homogeneity, and the harder heads saw WTO entry, for example, as a mutually beneficial wealth-creator, rather than a way to somehow create liberal democracy in China. The magnitude of Xi Jinping's move away from Deng Xiaoping's model and back toward a more Maoist approach (first in governance and foreign policy, and now also in approach to private enterprise) was not foreseen even by people in and close to China, though, see "How the West got China wrong", *The Economist*, 1st March 2018, https://www.economist.com/leaders/2018/03/01/how-the-west-got-china-wrong See also: G Rachman, "How China broke the Asian model," *Australian Financial Review*, 22nd June 2021: https://www.afr.com/world/asia/how-china-broke-the-asian-model-20210622-p58335
16. Apart from compulsory voting, preferential voting and the House of Lords, the UK might consider cleaning up some other peculiarities that Australians—who expect voting to be the best possible representation of the whole of the citizenry—find strange. These include voting on a Thursday rather than a

Saturday (one reason that one third of people, and an even higher proportion of working age people, don't get polled) and allowing citizens of other countries (in the Commonwealth) to vote as if they were the local people whose lives are being impacted by the election.

17. A Ford, "The Brexit Vote was never about 'head versus heart': new study", press release, 10th December 2020: https://www.sussex.ac.uk/broadcast/read/54093
18. Further, the *Referendum (Machinery Provisions) Act 1984* requires the Australian Electoral Commission (AEC) to distribute a pamphlet with a written argument for and against the passage of the referendum.
19. The majority of members of the House of Lords are "life peers" formally appointed by the monarch, with the remainder comprising members who have inherited their titles and bishops and archbishops of the Church of England. See: M. Russell, "House of Lords reform: navigating the obstacles", (Institute for Government, UK 2023), https://www.ucl.ac.uk/constitution-unit/news/2023/mar/launch-new-report-house-lords-reform-navigating-obstacles Legislation has been announced to remove the life peers in 2025.
20. See further, H Zaidy, "Britain's NHS was once idolized. Now its worst-ever crisis is fueling a boom in private health care", *CNN*, 6th February 2023: https://edition.cnn.com/2023/02/06/business/nhs-strikes-private-healthcare-uk/index.html
21. Australian Institute of Health and Welfare, "Australia's hospitals at a glance" (2023): https://www.aihw.gov.au/getmedia/8c50762e-f614-438d-86d5-713d19203686/aihw-hse-253-hospitals-at-a-glance-dec23.pdf
22. The UK has the lowest number of CT units per million population amongst comparator countries with approximately 10 units per million population, whereas Australia has approximately 59 units per million population, see T Lovell, "UK ranks lowest internationally for number of scanners per million", *Digital Health*, 16th July 2024: https://www.digitalhealth.net/2024/07/uk-ranks-lowest-internationally-for-number-of-scanners-per-million/#:~:text=News per cent2C per cent20Smart per cent20Health&text='Life per cent20sciences per cent20competitive per cent20indicators per cent202024similar per cent20levels per cent20of per cent20economic per cent20development Also: "Number of computer tomography (CT) scanners in selected countries as of 2021" (website), Statista, accessed 11th August 2024: https://www.statista.com/statistics/266539/distribution-of-equipment-for-computer-tomography/
23. C Rowland and N Davis, "Fixing public services: The criminal justice system" (Institute for Government): https://www.instituteforgovernment.org.uk/publication/fixing-public-services-labour-government/criminal-justice-system
24. For instance, whilst the UK's Financial Conduct Authority is independently established under law, it reports to the HM Treasury which appoints the FCA's board, while economic policy priorities are set by the chancellor. Meanwhile, the Australian Securities and Investment Commission was established under statute and its commissioners are independent statutory appointees. See: "Financial regulator's independence put to the test", *Flint Global*, 8th May 2024: https://flint-global.com/blog/financial-regulator-independence-put-to-the-test/#:~:text=How per cent20independent per cent20is per cent20the

per cent20FCA,on per cent20its per cent20approach per cent20to per cent20enforcement See also: "Australian Securities and Investments Commission investigation and enforcement" (Parliament of Australia 2024): https://www.aph.gov.au/Parliamentary_Business/Committees/Senate/Economics/ASICinvestigation/Report/Chapter_3_-_The_current_regulatory_system

25. "Former mining communities still scarred by past" BBC, 17th October 2019: https://www.bbc.com/news/uk-england-50069336

26. The Fraser government controlled the senate for approximately four years, gaining senate majority in 1975 until 1980, and the Howard government only controlled the senate from 2004 to 2007. See "Federal election results" (website), Parliament of Australia, accessed 11th August 2024: https://www.aph.gov.au/About_Parliament/Parliamentary_Departments/Parliamentary_Library/pubs/rp/rp1617/FederalElectionResults

27. The resources curse (also known as the paradox of the plenty) refers to countries with an abundance of natural resources having less economic growth and lower rates of economic stability. See "The Resource Curse: The Political and Economic Challenges of Natural Resource Wealth", Natural Resource Governance Institute, https://resourcegovernance.org/sites/default/files/nrgi_Resource-Curse.pdf See also: JA Frankel, "The Natural Resources Curse: A Survey of Diagnoses and Some Prescriptions", Chapter Two in *Commodity Price Volatility and Inclusive Growth in Low-Income Countries*, ed R Arezki et al. (International Monetary Fund, 2012), http://nrs.harvard.edu/urn-3:HUL.InstRepos:8694932.

CHAPTER 1. WHAT IS AN AUSTRALIAN?

1. B Bryson, *Down Under* (Penguin, 2000).
2. "Country Comparison Tool "(website), Hofstete Insights, accessed 11th August 2024: https://www.hofstede-insights.com/country-comparison-tool?countries=australia
3. J Rawls, *A Theory of Justice* (Harvard University Press, 1971).
4. E Tarnow, "Towards the Zero Accident Goal: Assisting the First Officer: Monitor and Challenge Captain Errors", *Journal of Aviation/Aerospace Education & Research*, 2000: https://doi.org/10.15394/jaaer.2000.1269
5. Qantas was ranked the safest airline among 385 in the analysis by AirlineRatings (taking into account airline crash and serious incident records, regulatory audits, safety initiatives and age of the fleet). Over 60 years, Qantas was either first or second airline to introduce 16 major safety enhancements, including technologies such as real-time engine monitoring and automatic landings using global navigation satellite systems. See L Bloom, "Ranked: The 25 Safest Airlines In The World, According To AirlineRatings.com", *Forbes*, 3rd January 2024: https://www.forbes.com/sites/laurabegleybloom/2024/01/03/ranked-the-25-safest-airlines-in-the-world-according-to-airlineratingscom/
6. Australia's average life expectancy is also well ahead of the OECD average of 80 years, see "International health data comparisons" (website), Australian Institute of Health and Welfare, accessed 11th August 2024: https://www.aihw.gov.au/reports/international-comparisons/international-health-data-comparisons

7. Covid contributed to a 16 per cent increase in the expected number of deaths in 2020 and the first half of 2021 across OECD countries. Life expectancy fell in 24 of 30 countries with comparable data, with drops particularly large in the US and Spain. See: *Health at a Glance 2021* (OECD, 2021): https://doi.org/10.1787/ae3016b9-en
8. The Economist Intelligence Unit's *Global Liveability Index 2023* ranked two of Australia's cities, Melbourne and Sydney, at third and fourth place. The EIU used a multivariate regression of factors, including stability, healthcare, culture and environment, education and infrastructure, Other studies have also ranked Australia at or close to the top in the world.
9. "Gambling in Australia" (website), Australian Institute of Health and Welfare: https://www.aihw.gov.au/reports/australias-welfare/gambling See also: "Countries with the largest gambling losses per adult worldwide in 2017" (website), Statista, 5th November 2024: https://www.statista.com/statistics/552821/gambling-losses-per-adult-by-country-worldwide/
10. "Overweight and obesity among Australian males", Australian Institute of Family Studies: https://aifs.gov.au/tentomen/insights-report/overweight-and-obesity-among-australian-males#:~:text=Australia per cent20had per cent20the per cent20third per cent20highest, per cent25) per cent20(AIHW per cent2C per cent202018)
11. "Household debt" (website), OECD 11th August 2024: https://www.oecd.org/en/data/indicators/household-debt.html?oecdcontrol-0c34c1bd70-var3=2021 See also: "Global Debt Database" (website), International Monetary Fund, accessed 11th August 2024: https://www.imf.org/external/datamapper/datasets/GDD
12. Australia ranks fourth in the world as the most tattooed nation globally, with around 43 per cent of people having at least one. See "Where Tattoos Are Most Popular" (website), Statista, accessed 11th August 2024: https://www.statista.com/chart/13942/where-tattoos-are-most-popular/
13. One in 20 babies in Australia are born through IVF. See "Almost one in 20 babies in Australia born through IVF," UNSW, media release, 6th September 2020: https://newsroom.unsw.edu.au/news/health/almost-one-20-babies-australia-born-through-ivf Meanwhile, Australia has the second-highest rate of vasectomies in the world, see D Colasimone, "More Australian men are getting vasectomies than ever before, despite some enduring myths," ABC News, 29th December 2020: https://www.abc.net.au/news/2020-12-29/getting-a-vasectomy-myths-australia/12917746
14. Australia is investing about 1.8 per cent of GDP in research and development, compared with 3 per cent for the US and 2.3 per cent across the OECD. See T Burton, "What to do about our poor innovation record," *Australian Financial Review*, 2nd September 2022: https://www.afr.com/politics/federal/what-to-do-about-our-poor-innovation-record-20220901-p5behb
15. S Grant, *Australia Day* (Harper Collins, 2019).
16. R Henderson, "Australian stocks lead the world in returns," *Australian Financial Review*, 5th March 2021: https://www.afr.com/markets/equity-markets/australian-stocks-lead-the-world-in-returns-20210305-p5784x Since federation, the Australian stock market has delivered average annual returns of 6.6 per

cent in US dollar real terms, placing it ahead of 22 other markets, partly due to dividends which accounted for more than half of the total returns. Also see: Credit Suisse, *Credit Suisse Global Investment Returns Yearbook 2021* (2021). Australian shares produced a total average annual compound return of 9.1 per cent over the past 30 years, easily eclipsing the 7.6 per cent returns of international shares, see J Collett, "Australian shares beating out global peers over the very long run," *Sydney Morning Herald*, 16th August 2023: https://www.smh.com.au/money/investing/australian-shares-beating-out-global-peers-over-the-very-long-run-20230814-p5dw98.html

17. The NBN was designed to deliver high speed internet to all Australians, but the project faced number of significant cost overruns, see P Smith, "Inside the bloody political war that led to a $31b NBN blowout," *Australian Financial Review*, 6th December 2022: https://www.afr.com/technology/inside-the-bloody-political-war-that-led-to-a-31bn-nbn-blowout-20221205-p5c3tr The NDIS's projected annual running cost in 2026 is more than double the initial projected annual cost of $22 billion, see M Read, "How the NDIS will blow out to $50b (in four charts)," *Australian Financial Review*, 25th October 2022: https://www.afr.com/politics/federal/how-the-ndis-will-blow-out-to-50b-in-four-charts-20221019-p5br1c See list of defence projects that have been delayed and over budget, A Tillett, "Australia's 10 major defence projects that are late and over budget," *Australian Financial Review*, 12th February 2024: https://www.afr.com/policy/foreign-affairs/australia-s-10-major-defence-projects-that-are-late-and-over-budget-20240212-p5f44g

18. Long-term thinking and planning is required to address future challenges including climate change, an aging population and escalating pressures on the health system, see *Australia to 2050: future challenges*, the 2010 Intergenerational Report (Commonwealth of Australia, 2010): https://treasury.gov.au/sites/default/files/2019-03/IGR_2010_Overview.pdf

19. B Salt quoted in C Middap, "Fortress Australia: how the pandemic strategy has divided us," *The Weekend Australian Magazine*, 26th June 2021: https://www.theaustralian.com.au/weekend-australian-magazine/fortress-australia-how-the-pandemic-strategy-has-divided-us/news-story/c287763f45e3bb16518f38b0546d8120

20. M Dalton, "NSW marks 50 years of mandatory seatbelts," *Nine News*, 2nd November 2021: https://www.9news.com.au/national/new-south-wales-celebrates-50-years-of-mandatory-seatbelts-automotive-history/4a63b2e3-739c-4c38-b38b-6cedbc930aa2

21. NDS, "2021 Federal budget sees increased funding for the NDIS," press release, 11th May 2021: https://www.nds.org.au/news/2021-federal-budget-sees-increased-funding-for-the-ndis

22. Following federation, when Australia introduced a system of federal elections, Australia, in 1902, became one of the first countries to grant women the right to vote at the federal level (comparatively, US and UK granted women the right to vote in 1920 and 1918, respectively). In 1924, Australia introduced compulsory voting, and in 1962 indigenous Australians gained the full right to vote in all states. See "A short history of federal electoral reform in Australia" (website),

Australian Electoral Commission: https://www.aec.gov.au/Elections/history-of-electoral-reform.htm
23. Australia is second behind Luxembourg in global minimum wage levels, see "Minimum Wage by Country 2021" (website), World Population Review, accessed 10th July 2021, https://worldpopulationreview.com/country-rankings/minimum-wage-by-country France, New Zealand and Germany have minimum wages next behind Australia.
24. Australia first introduced sick leave entitlement to an award in 1907. From 1935 to the 1970s, paid sick leave and annual leave were gradually introduced into federal awards until ten days' sick leave and four weeks' annual leave became standard, see "Australia's industrial relations timeline" (website), Fairwork Ombudsman, accessed 10th July 2021: https://www.fairwork.gov.au/about-us/legislation/the-fair-work-system/australias-industrial-relations-timeline#nineteen-thirty-five
25. 13 per cent of employees in Australia work very long hours, which is above the OECD average, see "Work-Life Balance" (website), *OECD Better Life Index*, accessed 16th August 2024: https://www.oecdbetterlifeindex.org/topics/work-life-balance/
26. See "Value of goods exported to leading trading partners from Australia in 2022" (website), accessed 28th May 2023: https://www.statista.com/statistics/622568/australia-export-partners-by-value/ According to the latest Australian Bureau of Statistics figures, Japan is now Australia's fourth most-visited overseas destination, see K Scott, "'Beyond crazy': Japan full of Aussies as we flock back", *Sydney Morning Herald*, 22nd April 2023: https://www.smh.com.au/traveller/travel-news/big-in-japan-what-s-reignited-our-travel-obsession-20230413-p5doal.html

CHAPTER 2. SUBURBIA & SPORT

1. S Turnbull, "Mapping the Vast Suburban Tundra: Australian comedy from Dame Edna to Kath and Kim," *International Journal of Cultural Studies*, 2008.
2. G Hugo, "Changing Patterns of Population Distribution in Australia", *Journal of Population Research and NZ Population Review* 2002: https://search.informit.org/doi/10.3316/informit.395273573294486
3. R Menzies, "The Forgotten People," (speech, 22nd May 1942).
4. See, for example, S Wright, "Why a vote in the country is worth more than the city," *The West Australia*, 28th February 2017: https://thewest.com.au/politics/state-election-2017/distorted-system-gives-rural-vote-more-weight-ng-b883987132
5. "Overseas Arrivals and Departures, Australia" (website), Australian Bureau of Statistics, accessed 17th August 17: https://www.abs.gov.au/statistics/industry/tourism-and-transport/overseas-arrivals-and-departures-australia/latest-release
6. "Largest cities by population 2024" (website), *World Population Review*, accessed 17th August 2024: https://worldpopulationreview.com/world-cities
7. The population in the South East Queensland region, comprising Brisbane, Gold Coast and Sunshine Coast, is 3.8 million in 2020 and forecast to reach more than 5.4 million by the 2040s, see "Population growth, housing and housing affordability in South East Queensland", Department of Infrastructure,

Transport, Regional Development, Communications and Arts: https://www.infrastructure.gov.au/department/media/publications/population-growth-housing-and-housing-affordability-south-east-queensland-placemats

8. "Countries by Population Density | Countries by Density 2023" (website), *World Population Review*, accessed 2nd June 2023: https://worldpopulationreview.com/country-rankings/countries-by-density

9. "Coasts" (website), Australia State of the Environment, accessed 17th August 2024: https://soe.dcceew.gov.au/coasts/pressures/population#:~:text=Australia per cent20is per cent20an per cent20urban per cent20coastal,now per cent20calling per cent20the per cent20coast per cent20home

10. "The city at a glance" (website), City of Sydney, accessed 17th August 2024: https://www.cityofsydney.nsw.gov.au/guides/city-at-a-glance See also "Manhattan borough, New York County, New York" (website), accessed 17th August 2024: https://data.census.gov/profile/Manhattan_borough,_New_York_County,_New_York?g=060XX00US3606144919

11. See, for example, L. Webster, "'Til it's done', let's make this the start of something," SGS Economics and Planning, 11th August 2023: https://sgsep.com.au/publications/insights/women-in-sport

CHAPTER 3. FAIR GO

1. Elizabeth Anderson argues for an approach she terms "democratic equality", as opposed to "luck egalitarianism". Whereas luck egalitarianism seeks to eliminate, as far as possible, the impacts of "bad luck" on people's lives, democratic equality seeks to end oppressive social relationships. The social conditions of democratic equality include equal respect and freedom to participate in a democratic government. See E Anderson, "What is the Point of Equality?", *Ethics* (1999): https://doi.org/10.1086/233897

2. M Ridley, "Innovation in Australia," Centre for Independent Studies, Paper 176, (2010): https://www.cis.org.au/app/uploads/2020/10/op176.pdf

3. "Australian population" (website), Worldometer, accessed 17th August 2024: https://www.worldometers.info/world-population/australia-population/#:~:text=Australia per cent20population per cent20is per cent20equivalent per cent20to,(and per cent20dependencies) per cent20by per cent20population

4. *The National Arts Participation Survey*, 2022.

5. *The Big Picture: public expenditure on artistic, cultural and creative activity in Australia*, A New Approach [ANA] thinktank with lead delivery partner the Australian Academy of the Humanities, 2019: https://www.humanities.org.au/wp-content/uploads/2020/06/ANA-InsightReportOne-FullReport_V0.1.pdf "About Australia Publishing" (website), Australian Publishers Association, accessed 17th August 2024: https://publishers.asn.au/Web/Web/About-Publishing/Overview.aspx

6. "Motion Picture and Video Production in Australia—Market Size, Industry Analysis, Trends and Forecasts (2024-2029)" (website), IBISWorld: https://www.ibisworld.com/au/industry/motion-picture-video-production/634/#TableOfContents

CHAPTER 4. SCEPTICAL PRAGMATISM

1. M. Oakehott, "On Being Conservative," in *Rationalism in Politics and Other Essays* (Basic Books, 1962).
2. *Parliamentary Library Briefing Book: Constitutional Reform* (Parliament of Australia, 2022): https://www.aph.gov.au/About_Parliament/Parliamentary_departments/Parliamentary_Library/pubs/BriefingBook47p
3. Hans Rosling dedicated his life to demonstrating with statistics and surveys that the vast majority of people systematically—and mistakenly—believe that the world is worse than it actually is and have not grasped the vast improvements in child mortality, wealth and life expectancy that have been made, see H Rosling, *Factfulness: Ten Reasons We're Wrong About the World—and Why Things Are Better Than You Think* (Flatiron Books, 2018).
4. A good discussion of the role of unions in award setting can be found in the Reserve Bank of Australia's Research Discussion Paper RDP 2019-02.
5. "Trade union membership" (website), Australian Bureau of Statistics: https://www.abs.gov.au/statistics/labour/earnings-and-working-conditions/trade-union-membership/latest-release#:~:text=Of per cent20the per cent2011.4 per cent20million per cent20employees,has per cent20generally per cent20declined per cent20since per cent201992 See also, "Countries with the highest per centage share of their workforce being members of labor unions worldwide as of 2020" (website), Statista, accessed 17th August 2024: https://www.statista.com/statistics/1356735/labor-unions-most-unionized-countries-worldwide/
6. See also, P Lewis, "Australia's Industrial Relations Singularity," in *Only in Australia*, ed WO Coleman (Oxford University Press, 2016): https://doi.org/10.1093/acprof:oso/9780198753254.003.0007

CHAPTER 5. THE FIRST AUSTRALIANS

1. "Indigenous Australian's right to vote" (website), National Museum Australia, accessed 18th August 2024: https://www.nma.gov.au/defining-moments/resources/indigenous-australians-right-to-vote
2. "Reforms to the native title system" (website), Australia Government: https://www.indigenous.gov.au/news-and-media/stories/reforms-native-title-system Indigenous people have legally recognised rights across 57 per cent of Australia; this is expected to reach 72 per cent by 2030, see *National Indigenous Land and Sea Strategy: 2023 to 2028*, prepared by the Indigenous Land and Sea Corporation (ILSC Group, 2023): https://www.ilsc.gov.au/wp-content/uploads/2023/06/FA-National-Indigenous-Land-and-Sea-Strategy-DIGITAL-3.pdf
3. Productivity Commission for the Steering Committee for the Review of Government Service Provision, *2017 Indigenous Expenditure Report* (Commonwealth of Australia, 2017): https://www.pc.gov.au/research/ongoing/indigenous-expenditure-report/2017/ier-2017-indigenous-expenditure-report.pdf
4. L Richards, *Aboriginal and Torres Strait Islander parliamentarians in Australia: a quick guide,* (Parliament of Australia, 2022): https://www.aph.gov.au/About_Parliament/Parliamentary_departments/Parliamentary_Library/pubs/rp/rp2223/Quick_Guides/IndigenousMPs2022#:~:text=Current per cent20representation,

NOTES AND FURTHER READING

per cent2C per cent2ostate per cent2oand per cent2oterritory per cent2oparliamentarians

5. *Closing the Gap Report 2022* (Australian Government, 2022): https://www.niaa.gov.au/resource-centre/indigenous-affairs/commonwealth-closing-gap-annual-report-2022/ 9.2 per cent of babies born to indigenous mothers were born with low birthweight compared with 4.9 per cent of babies born to non-indigenous mothers, see "Birthweight" (website), Australian Institute of Health and Welfare, National Indigenous Australians Agency, accessed 2nd June 2023: https://www.indigenoushpf.gov.au/measures/1-01-birthweight

6. In 2016, the unemployment rate for indigenous people of working age was 18.4 per cent, 2.7 times the non-indigenous unemployment rate (6.8 per cent), see *Closing the Gap Report 2018*, "Chapter 4: Employment" (website), Australian Government Department of Prime Minister and Cabinet, accessed 25th January 2021: https://www.pmc.gov.au/sites/default/files/reports/closing-the-gap-2018/employment.html According to *Closing the Gap Report 2020*, between 2008 and 2018–19, the national indigenous employment rate for those aged between 15 and 64 increased from 48.2 per cent to 49.1 per cent. The employment rate for non-indigenous Australians aged between 15 and 64 over the same period remained relatively stable at around 75 per cent. According to *Closing the Gap Report 2023*, improvements have been made but the outcomes are not on track. See also: "Indigenous education and skills" (website), Australian Institute of Health and Welfare, accessed 2nd June 2023: https://www.aihw.gov.au/reports/australias-welfare/indigenous-education-and-skills

7. Indigenous women were 32 times as likely to be hospitalised due to family violence as non-indigenous women, while indigenous men were 23 times as likely to be hospitalised as non-indigenous men, see *Family, domestic and sexual violence in Australia: continuing the national story* (Australian Institute of Health and Welfare, 2019), https://www.aihw.gov.au/reports/family-domestic-and-sexual-violence/family-domestic-sexual-violence-australia-2019/contents/summary

8. "Health" (website), United Nations Depart of Economic and Social Affairs, accessed 18th August 2024: https://www.un.org/development/desa/indigenouspeoples/mandated-areas1/health.html

9. *2022 Australian Reconciliation Barometer* (Reconciliation Australia, 2022): https://www.reconciliation.org.au/publication/2022-australian-reconciliation-barometer/

10. In the ten years since the first Closing the Gap programme began in 2008, two out of the seven targets were met or were on track to being met. These are: (1) 95 per cent of all indigenous four-year-olds enrolled in early childhood education by 2025, and (2) halve the gap in Year 12 or equivalent attainment rates by 2020. Other targets across literacy and numeracy, employment, child mortality, school attendance and life expectancy were not met. See *Closing the Gap Report 2020*. See also "Australian Universities Committed to Indigenous Opportunity" (website), Universities Australia, accessed 25th January 2021: https://www.universitiesaustralia.edu.au/media-item/australian-universities-committed-to-indigenous-opportunity/

11. See, for example, G McCubbing, "'Bureaucratic gobbledegook' holding up Closing the Gap," *Australian Financial Review*, 7th February 2024: https://www.afr.com/politics/bureaucratic-gobbledegook-holding-up-closing-the-gap-20240206-p5f2n9
12. J Nicholas et al, "Who Owns Australia?", *The Guardian*, 17th May 2021: https://www.theguardian.com/australia-news/ng-interactive/2021/may/17/who-owns-australia See also, H Hughes and M Hughes, "The Denial of Private Property Rights to Aborigines," *Quadrant Online*, 1st May 2012: https://quadrant.org.au/magazine/2012/05/the-denial-of-private-property-rights-to-aborigines/
13. J Cross, "Indigenous school attendance slipping in NSW schools," *National Indigenous Times*, 22nd September 2022: https://nit.com.au/29-09-2022/3981/indigenous-school-attendance-slipping-in-nsw-schools#:~:text=Indigenous per cent20school per cent20attendance per cent20slipping per cent20in per cent20NSW per cent20schools&text=An per cent20Auditor per cent20General's per cent20report per cent20this,52.7 per cent20per cent per cent20three per cent20years per cent20prior
14. N Pearson, *Radical Hope: Education and Equality in Australia*, (Black Inc, 2011).
15. Stanner, in his 1968 Boyer Lecture, pointed out that there was a "cult of disremembering", and the history of the dispossession had been obliterated from the national view. See P Adams, "WEH Stanner and the Great Australian Silence" (podcast) 26th March 2009: https://www.abc.net.au/radionational/programs/latenightlive/weh-stanner-and-the-great-australian-silence/3143396

CHAPTER 6. BORN BY BALLOT NOT BATTLEFIELD

1. J Hirst, "The Distinctiveness of Australian Democracy", *Papers on Parliament*, (Parliament of Australia, 2004): https://www.aph.gov.au/sitecore/content/Home/About_Parliament/Senate/Powers_practice_n_procedures/pops/pop42/hirst#:~:text=Question per cent20 per centE2 per cent80 per cent94 per cent20The per cent20two per cent20features per cent20of,changed per cent20with per cent2010 per cent20000 per cent20votes
2. J Brett writes that voting is compulsory in 19 countries but only 9 strictly enforce it. See J Brett, *From Secret Ballot to Democracy Sausage: How Australia got Compulsory Voting*. (Textpublishing, 2019). According to the *Democracy index*, as published by *The Economist*, 23 countries are regarded as "full democracies" where "not only basic political freedoms and civil liberties are respected, but which also tend to be underpinned by a political culture conducive to the flourishing of democracy"—of which Australia is one. Notably, only 8.4 per cent of the world's population lives in these full democracies. The vast majority of the global population lives in "flawed democracies" (representing 41 per cent of the world's population) and in authoritarian regimes (representing 35.6 per cent of the world's population), see *Democracy Index 2020—In sickness and in health?* (The Economist Intelligence Unit, 2021). See also, "Appendix G—Countries with compulsory voting" (website), Parliament of Australia, accessed 18th August 2024: https://www.aph.gov.au/Parliamentary_Business/Committees/Joint/Completed_Inquiries/em/electo4/appendixg

3. Australian elections stand out from the US and other counterparts largely because of the non-politicised federal administration body—the Australian Electoral Commission. Whereas powerful local authorities control elections in the UK, and electoral administration is controlled by individual states, rather than on a national level, in the US (with individual states using this power for some very imaginative boundary definitions), the Australian Electoral Commission's non-partisan, independent and centralised system is crucial to the integrity of Australian's electoral system, see B Mercurio and G Williams, "Australian Electoral Law: 'Free and Fair'?," *Federal Law Review*, 2004: http://classic.austlii.edu.au/au/journals/FedLawRw/2004/18.html#fn35

4. "Boix-Miller-Rosato (BMR) dichotomous coding of democracy 1800-2015 dataset", version 3.0, Michael K Miller, accessed 10th June 2023: https://sites.google.com/site/mkmtwo/data

5. "Share of the World Population Living in Democracies" (website), Our World in Data: https://ourworldindata.org/democracy#share-of-world-population-living-in-democracies See also "Population, Total—China" (website), The World Bank, accessed 10th June 2023: https://data.worldbank.org/indicator/SP.POP.TOTL?locations=CN

6. L Barber and H Foy, "Vladimir Putin: liberalism has 'outlived its purpose'", *Financial Times*, 18th September 2019, https://www.ft.com/content/2880c762-98c2-11e9-8cfb-30c211dcd229

7. The comments on correlation between liberalism and economic success (measured by GDP per capita) draw on the World Bank for indexation of "Voice and accountability" and the Heritage Foundation for "Economic freedom". As Martin Wolf points out (see M Wolf, "Liberalism will endure but must be renewed", *Financial Times*, 3rd July 2019: https://www.ft.com/content/52dc93d2-9c1f-11e9-9c06-a4640c9feebb), the two tend to go together, in part because both depend on the effective operation of the rule of law. This article also cites the comparison of Russian economic growth over the 20 years since the Soviet Union broke up to other post-Soviet States.

8. Studies show that enhanced political participation leads to increased spending on public healthcare with more positive outcomes, see E Ortiz-Ospina, "Does Democracy lead to better health?", Our World in Data, 2019: https://ourworldindata.org/democracy-health

9. An MIT study has shown that democracy significantly increases economic development. Countries changing to democratic regimes experience a 20 per cent increase in GDP over a 25 year period, see P Dizikes, "Study: Democracy fosters economic growth," *Massachusetts Institute of Technology*, 7th March 7 2019: https://news.mit.edu/2019/study-democracy-fosters-economic-growth-acemoglu-0307 Further studies have shown that democracies experience faster technological change and technology-induced growth than autocracies, which may be due to greater civil liberties facilitating free flow of ideas and dissemination of economically productive technologies, see CH Knutsen, "Why Democracies Outgrow Autocracies in the Long Run: Civil Liberties, Information Flows and Technological Change," *Kyklos*, 2015: https://doi.org/10.1111/kykl.12087

10. Regimes that are more democratic are more likely to be politically stable and less politically violent than more autocratic regimes, as well as more likely to have a smooth transition from one elected leader to the next without political violence, see RF Tusalem, "Democracies, Autocracies, and Political Stability," *International Social Science Review*, 2015): https://digitalcommons.northgeorgia.edu/cgi/viewcontent.cgi?article=1070&context=issr See also M Qvortrup, *Winners and Losers: Which countries are successful and why?* (Peter Lang Books, 2021).

CHAPTER 7. BOUNDLESS PLAINS TO SHARE

1. "Australian citizenship statistics" (website), Australian Government Department of Home Affairs, accessed 18th August 2024: https://www.homeaffairs.gov.au/research-and-statistics/statistics/citizenship-statistics
2. G Ballantyne & A Podkalicka, "Dreaming Diversity: Second Generation Australians and the Reimagining of Multicultural Australia", *M/C Journal*, 2020: https://doi.org/10.5204/mcj.1648
3. "Population Growth" (website), Our World in Data, accessed 18th August 2024: https://ourworldindata.org/population-growth#all-charts
4. At any time, there are around one million Australians living and working overseas, see "Going overseas to live or work" (website), *Smart Traveller*, accessed 10th June 2023: https://www.smartraveller.gov.au/before-you-go/activities/living-overseas
5. "Table 2: Total Movement, Departures—Category of Movement", Australian Bureau of Statistics: https://www.abs.gov.au/statistics/industry/tourism-and-transport/overseas-arrivals-and-departures-australia/latest-release#abs-stat-datasets
6. "Convicts" (website), National Library of Australia, accessed 10th June 2023, https://www.nla.gov.au/research-guides/convicts#:~:text=From per cent20January per cent201788 per cent2C per cent20when per cent20the,convicts per cent20were per cent20transported per cent20to per cent 20Australia Between 1851 and 1871, the Australian population quadrupled from 430,000 people to 1.7 million as migrants from across the world arrived in search of gold, see "Gold Rushes "(website), National Museum Australia, accessed 10th June 10 2023: https://www.nma.gov.au/defining-moments/resources/gold-rushes#:~:text=Migration per cent20boom&text=Between per cent201851 per cent20and per cent201871 per cent20the,arrived per cent20in per cent20search per cent20of per cent20gold
7. "Postwar Immigration Drive" (website), National Museum Australia, accessed 10th June 2023: https://www.nma.gov.au/defining-moments/resources/postwar-immigration-drive Between 1945 and 2000, most of Australia's population increase (59 per cent of the increase from 7.4 million to 19.1 million) has come from immigration, see "International Migration Transforms Australia" (website), Population Reference Bureau, last modified 1st June 2001, https://www.prb.org/internationalmigrationtransformsaustralia/
8. "Lowy Institute Poll 2024: Societal Issues" (website), Lowy Institute, accessed 18th August 18: https://poll.lowyinstitute.org/report/2024/societal-issues/#immigration

9. J O'Donnell, *Mapping Social Cohesion 2023* (Scanlon Foundation Research Institute, 2023): https://scanloninstitute.org.au/publications/mapping-social-cohesion-report/2023-mapping-social-cohesion-report

10. The consistent finding is that immigration has no harmful impacts on the number of jobs or wage levels overall. Immigrants bring expenditure into the host country and enhance demand for more labour to produce those goods and services. Skilled migration, especially those with skills complementary to those of existing workers, may increase productivity and wages and engender innovation through increased knowledge and bringing in international best practice. Across other jurisdictions with relatively high immigration rates, such as the UK and Canada, studies have similarly shown that immigration does not negatively affect local employment and wage levels. Studies agree that even if immigration results in short-term labour competition, the effects disappear in the long term (due to market elasticity). See, "Migrant Intake into Australia", *Inquiry Report*, 2016: https://www.pc.gov.au/inquiries/completed/migrant-intake/report/migrant-intake-report.pdf; R Chomik, J Piggott, and P McDonald, "The impact of demographic change on labour supply and economic growth: Can Apec meet the challenges ahead?", *ARC Centre of Excellence in Population Ageing Research*, Working Paper 2017: https://cepar.edu.au/sites/default/files/The_Impact_of_Demographic_Change_on_Labour_Supply.pdf; J Tu, "The Impact of Immigration on the Labour Market Outcomes of Native-Born Canadians", IZA Discussion Paper No. 5129 (2010): http://ftp.iza.org/dp5129.pdf; "The Labour Market Effects of Immigration" (website), The Migration Observatory at the University of Oxford: https://migrationobservatory.ox.ac.uk/resources/briefings/the-labour-market-effects-of-immigration/

11. "Engineers Australia responds to Government's new migration strategy and Infrastructure Australia Market Capacity Report," Engineers Australia, media release, 12th December 2023: https://www.engineersaustralia.org.au/news-and-media/2023/12/engineers-australia-response-governments-new-migration-strategy-and

12. S Dumitriu, A Stewart, *Job Creators: The Immigrant Founders of Britain's Fastest Growing Businesses*, (The Entrepreneurs Network, 2021): https://static1.squarespace.com/static/58ed40453a04116f46e8d99b/t/5d275769b2a56d00017deb2f/1562859421693/Job+Creators

13. P Legrain, *Them and Us: How Immigrants and Locals can thrive together* (Oneworld Publications, 2020).

14. YN Harari, *21 Lessons for the 21st Century* (Vintage, 2018).

15. E Hunt, "Barely half of population born in Australia to Australian-born parents," *The Guardian*, 27th June 2017: https://www.theguardian.com/australia-news/2017/jun/27/australia-reaches-tipping-point-with-quarter-of-population-born-overseas See also "Census reveals a fast changing, culturally diverse nation," Australian Bureau of Statistics, media release, 27th June 2017: https://www.abs.gov.au/ausstats/abs@.nsf/lookup/media per cent20release3

16. OM Hartwich, *Selection, Migration and Integration: Why Multiculturalism works in Australia (and fails in Europe)* (CIS Policy Monograph, 2011): https://library.

bsl.org.au/jspui/bitstream/1/2896/1/Selection per cent20migration per cent20and per cent20integration.pdf
17. J Phillips and H Spinks, *Boat Arrivals in Australia since 1976* (Parliament of Australia, 2013): https://www.aph.gov.au/about_parliament/parliamentary_departments/parliamentary_library/pubs/rp/rp1314/boatarrivals
18. D Goodhart, *The Road to Somewhere* (Hurst, 2017).
19. A survey conducted by Onepoll shows that 11 per cent of respondents in America have never travelled beyond the state in which they were born, and 40 per cent per cent have never left the country, see L Lane, "Percentage Of Americans Who Never Traveled Beyond The State Where They Were Born? A Surprise," *Forbes*, 2nd May 2019: https://www.forbes.com/sites/lealane/2019/05/02/per centage-of-americans-who-never-traveled-beyond-the-state-where-they-were-born-a-surprise/?sh=53ab1d452898
20. Data suggests that Australia is amongst the most mobile societies in the world, with 15 per cent of the population changing their address within Australia in the year prior to the 2016 Census, and 39 per cent changing their address in the five years prior to the Census. Across the globe, on average, 7.9 per cent of people move domestically each year, while 21 per cent move at least once every five years, see "Census of Population and Housing: Reflecting Australia—Stories from the Census" (website), Australian Bureau of Statistics, 2016: https://www.abs.gov.au/ausstats/abs@.nsf/Lookup/by per cent20Subject/2071.0~2016~Main per cent20Features~Population per cent20Shift: per cent20Understanding per cent20Internal per cent20Migration per cent20in per cent20Australia~69
21. "Brick by Brick: Building Better Housing Policies—Lifting Obstacles to Residential Mobility", OECD, accessed 19th August 2024: https://www.oecd-ilibrary.org/sites/b453b043-en/1/3/6/index.html?itemId=/content/publication/b453b043-en&_csp_=6c2144a214b333aaac200b082e70ed53&itemIGO=oecd&itemContentType=book#chapter-d1e8069
22. "Overseas Migration" (website), Australian Bureau of Statistics, accessed 18th August 2024: https://www.abs.gov.au/statistics/people/population/overseas-migration/latest-release
23. Immigration tends to provide a fiscal boost to Anglophone countries such as Australia, UK and US, and there are tangible benefits, see J Burn-Murdoch, "The Anglosphere has an advantage on immigration," *Financial Times*, 26th April 2024: https://www.ft.com/content/c6bb7307-484c-4076-a0f3-fc2aeb0b6112

CHAPTER 8. HEALTHY

1. *British Medical Journal*, August 2024 (see Chapter One for full citation).
2. According to the Commonwealth Fund cross-country analysis, Australia ranked highest on Healthcare Outcomes and Administrative Efficiency but lower on Equity (perhaps because of poor indigenous health outcomes). An OECD study observed that a good indicator of quality of hospital care is the 30-day mortality rate following a heart attack. The study shows that Australia has one of the lowest rates in the world, comparative with the likes of Iceland, Denmark and Norway (all lower than 4 per cent) and much lower than UK (at 8 per cent), see "Mortality following acute myocardial infarction (AMI)" (website),

NOTES AND FURTHER READING

OECD, accessed 16th August 2024: https://www.oecd-ilibrary.org/social-issues-migration-health/health-at-a-glance-2023_58ed1a63-en Cancer Australia research also showed that Australian women diagnosed with breast cancer had better survival rates than those for northern America and western Europe, see, "Breast cancer in Australia—an overview", Cancer Series (Australia Institute of Health and Welfare, 2012): https://www.aihw.gov.au/getmedia/5a35b0e1-c1fe-4842-8ad7-c33b2fad39ce/14225.pdf.aspx?inline=true

3. "Current health expenditure (website)", World Bank Group: https://data.worldbank.org/indicator/SH.XPD.CHEX.GD.ZS
4. D Scott, "Two Sisters: Two Different Journeys through Australia's health care system", *Vox*, 16th January 2020: https://www.vox.com/2020/1/15/21030568/australia-health-insurance-medicare
5. "Nursing in the UK vs Nursing in Australia", *Nursing Notes*: https://nursingnotes.co.uk/workforce/comparing-nursing-australia-nursing-uk/
6. "Australia's hospitals at a glance", Australian Institute of Health and Welfare.
7. Australians are also signing up in record numbers to private health insurance, with 55 per cent of the population now having private health insurance, see "Australians sign up to private health insurance in record numbers", Private Healthcare Australia, media release, 1st March 2023: https://www.privatehealthcareaustralia.org.au/australians-sign-up-to-private-health-insurance-in-record-numbers/
8. Almost 30 per cent of total health expenditure comes from non-government sources, see "Health expenditure" (website), Australian Institute of Health and Welfare: https://www.aihw.gov.au/reports/health-welfare-expenditure/health-expenditure See also "UK vs Australia: Which is better for Doctors?" (website), accessed 22nd August 2024: https://medrecruit.medworld.com/articles/uk-vs-australia-which-is-better-for-doctors
9. *How does the NHS compare to health care systems of other countries?* (The King's Fund, 2023).
10. Across all healthcare outcomes, the top-performing countries are Norway, the Netherlands and Australia, see EC Schneider et al, *Mirror, Mirror 2021—Reflecting Poorly: Health Care in the US Compared to Other High Income Countries* (The Commonwealth Fund, 2021): https://www.commonwealthfund.org/publications/fund-reports/2021/aug/mirror-mirror-2021-reflecting-poorly See also "Why do Australians live so long?" *The Economist*, 23rd August 2024: https://www.economist.com/graphic-detail/2024/08/23/why-do-australians-live-so-long
11. See also E Hayward, "The Secret to a longer, healthier life is… move to Australia," *The Times*, 13th August 2024: https://www.thetimes.com/uk/healthcare/article/the-secret-to-a-longer-healthier-life-is-move-to-australia-jn7std2ck
12. *Health at a Glance 2023* (OECD, 2023): https://doi.org/10.1787/7a7afb35-en
13. "Breast Cancer" (website), The Cancer Atlas, accessed 2nd July 2023, https://canceratlas.cancer.org/the-burden/breast-cancer/
14. Further see, E Hayward and B Lagan, "What Australia can teach Wes Streeting about healthcare," *The Times*, 11th July 2024: https://www.thetimes.com/uk/

healthcare/article/what-australia-can-teach-wes-streeting-about-healthcare-lz95t89f9

15. EC Schneider et al, *Mirror, Mirror 2021—Reflecting Poorly: Health Care in the US Compared to Other High Income Countries.*

16. "Percentage of population covered by public or private health insurance in the UK from 2000 to 2020" (website), Statista, accessed 18th August 2024: https://www.statista.com/statistics/683451/population-covered-by-public-or-private-health-insurance-in-united-kingdom/

17. D Campbell, "One in 20 patients in England wait at least four weeks to see GP, figures show," *The Guardian,* 25th January 2024: https://www.theguardian.com/society/2024/jan/22/patients-england-waiting-times-gp-appointments-nhs-figures

18. For instance, Australia has more hospital beds and physicians per 1,000 people than the UK. "Country Comparison: Australia and UK" (website), World Data, accessed 9th July 2023: https://www.worlddata.info/country-comparison.php?country1=AUS&country2=GBR#live

19. See H Nguyen et al., "The Covid-19 pandemic in Australia: Public health response, opportunities and challenges", *The International Journal of Health Planning and Management,* 2022: https://doi.org/10.1002/hpm.3326 Australia had one of the world's lowest excess mortality rates, but had only spent a fraction of the OECD's health spending during the 2020-2022 years, see L Thorne, "New Covid data shows how Australia's pandemic strategy compares with other countries," *ABC News,* 29th November 2023: https://www.abc.net.au/news/2023-11-29/australia-covid-data-on-masks-tests-deaths-spending/103160238

20. According to a report published by the Australian Medical Association, Australia faces a shortage of more than 10,000 GPs by 2031–32, with key contributing factors to the shortfall being disparity in remuneration between GPs and their hospital counterparts, negative perceptions/decreasing prestige, limited training opportunities and training not being prioritised in medical schools, see "The general practitioner workforce: why the neglect must end", Australian Medical Association, 2022: https://www.ama.com.au/articles/general-practitioner-workforce-why-neglect-must-end?check_logged_in=1

21. The federal government provides the majority of health funding, however funding is not necessarily correlated with the responsibility for its management or operation. For instance, whilst the federal government funds public hospitals, the states are responsible for management and regulation, see *Australia's Health 2018* (Australian Institute of Health and Welfare, 2018): https://www.aihw.gov.au/getmedia/7c42913d-295f-4bc9-9c24-4e44eff4a04a/aihw-aus-221.pdf

22. N May, "Rate of GPs bulk billing all patients in Australia drops to below one in four, data reveals," *The Guardian,* 2nd January 2024: https://www.theguardian.com/australia-news/2024/jan/08/rate-gps-bulk-billing-patients-australia-medicare See also, J Fisher, "Patients paying huge gap fees for diagnostic imaging," *Your Life Choices,* 23rd January 2024: https://www.yourlifechoices.com.au/health/patients-paying-huge-gap-fees-for-diagnostic-imaging/

23. The number of ICU beds in New South Wales far exceeds Queensland's total on a pro rata basis to population, see "Number of intensive care unit (ICU) beds

in Australia in 2020, by state and territory" (website), Statista, accessed 9th July 2023: https://www.statista.com/statistics/1106720/australia-number-of-icu-beds-by-state/

CHAPTER 9. WEALTHY

1. "Australia's economy is still booming, but politics is a cause for concern," *Economist* survey of Australia, 25th October 2018: https://www.economist.com/special-report/2018/10/25/australias-economy-is-still-booming-but-politics-is-a-cause-for-concern
2. Australia had the highest GDP per capita in the late 19th century, which fell more than 10 rankings in the 1960s, see: "GDP per capita" (website), Our World in Data, accessed 23rd August 2024, https://ourworldindata.org/grapher/maddison-data-gdp-per-capita-in-2011us-slopechart
3. A good study of Australia's economic history is by Ian Mclean, *Why Australia Prospered: The shifting sources of economic growth* (Princeton University Press, 2013).
4. Australia's burgeoning tech sector was addressed by J Smyth, "Australia's booming tech scene looks to make mark on global stage", *Financial Times*, 25th August 2021: https://www.ft.com/content/516ccobd-4ce2-4432-8401-8e128ebc5a8f The capitalisation of the technology sector on the Australian stock exchange has grown by multiples, see "S&P/ASX All Technology Index" (website), ASX, accessed 9th July 2023: https://www2.asx.com.au/markets/trade-our-cash-market/overview/indices/asx-all-technology-index
5. G Sawlani and B Trembath, "Singapore founding PM Lee Kuan Yew once warned Australia could be 'white trash' of Asia," *ABC News*, 24th March 2015, https://www.abc.net.au/news/2015-03-24/lee-kuan-yew-warned-australia-could-be-the-white-trash-of-asia/6342578
6. "Australia Population" (website), Worldometer, accessed 9th July 2023: https://www.worldometers.info/world-population/australia-population/#:~:text=Australia per cent20population per cent20is per cent20equivalent per cent20to,(and per cent20dependencies) per cent20by per cent20population; "Australia is a top 20 country" (website), World Economic Outlook database, International Monetary Fund, accessed 9th July 2023: https://www.imf.org/en/Publications/WEO/weo-database/2020/October See also, *"Australia is a top 20 country"*, (Australian government, 2022): https://www.dfat.gov.au/sites/default/files/australia-is-a-top-20-country-all-topics.pdf
7. Australia's 29-year run without a recession was well reported, see R Goncalves, J Blakkarly, N Razik, "Australia is in recession for the first time in 29 years—here's what it means for you", SBS News, 2nd September 2020: https://www.sbs.com.au/news/australia-is-in-recession-for-the-first-time-in-29-years-here-s-what-it-means-for-you
8. M Cranston and T McIlroy, "Just four countries fared better than Australia", *Australian Financial Review*, 2nd September 2020: https://www.afr.com/policy/economy/just-three-countries-fared-better-than-australia-20200902-p55rly See also, J Murphy, "Coronavirus crisis could leave Australia better off than many other nations", *Nationwide News*, 26th September 2020: https://www.news.

com.au/finance/economy/australian-economy/coronavirus-crisis-could-leave-australia-better-off-than-many-other-nations/news-story/685c0e0a01c11ec55f1af522da5c4cf1. Unemployment was lower within a year of Covid than it had been prior to the pandemic.

9. Income from natural resources as a percentage of Australia's GDP in 2011 was 10.7 per cent. This fell to 5.3 per cent in 2015, however overall GDP growth maintained at above 2 per cent, see "Australia: Natural resources income" (Website), The Global Economy.com, accessed 23rd August 2024: https://www.theglobaleconomy.com/Australia/Natural_resources_income/; "GDP Growth (annual per cent)—Australia" (Website), The World Bank, accessed 23rd August 2024: https://data.worldbank.org/indicator/NY.GDP.MKTP.KD.ZG?end=2019&locations=AU&start=2015

10. JA Frankel, "The Natural Resources Curse: A Survey of Diagnoses and Some Prescriptions".

11. P Keating, "'We knew we were in for it': Keating pays tribute to Hawke", *Australian Financial Review*, 14th June 2019: https://www.afr.com/politics/federal/we-knew-we-were-in-for-it-keating-pays-tribute-to-hawke-20190614-p51xrm

12. According to polling by the Harvard Institute of Politics, less than half (42 per cent) of 18 to 29 year-olds supported capitalism, while 51 per cent opposed it: https://iop.harvard.edu/youth-poll/30th-edition-summer-2016 Further, a more recent survey shows that over half of young people do not think businesses have a positive impact on society, see *2021 Millennial & Gen Z Survey* (Deloitte, 2021): https://www2.deloitte.com/au/en/pages/about-deloitte/articles/millennial-survey.html

13. B Flyberg, *How Bigs Things Get Done* (Macmillan, 2023) is a comprehensive analysis of how modular approaches to infrastructure and other big investments avoid the typical cost blowouts and wastage in big investments, both public and private.

14. "Ranking of OECD countries by real national minimum wage 2022" (website), Statista, accessed 3rd August 2024: https://www.statista.com/statistics/322716/ranking-of-oecd-countries-by-national-minimum-wage/

15. UK pension scheme comparisons are drawn against Australia's superannuation system, specifically observing that Australia's system delivers better outcomes, C Mahon and J Vitali, *Growing Pension Capital* (Policy Exchange, UK, 2024): https://policyexchange.org.uk/wp-content/uploads/PX7-Growing-Pension-Capital.pdf See also, "Super Statistics" (website), ASFA, accessed 23rd August 2024: https://www.superannuation.asn.au/resources/super-stats/; H Wootton, "Cap big super at 10pc of ASX companies: senator," *Australian Financial Review*, 20th May 2024: https://www.afr.com/markets/equity-markets/cap-big-super-at-10pc-of-asx-companies-senator-20240520-p5jf3j

16. Australia ranks as the 87th most complex country in the Economic Complexity Index (ECI) ranking in 2022, behind Uganda (86th) and Botswana (84th), and slightly above Cambodia (90th) and Kazakhstan (93rd). This index is based on the "the diversity and complexity of their export basket. High complexity countries are home to a range of sophisticated, specialized capabilities and are

therefore able to produce a highly diversified set of complex products." The index also claims to predict future growth better than any other single measure. It is claimed that "compared to a decade prior, Australia's economy has become less complex, worsening 5 positions in the ECI ranking. Australia's worsening complexity has been driven by a lack of diversification of exports," see "Australia" (website), Atlas of Economic Complexity, accessed 9th July 2023: https://atlas.cid.harvard.edu/countries/14

17. A Patrick, "Australia is rich, dumb and getting dumber", *Australian Financial Review*, 8th October 2019: https://www.afr.com/policy/economy/australia-is-rich-dumb-and-getting-dumber-20191007-p52y8i

18. Rio Tinto has launched its autonomous train fleet, which can carry one million tonnes of product from its 16 mines to port, and the automated train system means that there is no need to swap drivers during its multiday journeys, see H Hastie, "No more training wheels: Rio Tinto launches 'world's biggest robot'", *The Sydney Morning Herald*, 15th June 2019: https://www.smh.com.au/business/companies/no-more-training-wheels-rio-tinto-launches-world-s-biggest-robot-20190614-p51xxj.html Automated underground mining systems are used in Northparkes copper mine in New South Wales, see "Automation pays off for Northparkes", *Australia Mining*, 2019: https://www.australianmining.com.au/automation-pays-off-for-northparkes/

19. See further, A Triggs, "Is Australia too dumb and too China-dependent?", *East Asia Forum*, 14th November 2019: https://www.eastasiaforum.org/2019/11/14/is-australia-too-dumb-and-too-china-dependent/

20. Australia is well-positioned to compete in "interaction-rich" jobs, as it has high levels of skilled labour. By contrast, because of high labour costs, manufacturing cost in terms of hourly compensation is much higher than that of South Korea and US, see J Lydon, D Dyer and C Bradley, *Compete to Prosper: Improving Australia's global competitiveness* (McKinsey Australia, 2014). Further, the *Financial Review*'s *Rich Bosses List* is an illustration of how rapidly wealth in Australia is moving towards younger people in different industries. Half of the top 50 were in either technology or financial services and only six from the resources industry (compared to 12 ten years earlier), being the same number as got rich from retail. See J Sprague and J Thomson, "Richest executives are younger than ever," *Australian Financial Review*, 23rd July 2021: https://www.afr.com/work-and-careers/leaders/richest-executives-are-younger-than-ever-20210721-p58bre

21. *Australian Jobs 2019* (Australian Government Department of Jobs and Small Business): https://www.professions.org.au/wp-content/uploads/Australian-Jobs-2019_AustGovt_DJSB.pdf

22. E Ortiz-Ospina and D Beltekian, "How and why should we study 'economic complexity'?", Our World in Data, 19th March 2018, https://ourworldindata.org/how-and-why-econ-complexity

23. *Australian National Outlook* (CSIRO, 2019) identifies different scenarios of realisation of Australia's potential ("Outlook Vision") and failure to act on key challenges ("Slow Decline"). Its prescriptions include greater investment in skills and technology, investment in transport and urban infrastructure, developing

low-emission energy exports, more effective land use and encouraging greater risk-appetite and trust in political, business and social institutions.
24. The Australian market pays higher dividends at a yield of 4.4 per cent compared with global shares' 2.5 per cent, A Gluyas, "Why Australian shares look set to beat global stocks", *Australian Financial Review*, 8th February 2023: https://www.afr.com/wealth/personal-finance/why-australian-shares-look-set-to-beat-global-stocks-20230131-p5cguu
25. In Australia, IPOs of more than AU$50m may cost approximately 5 per cent or less of the funds raised, with underwriter fees in the 2-3 per cent range, see J Williamson-Noble, *The Float Guide: How to float a company on the Australian Securities Exchange*, (Gilbert+Tobin, 2009). In the US, average total costs for a new float fund raising of US$50-100m are approximately US$8.2m, equivalent to 8-16 per cent of funds raised, see "Considering an IPO? An insight into the costs post-JOBS Act", (PwC, 2015).
26. K Treece and C Jennings, "What Is The Average Real Estate Agent Commission?" *Forbes Advisor*, 22nd September 2022: https://www.forbes.com/advisor/mortgages/real-estate/real-estate-agent-commission/
27. S Pandey, "S&P upgrades outlook on Australia's AAA rating to stable from negative".
28. *The State of Australian Start Up Funding*, (Cut Through Venture, 2023): https://australianstartupfunding.com
29. *Australia's productivity slowdown* (Parliament of Australia, 2022): https://www.aph.gov.au/About_Parliament/Parliamentary_departments/Parliamentary_Library/pubs/BriefingBook47p
30. J Kay, "Mission Economy by Mariana Mazzucato — could moonshot thinking help fix the planet?", *Financial Times*, 13th January 2021: https://www.ft.com/content/86475b94-3636-49ec-9b3f-7d7756350b30 In this book review, Kay criticises that book's contention that capitalism would be invigorated by more moonshots. He points out that the Apollo mission was a success because "the objective was specific and limited, the basic science was well understood. and the political commitment [made] budget overruns almost irrelevant." These conditions do not apply to the many other "moonshot" proposals that are advanced as a rationale for greater Government "coordination" in economic life.
31. S Reinhardt and L Steel, "A brief history of Australia's tax system", presented at the 22nd Apec Finance Ministers' Technical Working Group Meeting, Khanh Hoa, Vietnam, 15th June 2006: https://treasury.gov.au/publication/economic-roundup-winter-2006/a-brief-history-of-australias-tax-system
32. See further, for a chronology of the GST debate, J Harrison, "The GST Debate—Chronology", Background Paper 1, (Economics, Commerce and Industrial Relations Group, 1997): https://www.aph.gov.au/About_Parliament/Parliamentary_Departments/Parliamentary_Library/Publications_Archive/Background_Papers/bp9798/98bp01
33. P Coggan, *More: The 10,000 year rise of the world economy* (The Economist Books, 2020) puts recent economic trends into the wider context of economic history.

CHAPTER 10. WISE

1. With the Education Act 1872, Victoria was one of the first regions in the world to offer free, secular and compulsory education, see "An educated community" (website), National Museum Australia, accessed 25th August 2024: https://digital-classroom.nma.gov.au/defining-moments/free-education-introduced Australia spends approximately 23 per cent more per full time equivalent student than the OECD average (adjusted for purchasing power and including expenditure on research and development), see "Australia—Overview of the education system (EAG, 2023)" (website), OECD, accessed 25th August 2024: https://gpseducation.oecd.org/CountryProfile?primaryCountry=AUS&treshold=10&topic=EO

2. In 1966, approximately three per cent of the population had either university or other tertiary qualification, whereas in 2016, close to one quarter of Australians had completed a bachelor's degree or above, see *Census of Population and Housing, Population: Single Characteristic, Part 6. Education Attainment*, vol. 1, (Commonwealth Bureau of Census and Statistics, 1966); "Census of Population and Housing: Reflecting Australia—Stories from the Census, 2016" (website), Australian Bureau of Statistics: https://www.abs.gov.au/ausstats/abs@.nsf/Lookup/by per cent20Subject/2071.0~2016~Main per cent20Features~Educational per cent20Qualifications per cent20Data per cent20Summary per cent20~65. See also, *Education at a Glance 2022: OECD Indicators* (2022): https://doi.org/10.1787/3197152b-en

3. P Hurley and N Van Dyke, *Australian investment in education: vocational education and training*, (Mitchell Institute, 2019): https://www.vu.edu.au/sites/default/files/australian-investment-in-education-vet-mitchell-institute.pdf See also, *National Agreement for Skills and Workforce Development Review Interim Report* (Productivity Commission, 2020): https://www.pc.gov.au/inquiries/completed/skills-workforce-agreement/interim/skills-workforce-agreement-interim.pdf

4. "Australians pursuing higher education in record numbers", Australian Bureau of Statistics, media release, 23rd October 2017: https://www.abs.gov.au/AUSSTATS/abs@.nsf/mediareleasesbyReleaseDate/1533FE5A8541D66CCA2581BF00362D1D

5. "World University Rankings 2024" (website), *Times Higher Education*, accessed 25th August 2024: https://www.timeshighereducation.com/world-university-rankings/2024/world-ranking

6. A Norton, "Key differences between Australian and British higher education: regional versus national markets and institutions," *Higher Education Commentary From Carlton*, 30th November 2020: https://andrewnorton.net.au/2020/11/30/key-differences-between-australian-and-british-higher-education-regional-versus-national-markets-and-institutions/

7. Australian universities such as UNSW, Monash or University of Sydney each have over 39,000, 45,000 and 40,000 domestic enrolments whilst Cambridge and Oxford each have approximately 14,000 domestic enrolments, see "Which university has the most domestic students in Australia?" (website),

StudyingAU, accessed 25th August 2024: https://www.studyingau.com/posts/which-university-has-the-most-domestic-students-in-australia; "Nationality / Domicile" (website), University of Cambridge, accessed 25th August 2024: https://www.information-hub.admin.cam.ac.uk/university-profile/student-numbers/nationalitydomicile; "Student numbers" (website), University of Oxford, accessed 25th August 2024: https://www.ox.ac.uk/about/facts-and-figures/student-numbers

8. University of Sydney, among the first in the world, admitted female students in 1881, see "Gender Equity" (website), University of Sydney, accessed 25th August 2024: https://www.sydney.edu.au/about-us/vision-and-values/diversity/gender-equity.html#:~:text=In%20per%20cent%201881%20per%20cent%20we%20per%20cent%20became%20per%20cent%20one,a%20per%20cent%20student%20per%20cent%20body%20per%20cent%20of%20per%20cent%2026%20per%20cent2C000

9. R Joseph, "ATAR's rising relevance: admission standards and completion rates", The Centre for Independent Studies: https://www.cis.org.au/wp-content/uploads/2023/02/AP44_-ATARs-rising-relevance-1.pdf

10. "Market snapshot: International student recruitment in China today" (website), ICEF Monitor: https://monitor.icef.com/2024/07/market-snapshot-international-student-recruitment-in-china-today/; S Sharma, "Top 10 Countries for Indian Students to Study Aboard: Universities, Opportunities and More," *The Times of India*, 1st June 2024: https://timesofindia.indiatimes.com/education/study-abroad/top-10-countries-for-indian-students-to-study-abroad-universities-opportunities-and-more/articleshow/110616360.cms

11. "Australia's Top 25 Exports" (Canberra: DFAT—Trade Investment Economics Branch, 2023): https://www.dfat.gov.au/sites/default/files/australias-goods-and-services-by-top-25-exports-2023.pdf

12. *Education at a Glance 2021: OECD Indicators*: https://doi.org/10.1787/b35a14e5-en

13. "Research and Experimental Development, Higher Education Organisations, Australia" (website), Australian Bureau of Statics: https://www.abs.gov.au/statistics/industry/technology-and-innovation/research-and-experimental-development-higher-education-organisations-australia/latest-release. See also, F Larkins and I Marshman, "$7.6 billion and 11 per cent of researchers: our estimate of how much Australian university research stands to lose by 2024," *The Conversation*, 22nd September 2020: https://theconversation.com/7-6-billion-and-11-of-researchers-our-estimate-of-how-much-australian-university-research-stands-to-lose-by-2024-146672

14. "Foreign students are pouring back into Australia," *The Economist*, December 2023: https://www.economist.com/asia/2023/12/07/foreign-students-are-pouring-back-into-australia

15. "Student numbers" (website), Australian Curriculum Assessment and Reporting Authority, accessed 25th August 2024: https://www.acara.edu.au/reporting/national-report-on-schooling-in-australia/student-numbers

16. "Private Schools and British Society" (website), UCL: https://www.ucl.ac.uk/ioe/research-projects/2023/dec/private-schools-and-british-society; "Elementary-Secondary Education Survey, 2020/2021" (website), Statistics Canada: https://www150.statcan.gc.ca/n1/daily-quotidien/221013/dq221013a-eng.

htm; "US public, private and charter schools in 5 charts" (website), Pew Research Centre: https://www.pewresearch.org/short-reads/2024/06/06/us-public-private-and-charter-schools-in-5-charts/; "Students in Germany Showing Growing Preference for Private Universities" (website), Study in Germany, accessed 25th August 2024: https://www.studying-in-germany.org/students-in-germany-showing-growing-preference-for-private-universities/; "How do private schools work in France?" *The Local*, 18th January 2024: https://www.thelocal.fr/20240118/how-do-private-schools-work-in-france

17. *Public Savings from Non-Public Schools* (Catholic Schools NSW, 2023): https://www.csnsw.catholic.edu.au/wp-content/uploads/2024/03/Public-Savings-from-Non-Public-Schools-4.pdf

18. S Thomson, "Aussie students are a year behind students 10 years ago in science, maths and reading," *The Conversation*, 3rd December 2021: https://theconversation.com/aussie-students-are-a-year-behind-students-10-years-ago-in-science-maths-and-reading-127013. See also, J Baker, "Alarm bells: Australian students record worst result in global tests," *Sydney Morning Herald*, 3rd December 2019: https://www.smh.com.au/education/alarm-bells-australian-students-record-worst-result-in-global-tests-20191203-p53gie.html

19. C Cassidy, "Australian students' Pisa scores still declining despite climb into OECD top 10," *The Guardian*, 5th December 2023: https://www.theguardian.com/australia-news/2023/dec/05/australian-students-2022-Pisa-scores-results-declining-oecd

20. *Education Policy Outlook in Australia*, OECD Education and Policy Perspectives (2023): https://www.oecd-ilibrary.org/docserver/ce7a0965-en.pdf?expires=1688878072&id=id&accname=guest&checksum=3C3EB982468B9B41CAE4D58977E43361

21. *The issue of increasing disruption in Australian school classrooms* (Parliament of Australia 2024): https://www.aph.gov.au/Parliamentary_Business/Committees/Senate/Education_and_Employment/DASC/Report/Chapter_1_-_Final_report

22. J Gleeson et al, *Supporting teachers to use research evidence well in practice* (Australian Education Research Organisation, 2022): https://www.edresearch.edu.au/sites/default/files/2022-12/supporting-teachers-to-use-research-evidence-aa_1.pdf

23. See also, P Gross, J Sonnemann, and J Nolan, *Attracting high achievers to teaching* (Grattan Institute, 2019): https://grattan.edu.au/wp-content/uploads/2019/08/921-Attracting-high-achievers-to-teaching.pdf which proposes recommended reforms that, if adopted, could potentially double the proportion of high achievers who choose teaching as a career within the next decade.

CHAPTER II. DIVERSE

1. P Adams, quoted from "Dog is Love", *The Australian*, 2nd June 2012: https://www.theaustralian.com.au/weekend-australian-magazine/dog-is-love/news-story/f091cb769598cd6c775508c98c2ce6c1

2. F Adamson, "Progress of women in diplomacy a point of pride for DFAT," *The Interpreter*, 10th July 2019: https://www.lowyinstitute.org/the-interpreter/progress-women-diplomacy-point-pride-dfat

3. TW Fitzsimmons, MS Yates and VJ Callan, *Towards Board Gender Parity* (University of Queensland Business School, 2021).
4. *Board Diversity Index 2021* (Watermark Search International, 2021).
5. *The Global Gender Gap Index 2022* rankings, World Economic Forum.
6. *2023 Edelman Trust Barometer*.

CHAPTER 12. DEMOCRATIC

1. "Worst form of government" (website), International Churchill Society, accessed 25th August 2024: https://winstonchurchill.org/resources/quotes/the-worst-form-of-government/
2. The Singapore Government is more responsive to public opinion than is perceived in Australia, but it can nonetheless be regarded as a success story of technocracy, as "public servants are expected to be technically minded, long-term thinkers and with a deep utilitarian streak. The late Lee Kuan Yew—a longsighted genius with a ruthless streak—is often credited with taking a small ex-British island expected to be a failed state and turning it into an economic powerhouse: an export-oriented manufacturer, a great port, a flight hub, a financial centre, a city-state with the third highest per capita income in the world. But Lee was just a man. Singapore's success came from its system of expert rule, focus on meritocratic talent and long-term thinking…" See D Hendrie, "In Praise of Technocracy: Why Australia Must Imitate Singapore", first published in *Meanjin Spring*, 2015: https://pursuit.unimelb.edu.au/articles/in-praise-of-technocracy-why-australia-must-imitate-singapore
3. Australia is ranked the 13th least corrupt out of 180 countries, see "Australia Country Data: (website), Transparency International, accessed 25th August 2024, https://www.transparency.org/en/cpi/2022/index/aus
4. For example, approximately one third of private income in election funding is undisclosed, see K Griffiths and I Chan, "Big money was spent on the 2022 election—but the party with the deepest pockets didn't win," *The Conversation*, 1st February 2023: https://theconversation.com/big-money-was-spent-on-the-2022-election-but-the-party-with-the-deepest-pockets-didnt-win-198780
5. The quote about the "currency of the internet" is from J Ganesh, "The BlackBerry and me", *Financial Times*, 25th September 2021: https://www.ft.com/content/d6def412-cb00-4a66-ba6c-30791e5c8438 Ganesh, an insightful observer of the sociology of modernity and the impact of the digital world, attributes this to the touchscreen and photographic capabilities introduced by the iPhone which made it harder and less appealing to type longer and more complex ideas.
6. E Higgins, *We are Bellingcat: An intelligence agency for the people* (Bloomsbury, 2021) is an excellent study of how technology can empower transparency and accountability, just as it can be used for disinformation and intimidation. The battle between open and authoritarian approaches is not qualitatively changed by technology, it just moves to a different field.
7. *The Economist* did the correlation between press freedom (measured by Reporters without Borders) and Ipsos MORI poll answers to the question of whether people are too easily offended or whether the way people talk needs to be more sensitive.

CHAPTER 13. ISLAND NATION

1. P Keating, "A Prospect of Europe", (speech, University of New South Wales, 4th September 1997).
2. T Marshall, *Prisoners of Geography* (Elliot & Thompson, 2016) and *The Power of Geography* (Elliot & Thompson, 2021). I had talked with the author about Australia after reading the first book, which helped to inform some of my thinking, and he specifically addresses Australia in the second.
3. A Santoreneos, "Another 400,000 Australians to become millionaires by 2028", *Forbes*, 11th July 2024: https://www.forbes.com.au/news/investing/wealth-australia-388-k-median-second-global/
4. J Diamon, *Guns, Germs and Steel: The Fates of Human Societies* (WW Norton & Company, 1997).
5. H White, *How to defend Australia* (La Trobe University Press, 2019).

CHAPTER 14. THE CHINA CHALLENGE

1. D Greenlees, "Asialink Milestones: John Howard Reflects on the China Challenge and Trump's Legacy," *Asialink*, 15th November 2020: https://asialink.unimelb.edu.au/insights/asialink-milestones-john-howard-reflects-on-the-china-challenge-and-the-trump-legacy
2. D Shambaugh and B Carson, "Vicious Cycle: the opening and closing of Chinese politics", 11th December 2018: https://warontherocks.com/2018/12/jaw-jaw-vicious-cycle-the-opening-and-closing-of-chinese-politics/
3. The Lowy Institute's annual Lowy Institute Poll has tracked Australian views on international policy for the last 17 years and is a fascinating in-depth analysis of how views about China, America and other issues have changed over that time. See "Lowy Institute Poll 2024" (website), accessed 30th August 2024: https://poll.lowyinstitute.org/report/2024/#report/
4. "Country comparison Australia vs China" (website), Country Economics, accessed 30th August 2024: https://countryeconomy.com/countries/compare/australia/china See also, "China GDP Growth Rate" (website), Trading Economics, accessed 30th August 2024: https://tradingeconomics.com/china/gdp-growth-annual
5. "Doing business with China" (website), Department of Foreign Affairs and Trade, accessed 30th August 2024: https://www.dfat.gov.au/trade/agreements/in-force/chafta/doing-business-with-china/doing-business-with-china
6. There is statistical association between GDP per capita and per capita income with democratisation, see C Boix, "Democracy, Development, and the International System," *American Political Science Review*, 2011: https://www.princeton.edu/~cboix/apsr per cent20- per cent20democracy, per cent20development per cent20and per cent20the per cent20international per cent20system.pdf See also, "GDP per capital vs type of political regime, 2015" (website), Our World in Data, accessed 23rd July 2023: https://ourworldindata.org/grapher/income-vs-type-of-political-regime.
7. G Raby, "Can Australia cope with China's new world order?" *Australian Financial Review*, 30th October 2020: https://www.afr.com/policy/foreign-

affairs/can-australia-cope-with-china-s-new-world-order-20201026-p568l6
8. Z Linetsky, "China Can't Catch a Break in Asian Public Opinion," *Foreign Policy*, 28th June 2023: https://foreignpolicy.com/2023/06/28/china-soft-power-asia-culture-influence-korea-singapore/
9. 60 per cent of China's iron ore imports are from Australia, followed by Brazil and India, see M Smith, "China's five-year plan to slash Australian iron ore imports," *Australian Financial Review*, 22nd May 2021: https://www.afr.com/world/asia/china-s-five-year-plan-to-slash-australian-iron-ore-imports-20210520-p57tq9 In 2019, Australia supplied more than 57 per cent of China's thermal coal and 40 per cent of its coking coal imports, see S Haselgrove, "Australian coal exporters brush Chinese ban aside", *Australian Mining*, 27th January 2021: https://www.australianmining.com.au/news/australian-coal-exporters-brush-chinese-ban-aside
10. *Index of FDI Restrictiveness 2024*, OECD. This index looks at four main types of restriction: foreign equity restrictions, discriminatory screening or approval mechanisms, restrictions on key foreign personnel and operational restrictions.
11. *Demystifying Chinese Investment in Australia* (KPMG, 2024): https://assets.kpmg.com/content/dam/kpmg/au/pdf/2024/demystifying-chinese-investment-in-australia-april-2024.pdf
12. "Statistics on who invests in Australia" (website), Department of Foreign Affairs and Trade, accessed 30th August 2024: https://www.dfat.gov.au/trade/trade-and-investment-data-information-and-publications/foreign-investment-statistics/statistics-on-who-invests-in-australia
13. "Education export income from Chinese students in Australia from financial years 2014 to 2019" (website), Statista, accessed 27th January 2021: https://www.statista.com/statistics/1086549/australia-education-export-income-chinese-students/; *Universities 2018 Audits* (Audit Office of New South Wales, 2019): https://www.audit.nsw.gov.au/sites/default/files/pdf-downloads/Final per cent20report_web per cent20version_Universities per cent202018 per cent20audits.pdf
14. "Sydney and Melbourne" (website), idcommunity, accessed 1st September 2024: https://profile.id.com.au/australia/ancestry?WebID=260
15. Japan's status as the world's third largest economy was achieved through significant growth in the second half of the 20th century, see "GDP, current prices" (website), International Monetary Fund, accessed 1st September 2024, https://www.imf.org/external/datamapper/NGDPD@WEO/OEMDC/ADVEC/WEOWORLD
16. Views are split between whether Australia should work with allies to deter China's use of military threat, even if it is at cost to relationship with China (45 per cent), or to strengthen the relationship with China (51 per cent), according to the Lowy Institute Poll 2024.

CHAPTER 15. AMERICAN UMBRELLA?

1. "A short history of America's economy since World War II" (website), Medium, accessed 30th August 2024: https://medium.com/the-worlds-economy-and-the-economys-world/a-short-history-of-americas-economy-since-world-war-ii-37293cdb640.

2. *US Relations with Australia* (US Department of State, 2024): https://www.state.gov/u-s-relations-with-australia.
3. "GDP based on market prices and on PPP, share of the world" (website), International Monetary Fund, accessed 30th August 2024: https://www.imf.org/external/datamapper/PPPSH@WEO/OEMDC/ADVEC/WEOWORLD/EEQ/EUQ
4. "US Population" (website), World Population Review, accessed 30th August 2024, https://worldpopulationreview.com/countries/united-states-population
5. LV Langenhove, "The Transformation of Multilateralism Mode 1.0 to Mode 2.0", *Global Policy*, 2010: https://doi.org/10.1111/j.1758-5899.2010.00042.x
6. "GDP based on PPP, share of the world" (website), International Monetary Fund.
7. The CPTPP has resulted in a number of benefits for Australia's exports, including elimination of more than 98 per cent of tariffs in the free trade area, see *CPTPP outcomes at a glance* (DFAT, 2021): https://www.dfat.gov.au/trade/agreements/in-force/cptpp/outcomes-documents/cptpp-outcomes-at-a-glance
8. "Good relations with the US and China" (website), Lowy Institute, accessed 30th August 2024: https://poll.lowyinstitute.org/charts/good-relations-with-us-and-china/ See also, "Potential conflict over Taiwan" (website), Lowy Institute, accessed 30th August 2024: https://poll.lowyinstitute.org/charts/potential-conflict-over-taiwan/
9. The Peace of Westphalia (signed in 1648) birthed the key tenets of the modern international system, as characterised by "non-interference in domestic affairs of other states; inviolability of borders; sovereignty of states; encouragements of international law." See H Kissinger, *World Order* (Penguin, 2014).

CHAPTER 16. ASCENDANT ASIA

1. P Keating, "Australian Labor Party Gala Federation Dinner Speech", (speech, Australian Labour Party Gala Dinner, 8th May 2001): http://www.paulkeating.net.au/shop/item/centenary-of-the-australian-labor-party---8-may-2001
2. D McDougall, "Australia's Growing Asian Minority: the Impact on Foreign Policy", *Australian Institute of International Affairs*, 2nd May 2019: https://www.internationalaffairs.org.au/australianoutlook/australias-growing-asian-minority-impact-foreign-policy/
3. PwC projects that there will be 450,000 Australians living and working in Asia by 2030, representing one third of the total expatriate community, up from approximately one fifth of the total currently, see *Our diaspora's got talent: Australia's advantage in Asia*, (PwC, 2016): https://advance.org/app/uploads/2020/08/PwC_our-diasporas-got-talent.pdf
4. "Cultural Diversity in Australia 2016" (website), Australian Bureau of Statistics, accessed 23rd July 2021: https://www.abs.gov.au/ausstats/abs@.nsf/Lookup/by per cent20Subject/2071.0~2016~Main per cent20Features~Cultural per cent20Diversity per cent20Article~60 Asian languages in the top 10 most widely spoken languages are Mandarin, Cantonese, Vietnamese, Hindi and Punjabi.
5. "Winning in Asia: Creating Long-Term Value" (website), Asialink, accessed 30th August 2020: https://asialink.unimelb.edu.au/stories/winning-in-asia-creating-long-term-value

6. "GDP based on PPP, share of the world" (website), International Monetary Fund, accessed 30th August 2024: https://www.imf.org/external/datamapper/PPPSH@WEO/OEMDC/ADVEC/WEOWORLD/EEQ/EUQ Based on IMF predictions, the collective GDP of Asia and the Pacific will reach 48 per cent of world GDP, measured on a PPP basis. McKinsey research also observes that while "in 2000, Asia accounted for just under one-third of global GDP (in terms of purchasing power parity), and it is on track to top 50 per cent by 2040". See O Tonby et al, *Asia's Future is Now*, (McKinsey Global Institute, 2019): https://www.mckinsey.com/~/media/McKinsey/Featured per cent20Insights/Asia per cent20Pacific/Asias per cent20future per cent20is per cent20now/Asias-future-is-now-final.pdf See also, "A short history of America's economy since World War II" (website), Medium: https://medium.com/the-worlds-economy-and-the-economys-world/a-short-history-of-americas-economy-since-world-war-ii-37293cdb640
7. "Business, Asean-Australia" (website), Department of the Prime Minister and Cabinet, accessed 30th August 2024: https://aseanaustralia.pmc.gov.au/resources/business
8. N Farrelly et al, "Fifty years of Asean-Australia ties show value of consistent cooperation," *Asialink*, 4th March 2024: https://asialink.unimelb.edu.au/insights/fifty-years-of-asean-australia-ties-show-value-of-consistent-cooperation
9. M Wesley, *There goes the neighbourhood: Australia and the rise of Asia* (New South, 2011).
10. J Clemente, "China Is The World's Largest Oil & Gas Importer", *Forbes*, 17th October 2019: https://www.forbes.com/sites/judeclemente/2019/10/17/china-is-the-worlds-largest-oil--gas-importer/ 45 per cent of China's LNG imports come from Australia, see Reuters, "China-Australia relations: LNG imports hit record in April due to industrial demand, climate change pledge," *South China Morning Post*, May 22, 2021, https://www.scmp.com/economy/china-economy/article/3134361/china-australia-relations-lng-imports-hit-record-april-due.
11. *Trade and Investment at a Glance* (Department of Foreign Affairs and Trade, 2019): https://www.dfat.gov.au/sites/default/files/trade-and-investment-at-a-glance-2019.pdf "Statistics on who invests in Australia" (website), Australian Government Department of Foreign Affairs and Trade, accessed 31st August 2024: https://www.dfat.gov.au/trade/resources/investment-statistics/statistics-on-who-invests-in-australia
12. J Eyers, "Macquarie, ANZ and Canva CEOs help power Australia's India push", *Australian Financial Review*, 25th April 2024, https://www.afr.com/companies/financial-services/macquarie-anz-and-canva-ceos-help-power-up-australia-s-india-push-20240425-p5fmga
13. Korea's electric vehicle manufacturers and battery suppliers are driving demand for Australia's critical minerals. More than $500m in investments has been committed by Korean corporates for Australian mining projects in recent years, see *Opportunities in Korea for Australian critical minerals* (Commonwealth of Australia, 2023).
14. N Burns, "The Diplomat as Gardener," *Foreign Affairs*, 19th February 2021, https://www.foreignaffairs.com/articles/united-states/2021-02-19/diplomat-gardener

15. C Anstey, "Summers Warns US Is Getting 'Lonely' as Other Powers Band Together", *Bloomberg*, 15th April 2023: https://www.bloomberg.com/news/articles/2023-04-14/summers-warns-us-getting-lonely-as-other-powers-band-together?embedded-checkout=true
16. O Tonby et al, *Asia's Future is Now*.
17. F Duate, "Countries with the Highest Number of Internet Users (2024)", *Exploding Topics* (blog), 7th May 2024: https://explodingtopics.com/blog/countries-internet-users
18. "Trust in government, policy effectiveness and the governance agenda", in *Government at a Glance 2013* (OECD, 2013): https://doi.org/10.1787/gov_glance-2013-6-en Trust in government in Singapore, India and Indonesia is much higher than in Sweden, Germany and Australia, see CH Min, "Government remains most trusted institution in Singapore, amid global trend of societal polarisation: Survey", *CNA*, 15th March 2023: https://www.channelnewsasia.com/singapore/edelman-trust-barometer-2023-government-business-polarisation-inequality-3345571
19. P Srinivasan and V Harrison, "Mapped, the vast network of security deals spanning the Pacific, and what it means", *The Guardian*, 9th July 2024.
20. According to Lowy Institute analysis, Australia placed second to the US in defensive networks and "exerts more influence in the region than expected given its available resources", see *Asia Power Index 2023* (Lowy Institute, 2023): https://power.lowyinstitute.org/downloads/lowy-institute-2023-asia-power-index-key-findings-report.pdf

CHAPTER 17. DIPLOMACY IN THE 21ST CENTURY

1. A Albanese, "Australia in the world" (speech, 2023 Lowy Lecture, Sydney, 19th December 2023): https://www.pm.gov.au/media/australia-world-2023-lowy-lecture
2. Philippines has praised the Aukus deal, whilst Malaysia has warned against provocation that could trigger an arms race in the region, see RJ Heydarian, "Philippines: The best friend for Aukus in Southeast Asia", *The Interpreter*, 27th March 2023: https://www.lowyinstitute.org/the-interpreter/philippines-best-friend-aukus-southeast-asia
3. The UK is now more strategically aligned with Australia now than any time since the 1960s, see E Graham, "Australia and Britain deepen defence cooperation, but are they allies?" *The Strategist*, 25th March 2024, https://www.aspistrategist.org.au/australia-and-britain-deepen-defence-cooperation-but-are-they-allies/
4. "World University Rankings 2024" (website), *Times Higher Education*.
5. D Webb, *UK-Australia free trade agreement* (House of Commons Library, 2023): https://commonslibrary.parliament.uk/research-briefings/cbp-9484/ See also, "Statistics on where Australia invests" (website), Department of Foreign Affairs and Trade, accessed 1st September 2024: https://www.dfat.gov.au/trade/trade-and-investment-data-information-and-publications/foreign-investment-statistics/statistics-on-where-australia-invests
6. "US expenditure on foreign economic aid, Percent of GDP" (website), World Bank Group, Prosperity Data 360, accessed 1st September 2024: https://

prosperitydata360.worldbank.org/en/indicator/IMF+GFSCOFOG+GEGPF_G14_GDP_PT
7. JJ Linz, "The perils of Presidentialism", *Journal of Democracy*, 1990.
8. D Torrance, "The King's style and titles in the UK and the Commonwealth" (UK Parliament, 2024): https://commonslibrary.parliament.uk/the-kings-style-and-titles-in-the-uk-and-the-commonwealth/
9. K Amadeo, "Largest Economies in the World", *The Balance*: https://www.thebalance.com/world-s-largest-economy-3306044 See also, "The 10 largest economies in the world" (website), CMC Markets, accessed 1st September 2024: https://www.cmcmarkets.com/en/trading-guides/largest-economies-in-the-world
10. N Okonjo-Iweala, "Why the world still needs trade", *Foreign Affairs*, 2023
11. "Lowy Institute Poll 2024? (website), Lowy Institute.
12. PwC, *Out of sight, out of mind? Australia's diaspora as a pathway to innovation* (PricewaterhouseCoopers, 2018): https://www.pwc.com.au/publications/pdf/the-australian-diaspora.pdf

CHAPTER 18. MAKING IT LAST

1. "Australia: CO2 Country Profile" (website), Our World in Data, accessed 23rd July 2023: https://ourworldindata.org/co2/country/australia?country=AUS~OWID_WRL See also, "CO2 and Greenhouse Gas Emissions" (website), Our World in Data, accessed 1st September 2024: https://ourworldindata.org/co2-and-greenhouse-gas-emissions#all-charts
2. "Solar Energy" (website), Australian Renewable Energy Agency, accessed 1st September 2024: https://arena.gov.au/renewable-energy/solar/ See also, "Solar Energy" (website), Geoscience Australia: https://www.ga.gov.au/scientific-topics/energy/resources/other-renewable-energy-resources/solar-energy
3. *Australia's Long-Term Emissions Reduction Plan* (Department of Industry, Science, Energy and Resources, 2021): https://unfccc.int/sites/default/files/resource/Australias_LTS_WEB.pdf See also, "Interactive Charts on CO2 and Greenhouse Gas Emissions" (website), accessed 8th September 2024: https://ourworldindata.org/co2-and-greenhouse-gas-emissions#all-charts
4. *Australian Energy Update 2023* (Department of Climate Change, Energy, the Environment and Water): https://www.energy.gov.au/sites/default/files/Australian per cent20Energy per cent20Update per cent202023_0.pdf See also, R Thomas, "The 82 per cent national renewable energy target—where did it come from and how can we get there?", Australian Energy Council, 17th August 2023: https://www.energycouncil.com.au/analysis/the-82-per-cent-national-renewable-energy-target-where-did-it-come-from-and-how-can-we-get-there/
5. *2024 Integrated System Plan for the National Electricity Market* (Australian Energy Market Operator, 2024): https://aemo.com.au/energy-systems/major-publications/integrated-system-plan-isp/2024-integrated-system-plan-isp
6. The Clean Energy Finance Corporation is established to "facilitate increased flows of finance into the clean energy sector". According to an audit conducted by the Australian National Audit Office for FY19–20, the CEFC's core portfolio, since inception, has preserved the capital granted to it and made an annual rate

of return of 4.8 per cent, see Australian National Audit Office, *Investments by the Clean Energy Finance Corporation*, Auditor-General Report (Commonwealth of Australia, 2020): https://www.anao.gov.au/work/performance-audit/investments-by-the-clean-energy-finance-corporation
7. See, for instance, "Eliminating fossil fuel diesel across Lendlease's UK construction projects with new Alternative Fuels Policy", Lendlease, media release, 15th July 2021: https://www.lendlease.com/better-places/eliminating-fossil-fuel-diesel-across-lendleases-uk-construction-projects-alternative-fuels-policy/
8. The CSIRO launched a Hydrogen Industry Mission, which aims to drive down the cost of hydrogen production, which, when mixed with oxygen, can be used as emissions-free fuel source to generate electricity, power or heat, see CSIRO, "A new Hydrogen Industry Mission launched today by CSIRO, Australia's national science agency, will help support the world's transition to clean energy, create new jobs and boost the economy," media release, 26th May 2021: https://www.csiro.au/en/news/News-releases/2021/Fuelling-a-clean-and-bright-future
9. *Education at a Glance 2021* (OECD, 2021): https://doi.org/10.1787/b35a14e5-en
10. L Walsh et al, "What are young Australians most worried about? Finding affordable housing, they told us", *The Conversation*, 29th November 2024: https://theconversation.com/what-are-young-australians-most-worried-about-finding-affordable-housing-they-told-us-218426
11. Sydney and Melbourne's total population is approximately 10 million, representing about 40 per cent of Australia's total population, whereas the total population of New York City and Los Angeles is only about 4 per cent of the total US population, while the combined population of Beijing and Shanghai is approximately 3.5 per cent of China's total population. Berlin and Hamburg are Germany's most populous cities, which represent about 7 per cent of its total population. "Largest cities by population 2024" (website), World population review.
12. Australia's progressive tax and highly targeted transfer system substantially reduce inequality, see *Rising inequality? A stocktake of the evidence* (Productivity Commission, 2018): https://www.pc.gov.au/research/completed/rising-inequality/rising-inequality.pdf
13. M Zorbas, "How to fix the housing supply nightmare", *Australian Financial Review*, 28th January 2024: https://www.afr.com/property/residential/how-to-fix-the-housing-supply-nightmare-20240128-p5fojm

CHAPTER 19. STILL LUCKY, STILL WORKING

1. D Acemoglu and JA Robinson, *Why Nations Fail* (Profile Books, 2012).
2. S Pinker, *Enlightenment Now* (Penguin, 2019) is one of the best summaries of the Enlightenment and historical progress of the last 200 years.
3. See A Low et al, *Australia as a Finance and Technology Centre Advisory Group (AFTCAG) Report* (2021).
4. D Horne, *The Lucky Country*.

ABOUT THE AUTHOR

ANDREW LOW's interest in Australia's unique culture, institutions and place in the world started when he grew up in the small town of Mount Isa in the Queensland Outback, having migrated from Namibia. He went on to become head of Asia for Macquarie Capital, global head of Macquarie's Telecom, Media, Entertainment & Technology and Financial Services practices, chief operating officer for Macquarie Capital Advisers, chief executive of RedBridge Grant Samuel, and then global head of investment banking for the international arm of China's largest securities firm, CITIC Securities.

Andrew is, or has been, a chair or director for organisations such as Advance Global Australians, Asia Society Australia, the Australia Foundation UK, the Australian British Chamber of Commerce, the Australian Ballet Foundation UK, the Australia–Japan Business Cooperation Committee, the Bell Shakespeare Company, the Europe Australia Business Council, Genea Biomedx and PRP Diagnostic Imaging. He has degrees in Economics and Asian Studies, and has also studied at Tsinghua University and at the Harvard Business School.

INDEX

Asean:
   and the US, 195–198
   region and politics, 194–198
Australia:
   characteristics and identity, xii, xiii, xiv–xvi, 146, 148
   economic stability, resilience, xvii, xviii–xix, 7, 133, 175
   geopolitical influence, Asia-Pacific focus, xxvi, xxvii–xxviii, 8–9, 120
   egalitarian nature, vi, vii, viii–ix, 21, 23, 148
   individualism and cultural impact, x, xi–xii, 23, 29, 148
   indulgence vs. restraint, cultural preferences, xiii, xiv–xv, 24, 36, 148
   safety orientation, societal implications, xviii, xix–xx, 27, 97, 148
   competitive nature, economic implications, xxi, xxii–xxiv, 28, 148
Australian values:
   overview and global perspective, xxiv, xxv, xxvi, 90–92, 148
   in foreign policy, xxvii, xxviii–xxix, 128–130
Australian Dream:
   definition, cultural roots, xxxi, xxxii–xxxiv, 45–88, 132–142
   historical significance, xxxiii, xxxiv, 46–49
   immigration's impact, contemporary relevance, 62–65, 157
   multicultural aspects, societal integration, 63, 65–66, 168
   democratic framework, xxxiii, 53–55, 168

B
Binary choices:
   in foreign policy, avoiding pitfalls, xxxii–xxxiii, 128–130, 130–132

Britain/United Kingdom:
   diplomacy, 202–206
   healthcare, xxiv, 102, 103–105
   parliamentary democracy, 68, 205–209
   voting, 68–74, 113–115

C
China:
   economic partnerships, 104–105, 163–166
   geopolitical tensions, strategic challenges, 110–113, 166–170
Compulsory voting:
   benefits, international comparison, 70–73
Cultural identity:
   detailed analysis, 20–44, 95–99
   implications for national policy, 98–100, 148–176

D
Democratic institutions:
   modern challenges, reform needs, 13, 90–92, 118–120
   comparative global analysis, 121–123, 168
Diagnostics:
   healthcare emphasis, 13, 67–69, 100–102, 159

E
Economic strategies:
   current evaluation, future prospects, 133, 175, 213–217
   superannuation, wealth distribution, 72–75, 112–114, 161
Education system:
   strengths, weaknesses, reforms, 80–82, 123–126, 165
   high schools vs. universities, comparative insights, 82, 127–130

INDEX

F

Fair Go:
  conceptual exploration, practical implications, xxxix, xl, xli–xliii, 36–38, 152

Foreign policy:
  strategic decisions, 17, 128–130, 181–186
  binary choices, implications, 128–130, 133–136

G

Gender equality:
  discussions and policy implications, 86, 136–139

H

Healthcare system:
  overview of strengths, areas for improvement, 67–70, 100–105, 159
  public vs. private sector roles, 75, 106–108

I

Immigration:
  debate and societal impacts, 62–65, 82–84
  integration challenges and successes, 85–87, 157

Individualism:
  influence on culture, policy making, x, xi–xii, 23

L

Lessons from Australian model:
  detailed analysis, global relevance, 12–18, 228–230

M

Media:
  role and influence in society, 88, 230–232
  effects of polarisation, implications for democracy, 88, 233–235

P

Political systems:
  Australian vs. global comparisons, practical implications, 90–92, 122–125

Productivity:
  policy, xxx, 229–231
  exports, 116–177, 231–233

R

Recognition of First Australians:
  historical overview, current initiatives, 46–49, 95–99

S

Safety:
  cultural emphasis, comparison with global norms, xviii–xx, 27, 97

Sport:
  societal role, cultural significance, xxix–xxxi, 34

Superannuation:
  system, 112–113

T

Technology:
  societal impacts, challenges, and opportunities, 94, 201–204

U

U.S. relations:
  strategic and economic considerations, 115–118, 181–183
  influence on Australian foreign policy, 117, 185–187

United Kingdom/Britain:
  diplomacy, 202–206
  healthcare, xxiv, 102–105
  parliamentary democracy, 68, 205–209
  voting, 68–74, 113–115

W

Wages and unions:
  economic implications, role in social stability, 43, 129–131

Wealth distribution:
  policy implications, economic analysis, 72–75, 112–114, 213–215
  superannuation impacts, future planning, 75, 112–114